An Introduction to Historical Comparison

An Introduction to Historical Comparison

Mikhail Krom
Translated by Elizabeth Guyatt

BLOOMSBURY ACADEMIC
LONDON • NEW YORK • OXFORD • NEW DELHI • SYDNEY

BLOOMSBURY ACADEMIC
Bloomsbury Publishing Plc
50 Bedford Square, London, WC1B 3DP, UK
1385 Broadway, New York, NY 10018, USA

BLOOMSBURY, BLOOMSBURY ACADEMIC and the Diana logo are trademarks of
Bloomsbury Publishing Plc

First published in Great Britain 2021
Paperback edition published 2022

Copyright © Mikhail Krom, 2021

Copyright in the original Russian language edition © European University at St. Petersburg, 2015

Mikhail Krom has asserted his right under the Copyright, Designs and Patents Act,
1988, to be identified as Author of this work.

Cover design: Terry Woodley
Cover image: The storming of the Winter Palace, St Petersburg, October 1917. (Photo by Ann
Ronan Pictures/Print Collector/Getty Images). 1960's China Cultural Revolution Era Chinese poster
(Shawshots/Alamy Stock Photo). Jean-Victor Schnetz, *The Battle for the Town Hall*, 28 July 1830
(ART Collection/Alamy Stock Photo)

All rights reserved. No part of this publication may be reproduced or transmitted in any form or
by any means, electronic or mechanical, including photocopying, recording, or any information
storage or retrieval system, without prior permission in writing from the publishers.

Bloomsbury Publishing Plc does not have any control over, or responsibility for, any third-party
websites referred to or in this book. All internet addresses given in this book were correct at the
time of going to press. The author and publisher regret any inconvenience caused if addresses
have changed or sites have ceased to exist, but can accept no responsibility for any such changes.

Every effort has been made to trace copyright holders and to obtain their permissions for the use
of copyright material. The publisher apologizes for any errors or omissions and would be grateful
if notified of any corrections that should be incorporated in future reprints or editions of this book.

A catalogue record for this book is available from the British Library.
Library of Congress Cataloging-in-Publication Data
Names: Krom, M. M. (Mikhail Markovich), author. | Guyatt, Elizabeth, translator.
Title: An introduction to historical comparison / Mikhail Krom; translated by Elizabeth Guyatt.
Other titles: Vvedenie v istoricheskuiu komparativistiku. English.
Description: London; New York: Bloomsbury Academic, [2021] |
Translation of: Vvedenie v istoricheskuiu komparativistiku: uchebnoe posobie. |
Includes bibliographical references and index. Identifiers: LCCN 2020035939 (print) |
LCCN 2020035940 (ebook) | ISBN 9781350123328 (hardback) | ISBN 9781350202115
(paperback) | ISBN 9781350123335 (ebook) | ISBN 9781350123342 (epub)
Subjects: LCSH: History–Methodology. | Historiography–Comparative method.
Classification: LCC D16 .K89413 2021 (print) | LCC D16 (ebook) | DDC 907.2–dc23
LC record available at https://lccn.loc.gov/2020035939
LC ebook record available at https://lccn.loc.gov/2020035940

ISBN: HB: 978-1-3501-2332-8
PB: 978-1-3502-0211-5
ePDF: 978-1-3501-2333-5
eBook: 978-1-3501-2334-2

Typeset by Deanta Global Publishing Services, Chennai, India

To find out more about our authors and books visit www.bloomsbury.com and
sign up for our newsletters.

Contents

List of table	vi
Acknowledgements	vii
Introduction: The paradoxes of historical comparison	1

Part I Key milestones in the development of historical comparison

1	Comparison in history: From antiquity to the Enlightenment	7
2	Historicism and the comparative method (nineteenth century to early twentieth century)	13
3	The lessons of Max Weber and Marc Bloch	23
4	The rise of historical comparison in the later twentieth century	38
5	New challenges: Cultural transfers, *histoire croiseé*, transnational history and criticism of traditional comparison	54
6	Comparative historical sociology	61

Part II Historical comparison in search of a method

7	Does method exist?	71
8	The functions of comparison and its specifics in historical research	80
9	Selection of objects for comparison and types of historical comparison	90
10	Recommendations for newcomers to historical comparison	97

Part III Themes of comparative historical research

11	Comparison in economic history	105
12	Comparison in political history	109
13	Comparison in social history	118
14	Comparative research on nationalism, empire and colonialism	128
Conclusion		135
Bibliography		137
Index		149

Table

1 Differences between Methods and Approaches Used in Historical Research   77

Acknowledgements

I have received help and support from many colleagues and institutions at every stage of my work on this book. First and foremost, I would like to express my sincere gratitude to the Rector's Office and Academic Council of the European University at St. Petersburg (EUSP), who supported my initiative for developing historical comparison at EUSP and founded a professorship in this unusual discipline.

I am grateful to the master's and PhD students at the EUSP Department of History who attended my course on historical comparison: our lively discussions led to many new insights and helped me hone the arguments on which this book is based.

Attending a summer school at the European University Institute in Florence in September 2012 – and Jan de Vries and Miroslav Hroch's lectures, in particular – significantly shaped my original idea for an academic course and the subsequent book.

I am very grateful to my colleague Mikhail Sokolov of the EUSP Department of Sociology, who introduced me to historical sociology, and also to Andrei Volodin, associate professor at Moscow State University, who in turn acquainted me with comparative economic and comparative labour history.

I am indebted to Wladimir Berelowitch of the School of Advanced Studies in the Social Sciences (EHESS) in Paris, Vera Kaplan of Tel Aviv University, Aleksandr Lavrov of the Sorbonne University and Matthias Middell of Leipzig University for their invaluable bibliographical advice and generously helping me access the literature I required.

It would have been impossible to write a book such as this without a modern and well-equipped academic library: I wish to thank Ona Lapenayte, director of EUSP's library, and her wonderful colleagues for their constant help and support.

Preparing the English edition has extended the list of acknowledgements further still. Jeroen Duindam of the University of Leiden encouraged me to publish the book in English and guided my search for a publisher. Valerie A. Kivelson of the University of Michigan kindly read the first draft of the translation of Part II and shared her observations. I am also grateful to the anonymous reviewers at Bloomsbury whose feedback helped me improve the manuscript.

Mollie Zuckermann prepared the first draft of the translation of Part II. The full translation of the book is the result of substantial and painstaking work by Elizabeth Guyatt, to whom I express my sincere gratitude.

Finally, I would like to thank Abigail Lane at Bloomsbury, with whom it was an immense pleasure to work.

Introduction

The paradoxes of historical comparison

This book is an attempt to analyse the theory and practice of comparative historical research, drawing on accumulated academic experience from around the world up to the beginning of the twenty-first century.

Comparison is an intrinsic part of everyday life: when we arrive in a new country, we cannot avoid comparing what we see with what we are used to at home and what we remember from our previous travels. When we take an important decision, we compare the options available.

Turning from everyday cognition to the academic level, we can see that comparison is essential for both natural and social scientists: whether it be testing new medicines or studying population migrations, the comparative method has a universal and very important role in contemporary research.

In this context, historians' attitude to comparison appears curious and even paradoxical.

The first paradox is that comparison has been used in history since the time of Herodotus: since comparison is a fundamental tool of human cognition, all historians compare their subjects in some way. We are often told, however, that the comparative study of history, or as it is more often called, 'comparative history', is very recent: 'Comparative history is still in its infancy,' as Carlo Ginzburg recently remarked.[1] Heinz-Gerhard Haupt explained that although the 'comparative perspective' had repeatedly featured in historiography, it was only in the 1930s that it started to become established as an example of a 'methodological instrument of explanatory theoretical comparison'.[2] What Haupt has in mind is conscious, focused comparison as opposed to implicit and ad hoc comparison, which historians have used since ancient times. But even if one takes this useful clarification into account, it remains unclear why scholars who make broad use of historical comparison, by their own acknowledgement, form a distinct minority among historians, despite the growth in comparative historical research in the twentieth century, which has been particularly prominent in recent decades.[3]

As Raymond Grew, the long-time editor of *Comparative Studies in Society and History* noted, it is something of an enigma that admiration of comparison is far

---

[1] Carlo Ginzburg's comment made at the seminar organized by the *Res Publica* Research Center, European University at St. Petersburg, 3 October 2013.
[2] Haupt (2001): 2397.
[3] See Cohen (2004): 57–8; Haupt and Kocka (2004): 25; etc.

more widespread among historians than its actual practice.[4] The attitude of historians to comparative research reminds Grew of the ambivalent relationship of the 'good bourgeois' to fine wines: 'To understand them – a sign of good taste, but to permit oneself to partake of them – this already feels like the manifestation of debauchery and extravagance.'[5]

Despite paying lip service to its usefulness, many historians mistrust comparison in practice; this appears particularly strange given the crucial role that it plays in the social sciences and humanities. The success of comparative linguistics, folklore studies or comparative political science is often based on the systematic application of the comparative method; this is another paradox of historical comparison that demands explanation.

Finally, what is known as the 'comparative historical method' has itself recently prompted a number of questions. Some historians are not now as confident about the existence of this method as so many of their predecessors were in the 1920s and even in the 1960s.[6] Thus, Grew stated plainly in 1980 that 'there is no comparative method in history'. Explaining his stance, he emphasized that ' historical comparison is no more attached to a single method than is the discipline of history itself'.[7] Later, several of Grew's colleagues – in particular Peter Kolchin[8] – aligned themselves with his opinion, and more recently Marta Petrusewicz characterized the current epistemological position well when she acknowledged in 2004 that 'we are not even sure what comparative history means: an approach? a method? a tool?' Petrusewicz appears inclined to believe that comparative history 'may be a combination of many things, approach, method, and tool'.[9] In other words, the present status of comparison in academic history is admittedly uncertain.

In this book, I have attempted to shed light on the methodology of historical comparison, drawing on both theoretical pronouncements and assertions by scholars such as those mentioned earlier and on prominent examples of specific comparative research.

As readers will see, there are a whole range of historical problems that require the use of comparison to solve them, or at least to discuss them fruitfully: Why was Britain the first country to successfully industrialize at the turn of the eighteenth to the nineteenth century? How true are claims that Germany, Russia or any other country has a special course of development? Is there a set of common features that impart meaning to concepts such as the modern state, nationalism or fascism? In each of these cases, we cannot escape the need for comparison.

A few words are probably needed to explain the title, scope and structure of this book: in selecting the term 'historical comparison' instead of the more familiar 'comparative history', I have aimed to avoid the ambiguity inherent in the latter term, a concept which is perceived as a particular variety or sub-type of history. It is, however,

---

[4] Grew (1980): 768.
[5] Grew (1980): 763.
[6] See Bloch ([1928] 1953); Sewell (1967).
[7] Grew (1980): 776.
[8] Kolchin (1982): 75.
[9] Petrusewicz (2004): 146.

neither a new trend nor a special field of historical research: historians have used comparison for many centuries; the fact that comparison has been used for different purposes and with varying results in different historiographical periods is another matter. Reflection on the functions of comparison in the work of historians is one of the main themes of this book.

But there is another important reason to place reflections on the comparative method in history under the 'umbrella' of historical comparison: for some time now, sociologists have been as interested as historians in studying the past and in doing so, they have taken a comparative approach. One need only mention figures such as Max Weber, Norbert Elias, and, more recently, Barrington Moore Jr., Charles Tilly, Jack Goldstone and other prominent sociologists. Historical comparison today is therefore an interdisciplinary field, although as will be shown in the book, comparison is used in distinct ways within the two disciplines.

The first edition of this book was aimed at Russian readers, and one of its emphases was therefore on subjects such as the history of Russia from a comparative perspective and the development of comparative research in Russia. In preparing the English-language edition I have attempted to make the book more relevant to a wider audience. The Russia-oriented chapters have been removed but, conversely, material has been added which relates to other parts of the world. The bibliography has also been substantially expanded. Nevertheless, I am under no illusion that I have been able to make the book truly global in its scope. As readers will see, the majority of the authors I have cited were born in Europe or the United States, and most of the phenomena or events I mention relate to Europe. The book also includes episodes from the histories of the United States, Latin America, India, China and Japan, although these are far fewer in number.

The limitations of the book – or at least its European slant – stem in many ways from the fact that my original specialization was the history of Eastern Europe. There is an additional, objective reason, however: until recently, comparative history was practised predominantly in Europe and the greatest comparativists of the twentieth century, including Weber, Hintze, Bloch, and, later, Gerschenkron and Hroch, remained Eurocentric in their focus. My main argument, however, is that because it is a method, historical comparison is not bound to any particular place. I therefore hope that in this book, historians all over the world will be able to find powerful ideas and revealing examples of the method's use, which will spur on their own comparative studies in various areas.

The book is in three parts. In the first, I trace the change in form and function of historical comparison from Herodotus to the present day, focusing on the period from the middle of the twentieth to the beginning of the twenty-first century, which has seen a significant growth in comparative historical research worldwide. The second part focuses on the problem of method, which is directly linked to the specific features of history as a discipline. Finally, the third part is a guide to contemporary historical comparison, designed to familiarize the reader with the main themes and trends in comparative historical research.

Part I

Key milestones in the development of historical comparison

1

Comparison in history

From antiquity to the Enlightenment

Comparison has existed in history as long as history itself. This does not mean that historians in ancient times developed a particular 'comparative historical' method: before the eighteenth century there were no discernible attempts to develop a theory of comparison that could be applied to society and its history. Rather, comparison is an integral part of any thought, whether on an everyday or a scholarly level. In Herodotus' time, the boundary between these levels was highly unstable and his work is an example of how an immense collection of historical and geographical information about the entire known world of the time was formed both from ordinary curiosity – through interviews with eyewitnesses to events and inhabitants of the countries he visited – and from his own observations and travel notes. In all this, Herodotus constantly resorts to comparison, particularly when describing the customs of various peoples: the 'father of history' could equally be considered the 'father of ethnography'. It is entirely natural that in these cross-cultural comparisons as we would call them now, the customs of Hellas, with which Herodotus and his readers were very familiar, serve as a kind of standard and an essential element of comparison. Thus, he writes of the Egyptians (*Histories*, II: 79–80),

The Egyptians keep to their native customs and never adopt any from abroad. Many of these customs are interesting, especially, perhaps, the 'Linus' song. This person, under different names, is celebrated in song not only in Egypt but in Phoenicia, Cyprus, and other places, and appears to be the person whom the Greeks celebrate as Linus....

There is another point in which the Egyptians resemble one section of the Greek people – the Lacedaemonians: I mean the custom of young men stepping aside to make room for their seniors when they meet them in the street, and of getting up from their seats when older men come in. But they are unlike any of the Greeks in that they do not greet one another by name in the streets, but make a low bow and drop one hand to the knee.[1]

---

[1] Herodotus ([1954] 1966): 131, 132.

Elsewhere in his *Histories* (VI: 58–9), Herodotus compares the burial customs of the Spartans with those of the Persians.[2] At times, he is even ready to believe on the basis of outward similarity that the Greeks had borrowed certain elements of their religious rites from the 'barbarians'; he makes such an assumption – mistaken as it happens – about a Libyan origin of the clothing and shield on a statue of Pallas Athena (IV: 189).[3]

Comparison also plays an important compositional role in Herodotus' work. In the first, 'ethnographic' books of his *Histories*, it helps organize heterogeneous material on the principle of the similarity and differences of the customs described with those of the Hellenes; when he reaches the central theme of the Graeco–Persian Wars and the opposition of a small but freedom-loving people to the vast hordes of barbarians led by King Xerxes, it becomes a leitmotif of the narrative.

It should be noted that the use of comparison in ancient historiography correlates with the chosen scale of research. The setting of Herodotus' *Histories* is the entire known world of the time, and it is thus unsurprising that comparison is his preferred method. Meanwhile, Thucydides makes virtually no use of comparison. This can be explained by the limited scale of his work; Thucydides's *Histories*, one of the masterpieces of ancient Greek historical thought, is devoted entirely to the events of the Peloponnesian War, in essence being a monographic analysis of the war. But when in the Hellenistic period, a few centuries later, Polybius first undertook an attempt to write a universal history, naturally he could not avoid the need to make comparisons.

Explaining his project, Polybius writes:

> Previously the doings of the world had been, so to say, dispersed, as they were held together by no unity of initiative, results, or locality; but ever since this date [140th Olympiad, 220–216 BC – MK] history has been an organic whole, and the affairs of Italy and Libya have been interlinked with those of Greece and Asia, all leading up to one end. And this is my reason for beginning their systematic history from that date.[4]

Polybius saw the meaning of events that had taken place as lying in the establishment of Rome's dominion over the world at that time. Justifying the importance of the subject he had chosen to study, he compared the might of the Romans with earlier great powers – the Persians and Macedonians – and naturally the comparison was in favour of the new conquerors.

Not satisfied with this, in the sixth book of his *Histories*, which constituted a genuine political treatise, Polybius tried to explain the successes of the Romans through particular features of their state's structure, and to this end compared the Roman Republic with the city states of the Cretans and Spartans and with Carthage, noting the advantages of the Roman army, social customs and religion.[5] Interestingly, Polybius does not include Plato's ideal state in this comparison for the following reason:

---

[2] Herodotus ([1954] 1966): 379–80.
[3] Herodotus ([1954] 1966): 305.
[4] Polybius ([1922] 1998), I: 7, 9.
[5] Polybius ([1923] 1979), III: 367–97.

Nor again is it fair to introduce Plato's republic, which also is much belauded by some philosophers. ... Up to the present it would be just the same thing to discuss it with a view to comparison with the constitutions of Sparta, Rome, and Carthage, as to take a statue and compare it with living and breathing men. For even if the workmanship of the statue were altogether praiseworthy, the comparison of the lifeless thing with a living being would strike spectators as entirely imperfect and incongruous.[6]

As we see, even in his theoretical analyses, Polybius strongly favoured real experience of the state structures of different eras and peoples over philosophers' abstract models.

As for Roman historiography, this did not succeed in overcoming the confines of ethnocentrism: neither Livy, Tacitus nor any other great Roman historian displayed interest in the fate of any people or state other than their own. Comparison is therefore virtually non-existent in their works.

At the end of antiquity, a work appeared that was entirely constructed on historical comparisons and was at the same time utterly unhistorical in its spirit, namely Plutarch's *Parallel Lives*. Comparing the biographies of famous Greeks and Romans – twenty-two of these paired biographies are extant – Plutarch discusses which of each pair displayed more skill in his affairs and showed greater virtue. In this, the differences in the periods when each figure had lived and their respective historical contexts were entirely glossed over. This is not surprising: in Plutarch's time – from the first to the beginning of the second century AD – the view of history as a collection of edifying examples or as 'life's teacher' (*magistra vitae*) as Cicero put it, was already firmly established.

Thus, the ancient historians – principally the Greeks – used comparison readily and for various purposes: as a descriptive or rhetorical method; as an element of causal analysis (Polybius); or as an exercise in moral philosophy (Plutarch).

Historical comparison did not develop further in the medieval period; the reasons for this are found primarily in provincialism and the narrow outlook of chroniclers whose interests, like those of their readers, did not go beyond the boundaries of distinct cultural domains.[7]

The genre of universal history is revived only with the beginning of the modern era. In his treatise *Method for the Easy Comprehension of History*, the French scholar Jean Bodin (1530–96) made active use of comparison, comparing different geographical regions and inferring the characters of the peoples inhabiting them from the features of the climate, and also analysing the forms of government of states that had existed in antiquity and the recent past.

Reflections on the course of world history, including comparative observations, were widely disseminated during the Enlightenment. Many eighteenth-century thinkers were given to attempting to widen the framework of historical knowledge and overcome traditional Eurocentrism. Thus, in an article about history published

---

[6] Polybius ([1923] 1979), III: 377.
[7] See Guenée (1980): 307–14 on the fragmentation of historical knowledge in the Middle Ages into cultural and geographical domains.

in Diderot's *Encyclopédie* (1765), enumerating the growing demands on 'the modern historian' Voltaire remarked:

> The history of a foreign country should be formed on a different model to that of our own.
>
> If we compose a history of France, we are under no necessity to describe the course of the Seine and the Loire; but if we publish a history of the conquests of the Portuguese in Asia, a topographical description of the recently explored country is required. It is desirable that we should, as it were, conduct the reader by the hand round Africa, and along the coasts of Persia and India; and it is expected that we should treat with information and judgement, of manners, laws, and customs so new to Europe.[8]

Another renowned French philosopher, Montesquieu, drew examples for his *The Spirit of the Laws* (1748) not only from the history of ancient Greece and Rome and the Europe of his day but also from the history of Turkey, Persia, China and Russia.

At the end of the eighteenth century, linking natural history with the history of society's development in his main work *Outline of a Philosophical History of Humanity*, Herder compared the structure and physical characteristics of different peoples – from Greenlanders and Eskimos living near the North Pole to African tribes and the native people of America – and came to the conclusion that '*all mankind are only one and the same species*'[9] (Herder's emphasis, MK).

In subsequent parts of his book he gave a brief sketch of the history of the peoples of the Middle East and Far East, of ancient Greece and Rome, and also of medieval Europe. In Herder's opinion, the history of humanity constitutes a forward movement and a gradual spreading of humanism and culture.[10]

Commenting on the views of Enlightenment thinkers, Theodor Schieder notes that in the historiography of the Enlightenment, comparing European and non-European cultures and historical processes had the function of revealing the homogeneity of the human race in any historical incarnations. The fact that this forever homogeneous human being was none other than a person of Enlightenment culture constituted a cognitive problem of the first order, which the eighteenth-century historians themselves could not appreciate.[11] He goes on to remark accurately that, in fact, it was not a fully developed method of comparison. The latter was still used almost instinctively as a means of paradigmatic proof of some basic ideas.[12]

Indeed, eighteenth-century scholars did not as a rule ponder the legitimacy of the parallels they presented between the customs and institutions of peoples who had lived at various periods and in various parts of the world: they simply formulated patterns they had perceived in the development of society and proceeded to select a number of historical examples that in their view supported these. In particular, it was precisely

---

[8] Voltaire ([1765] 1901): 91.
[9] Herder ([1784–91] 1966): 164.
[10] Herder ([1784–91] 1966): 457–62.
[11] Schieder (1968): 198.
[12] Schieder (1968): 199.

this method of reasoning that Montesquieu used in his book *The Spirit of the Laws*, in which he put forward the theory of geographical predetermination of the customs and political systems of different countries. Alluding to the natural qualities of the body and even to experiments that he himself had carried out, Montesquieu asserted that heat has an enervating effect on people's bodies and souls, making them cowardly and apathetic:

> The peoples in hot countries are timid like old men; those in cold countries are courageous like young men.[13] Therefore, one must not be surprised that the cowardice of the peoples of hot climates has almost always made them slaves and that the courage of the peoples of cold climates has kept them free. This is an effect that derives from its natural cause.[14]

Believing that he had established the 'major reason for the weakness of Asia and the strength of Europe, for the liberty of Europe and the servitude of Asia', Montesquieu then adduces a number of historical events which he assures his readers confirm his point of view. He points out the ease with which various conquerors had subdued Asia: by his calculations, this had happened thirteen times in all, while in its entire history Europe had experienced only four 'great changes': the first was caused by the Roman conquests; the second by the barbarian invasions; the third by Charlemagne's victories; and the fourth by the Norman raids.[15]

Although similar historical examples are scattered throughout Montesquieu's book, these merely illustrate individual tenets of his social theory, which was founded on contemporary ideas about natural science.

Historical parallels play a more serious role in the Italian philosopher Vico's *Principles of the New Science about the Common Nature of Nations* (1725). If Montesquieu had compared certain historical events, as well as the law and forms of government of European and Asian countries, then Vico found analogies between whole eras of world history. He observed that people of all eras go through three successive stages – which he calls 'ages' – in their development; each age has a corresponding form of government and law, language and culture. After the 'age of the gods', when people believed that they were ruled by deities and obeyed oracles and auspices, came the 'age of the heroes', in which the supremacy of the aristocracy was established; finally, the advent of the 'age of men' saw the establishment, first, of government by the people, or 'the popular commonwealths' and then the monarchies.[16] There is a cycle of development in which all three of these stages are repeated afresh: Vico likens the era that began after the fall of Rome, when the barbarians invaded Europe to the ancient 'times of the gods', and likens the subsequent feudal period to the aristocratic 'age of the heroes' and so forth.[17]

Although comparison has a far more systematic character in Vico's book than in any other historical work published in the eighteenth century, Schieder's assessment of

---

[13] Montesquieu ([1748] 1989): 232.
[14] Montesquieu ([1748] 1989): 278.
[15] Montesquieu ([1748] 1989): 280, 281.
[16] Vico ([1744] 1968): 20.
[17] Vico ([1744] 1968): 397–415.

comparison in the Enlightenment as a whole still applies to it: for Vico, too, historical comparison mainly fulfils a paradigmatic function, since his theory is expounded in the form of axioms at the very beginning of the work, and the rich historical and cultural material that is cited thereafter is drawn on to clarify and develop these initial theses. But in the concluding part of *The New Science*, we encounter different uses of comparison when Vico, talking about the times of the 'second barbarism' which began after the fall of the Roman empire, notes that light could be shed on these 'dark' ages by what we know of the 'first barbarism' from the works of classical authors.[18] In other words, he is suggesting the possibility of filling in gaps in our knowledge using historical analogy. Subsequently, Schiller recommended the method of conclusion by analogies in his introductory speech on the meaning and function of universal history given at the University of Jena in 1789.[19]

Returning to the assessment of historical comparison in the eighteenth century, it should be emphasized that the works considered earlier belong to the category of philosophy of history. This category was conceived by Voltaire, who, as Collingwood explains, understood the term to mean simply 'critical or scientific history, a type of historical thinking in which the historian made up his mind for himself instead of repeating whatever stories he found in old books'.[20] It is not merely that thinkers such as Voltaire wished to avoid imitating the authors of numerous rehashes in their historical works, however: there was a break between the philosophically conceived 'reasoning' history – whose models have been passed down to us by eighteenth-century scholars such as Vico, Voltaire and Herder – and the work of the polymath historians of the same era, like Mabillon, de Montfaucon and Muratori, who were concerned with seeking and publishing new sources and with the development of critical methods for interpreting these. It is far from coincidental that at that time, historical comparison was practised by broadly educated philosophers and not by polymath experts in various sources. The main issue is that social science in the era was not yet distinct from history and every social theory inevitably took a historical form. This separation happened in the nineteenth century; it turned out then that with their theories of generalizing comparisons, the closest successors to Vico, Montesquieu and Herder were not historians but sociologists, philosophers, anthropologists and linguists.

In studying the fortunes of comparison in the nineteenth century, it is helpful to remember this legacy.

---

[18] Vico ([1744] 1968): 397–9, 404–5, 409–10.
[19] See Schieder (1968): 199.
[20] Collingwood ([1946] 1961): 1.

2

Historicism and the comparative method (nineteenth century to early twentieth century)

The nineteenth century was a highly successful period for the comparative method, which became firmly established in every area of the natural and social sciences and the humanities – except for history.

As an essential part of any experiment, comparison had long since become the practice in the experimental sciences such as physics and chemistry. But at the beginning of the nineteenth century comparison established itself in scientific fields where direct experiment is not possible, for example, in comparative anatomy and palaeontology, to establishing which Georges Cuvier (1769–1832) made a decisive contribution. Having established the principle of 'correlation of parts', he was able to infer the skeletal structure of dozens of kinds of fossilized animals from a few preserved bones. In their turn, Cuvier's discoveries influenced the linguists of the time, creating an impulse for the development of comparative linguistics; they also influenced the forefather of sociology, Auguste Comte, to whom sociology largely owes its present name. Inspired by the successes of comparative anatomy, Comte believed that various stages of the development of humankind could be discovered in a reproduced form among the diverse modern-day peoples of the world; he believed that a scientific reconstruction of human history could be achieved using systematic historical and ethnographical comparison.[1]

John Stuart Mill had amply demonstrated the role of comparison as the logical basis of experimental research in the natural sciences in his classical work *A System of Logic* (1843). He described four methods of induction, all of which were aimed at establishing the causes (invariable laws) of phenomena. The first method, which Mill called the method of agreement, applies to situations where two or more instances of a phenomenon display similarity in one circumstance only: this circumstance is the cause of the phenomenon concerned. The second method, to which Mill ascribed crucial importance and which he called the method of difference, is used when an instance in which the phenomenon occurs and another in which it does not occur are similar in all respects except one, which is only observed in the first instance: the single factor, by which the two instances differ from each other, indicates the cause of the phenomenon. Along with these main methods of induction, Mill indicated

---

[1] Cited in Blue (1998): 193.

two additional methods: the method of residues (if the causes of certain parts of a phenomenon have already been ascertained as a result of previous inductions, then the remaining parts will be a consequence of the remaining factors present) and the method of concomitant variations (if a certain phenomenon changes in a particular way each time that another phenomenon changes in a certain way, then a causal link exists between the phenomena).[2]

However, Mill deliberately stressed that the inductive methods developed for the experimental sciences were not suitable for the social sciences; the reasons for this included the complexity of the life of society – which has numerous factors operating within it, meaning that the same phenomenon can arise from different causes – and the impossibility of performing an artificial scientific experiment on human beings.[3]

The problem posed by Mill is directly related to the key theme of this book, the comparative study of human communities in history, and we will return to it repeatedly. But for now, it is essential to note that by the point at which *A System of Logic* was published in the 1840s, comparison was being used successfully not only in the natural sciences but also in some of the humanities – in particular, in linguistics.[4]

Franz Bopp, one of the founders of the new approach in linguistics, compared the verb forms of Sanskrit with their equivalents in the Greek, Latin, Persian and Germanic languages (1816). At the same time, Rasmus Rask explained the origin of the Icelandic language and its relationship with Germanic and other European languages (1818). The publication of Wilhelm von Humboldt's *On the Comparative Study of Languages in Connection with Various Stages of their Development* (1820), Bopp's comparative grammar of Indo-European languages (1833) and Jacob Grimm's four-volume grammar of Germanic languages (1819–37) consolidated the position of comparative historical linguistics in academia.

By the middle of the nineteenth century, evolutionary theory and the comparative method had penetrated archaeology, anthropology and the history of law – the fields of academic knowledge which bordered directly on the 'domains' of historians. The jurist Henry Maine tried to provide an overview of the origin of law and the establishment of social institutions such as the family and property among Indo-European peoples drawing on the codes of Roman law, in which he had great expertise, and comparing them with records of Irish, Germanic, Slavic and Indian laws.[5]

Maine's views on the origin of the family drew criticism from the scholar and lawyer John McLennan. Having amassed extensive ethnographical material, he disputed Maine's thesis about the primacy and universality of the patriarchal family known from the relics of Roman law. As the anthropologist E.E. Evans-Pritchard remarked a century later, McLennan's book *Primitive Marriage* (1865) was 'the first really systematic attempt to make a comparative study of primitive societies on a world-wide scale'.[6] McLennan had tried to argue – not entirely convincingly according to subsequent scholars – that

---

[2] Mill ([1843] 1874): 278–91.
[3] Mill ([1843] 1874): 324, 608–13.
[4] On the rise of comparative linguistics and the application of comparison to the studies of religions, politics and law in the nineteenth century, see Redlich (1958): 364–72.
[5] Maine ([1861] 1908).
[6] Evans-Pritchard (1963): 4.

institutions such as totemism, exogamy (the prohibition of marriages between men and women within one familial group) or marriage by abduction were characteristic of all peoples at a particular stage of their development.[7]

The comparative method was used actively by other proponents of evolutionary theory in anthropology, including Edward Burnett Tylor, the author of *Primitive Culture* (1871). In the first chapter he gives a detailed description of the research methods he had used. 'A first step in the study of civilization', Tylor thought, 'is to dissect it into details, and to classify these in their proper groups.'[8] He considered weapons, textile products, myths and rites among the entities that could be classified. Characteristically, Tylor drew an analogy between cultural phenomena and species of plants and animals studied by naturalists:

> To the ethnographer the bow and arrow is a species, the habit of flattening children's skulls is a species, the practice of reckoning numbers by tens is a species. The geographical distribution of these things, and their transmission from region to region, have to be studied as the naturalist studies the geography of his botanical and zoological species. . . . Just as the catalogue of all the species of plants and animals of a district represents its Flora and Fauna, so the list of all the items of the general life of a people represents that whole which we call its culture.[9]

Likening the work of an ethnographer to a naturalist's research was, of course, not coincidental. The scholars of the nineteenth century had inherited the approach of the natural sciences to the study of society from Enlightenment thinkers. Comte, founder of the so-called 'positive philosophy' as the ultimate stage of human intellectual development, free from religious prejudice and superfluous metaphysics (the concept of positivism itself also derives from this), believed that the new science of sociology that he proposed should be the pinnacle in a hierarchy of sciences that began with the most 'simple' disciplines, mathematics and astronomy, and ascended through physics, chemistry and biology to the most complex science of all, which concerned society. In his work *Foundations of Sociology*, Comte's successor Herbert Spencer systematically drew an analogy between biological and social bodies. The orientation of positivist social studies towards the natural sciences was evident in its methods, which included induction and comparison.

Let us, however, return to Tylor's work. In his opinion, the sets of classifications he proposed not only provided evidence of the similarity of cultural phenomena in different parts of the world but also served as an effective means of testing the reliability of sources of ethnographical information such as the accounts of travellers and missionaries.[10]

Aiming for greater rigour in the methods he used, Tylor included qualitative parameters in the comparison process for the first time. Having studied literature on

---

[7] See Evans-Pritchard (1981): 61–8 for a critical study of McLennan's work.
[8] Tylor ([1871] 1920): 7.
[9] Tylor ([1871] 1920): 8.
[10] Tylor ([1871] 1920): 6–10.

marriage customs and kinship in 350 peoples, he therefore meticulously recorded the number of known instances of each phenomenon and noted all the data obtained in tables, subsequently comparing the rows obtained with a view to discovering correlations. But his contemporaries had already noticed a number of shortcomings in the comparative method Tylor had developed. In particular, Francis Galton pointed to the desirability of information about whether there was a relationship between the tribes being compared since the same customs could simply have been replicated during descent from common ancestors – this is known as Galton's problem. Should monogamy among the Vedda in Ceylon (as it was known at the time) and monogamy in Western Europe, and monotheism in Islam and the monotheism of pygmy tribes, be considered phenomena of the same order?[11] At the very end of the nineteenth century, Franz Boas made a general criticism of the evolutionary approach and the comparative method that was being applied to construct a universal scheme of cultural development.[12]

If historians of law and anthropology began to introduce the comparative method to the study of humanity's earliest history, sociologists, representatives of a new, independent discipline that had arisen in the nineteenth century used the method to study the society of their day. Comte and Spencer devoted a large part of their work to comparison.[13] Émile Durkheim, who continued the same positivist tradition and founded the French School of Sociology took the comparative method to an even higher level, calling it 'the only one that suited to sociology'[14] and said the following of the discipline itself: 'Comparative sociology is not a particular branch of sociology; it is sociology itself, in so far as it ceases to be purely descriptive and aspires to account for facts.'[15]

Durkheim formulated several rules for applying the comparative method in social science. He considered the purpose of comparison to be to identify the causes of observed phenomena. Of Mill's four methods of induction (Durkheim categorically rejected Mill's thesis about the unsuitability of these methods for studying the life of society), he had a strong preference for the method of concomitant variations, seeing in it 'the instrument par excellence of sociological research'.[16] At the same time, Durkheim cautioned against simple illustration of hypotheses using more or less numerous examples:

> It is necessary to compare not isolated variations but a series of systematically arranged variations of wide range, in which the individual items tie up with one another in as continuous a gradation as possible. For the variations of a phenomenon permit inductive generalizations only if they reveal clearly the

---

[11] For a detailed analysis of the merits and shortcomings of Tylor's comparative method, see Evans-Pritchard (1963): 8–10; Evans-Pritchard (1981): 91–4.
[12] Boas ([1896] 2006).
[13] See Evans-Pritchard (1963): 6–7 regarding Spencer's contribution to the development of the comparative method.
[14] Durkheim ([1895] 1966): 125.
[15] Durkheim ([1895] 1966): 139.
[16] Durkheim ([1895] 1966): 132.

manner in which they develop under given circumstances. There must be between them the same sequence as between the different stages of a given natural evolution; and, in addition, the evolutionary trend that they establish ought to be sufficiently extended as to lend some certainty to its direction.[17]

There is an overt orientation in this quotation towards the canons of the natural sciences, on whose model and likeness the new science of society was founded – hence also the preoccupation with deducing new laws governing the observed phenomena of the life of society. The evolutionary approach that was characteristic of Durkheim's sociological theory had the same origin. Therefore, he particularly recommended 'to consider the societies compared at the same period of their development', contrasting 'young societies' with those that were in a state of decline.[18]

Thus, by the end of the nineteenth century, the humanities and social sciences had already accumulated a great deal of experience of practical comparative research and also a certain stock of theoretical generalizations on the possibilities and limitations of the use of the comparative method. But history, which had gone through a process of professionalization and institutionalization in the nineteenth century, was the one outcrop among these swirling comparative currents that remained impervious to the prevailing approach in academic thought.

Examples of comparison can, of course, be found in the works of major historians of the nineteenth century, in particular those of Leopold von Ranke.[19] This is understandable since as mentioned earlier, no kind of knowledge is possible without comparison, academic least of all. But the problem lies in the fact that European historians of the nineteenth century did not attach importance to comparison, did not use it systematically or purposefully in their research and, in contrast to their counterparts in other disciplines, did not try to develop a particular comparative method. There are also well-known cases of influential scholars explicitly rejecting comparative methods in history, seeing in them superficial analogies leading to dubious and short-lived conclusions.[20]

Textbooks on methodology, which began to appear in the second half of the nineteenth century, are clear evidence of the academic priorities of the professional history community. One of the first examples of the genre are the lectures of Johann Gustav Droysen, entitled *an Encyclopaedia and Methodology of History*, which were given in the 1850s but published only in 1937. The focus in the methodology section is on the characterization of sources and critical methods of working with them, but under the 'Pragmatic Interpretation' heading, there is a cursory examination of the possibility of inferences by analogy, in the spirit of the analogical comparison that Schiller had recommended back in the eighteenth century. As an example, Droysen cites the disappearance of the peasantry in England which (in a hypothetical case

---

[17] Durkheim ([1895] 1966): 135–6.
[18] Durkheim ([1895] 1966): 139–40.
[19] For examples of comparison in Ranke's works, see Schieder (1968): 207–9.
[20] Thus, Georg von Below criticized the comparative method, to which a hypothesis concerning the universal distribution of communal land ownership that he had rejected owed its existence (cited in Schieder (1968): 203–4).

of lack of evidence) could have been inferred by analogy with agrarian relations in Mecklenburg, Brandenburg and Pomerania, where landlords had also destroyed the peasant class. In this case, Droysen concludes, the comparative method that we use to explain a partially known phenomenon is so clear that a mere description of analogies will be enough to prove the correctness of equivalence.[21]

Later too, until the beginning of the twentieth century, the comparative method failed to attract serious attention from German historians. In his popular 1908 textbook *An Introduction to Historical Science,* Bernheim readily mentions comparison as an essential method for examining sources[22] but at the same time cautions against the comparative method in a wider sense, pointing to the danger of analogies (here Bernheim refers to works of comparative ethnology), which often led to incorrect conclusions.[23]

The comparative method also does not receive particular attention in English and French textbooks on the methodology of history. Thus, the greater part of Oxford professor Edward Freeman's *Methods of Historical Study,* a course of lectures published in 1886, is taken up with a description of ancient and medieval sources, but there is no mention at all of comparative history.[24] Paradoxically, however, Freeman himself had previously published a lecture cycle entitled *Comparative Politics*[25] – thanks to which he is now considered one of the founders of comparative political science. Clearly, the academic interests of individual historians can be very wide but in textbooks on their specialism they are able to include only those methods that are recognized within the academic community of the time.

A similar situation occurred at the very end of the nineteenth century. In 1890 the French historian Charles-Victor Langlois published a short article in *The English Historical Review* in which he called on his fellow English and French medievalists to undertake a comparative study of the medieval history of the two countries.[26] Interestingly, while Langlois was trying to convince historians of the value of comparison, British anthropologists, as indicated earlier, were actively discussing the quantitative method for comparative analysis of the marriage customs of different peoples proposed by Tylor. The contrast in the attitude of the two disciplines to comparison is evident. But even more telling is the fact that when eight years later in 1898 Langlois published the textbook *Introduction to the Study of History* with Charles Seignobos, no trace remained of his earlier optimism about the comparative method.

The authors of this textbook, which quickly achieved widespread popularity in France and beyond, mention the comparative method only once, when discussing problems of causal analysis of historical events, and even then, the term is in quotation marks.

Langlois and Seignobos consider the comparison of parallel rows of facts with a view to studying the development of a particular phenomenon (such as a custom,

---

[21] Droysen (1937): 160.
[22] Bernheim (1908): 372, 390, 393, 401.
[23] Bernheim (1908): 609–13.
[24] Freeman (1886).
[25] Freeman (1873).
[26] Langlois (1890).

institution, belief or law) and identifying its cause 'the classical procedure of the natural sciences' that can be used in history. According to them, this is how comparative linguistics, mythology and law began. They also mention attempts to increase the accuracy of comparison with the help of a statistical method and similarity tables, evidently alluding to Tylor's experiments. However, the authors express doubt about the ability of this method to yield results. In their words, 'The defect of all such methods is that they apply to abstract and partly arbitrary notions, sometimes to merely verbal resemblances, and do not rest on a knowledge of the whole of the conditions under which the facts occur.'[27] In other words, Langlois and Seignobos were reproaching the proponents of comparison in the humanities and social sciences for ignoring the context from which the facts being compared were drawn.

As for larger-scale comparisons, in which societies as a whole rather than particular phenomena are subjected to comparison, Langlois and Seignobos rejected this research method outright:

> We can conceive a more concrete method which, instead of comparing fragments, should compare wholes, that is entire societies, either the same society at different stages of its evolution (England in the sixteenth, and again in the nineteenth century), or the general evolution of several societies, contemporary with each other (England and France), or existing at different epochs (Rome and England). Such a method might be useful negatively, for the purpose of ascertaining that a given fact is not the necessary effect of another, since they are not always found together (for example, the emancipation of women and Christianity). But positive results are hardly to be expected of it, for the concomitance of two facts in several series does not show whether one is the cause of the other, or whether both are joint effects of a single cause.[28]

As can be seen, by the end of the nineteenth century, the position of leading French historians in relation to the comparative method was just as sceptical as that of their German counterparts.

The state of affairs in nineteenth-century academic history described earlier can be viewed as a direct continuation of certain tendencies that had existed since the Enlightenment. As shown in the previous chapter, a sharp division appeared even then between the 'philosophy of history' of Voltaire and other Enlightenment thinkers on the one hand and the factual history of the polymath experts on the other. Having seen an important claim for the scientific approach of their activities in the 'critical method' of source analysis, the historians of the nineteenth century acted as the direct descendants of the polymaths. But practitioners of the social sciences that developed in the nineteenth century – primarily in sociology and anthropology – inherited the methods of comparison and a drive towards generalization from the philosophers of the eighteenth century.

---

[27] Langlois and Seignobos ([1898] 1912): 291.
[28] Langlois and Seignobos ([1898] 1912): 291.

A cult of sources blended with the cult of the nation state in historians' world view. To many scholars, the political borders of the time seemed natural frameworks for writing history, and tracing the fates of their own state from roots deep in history to the present day appeared a topical and noble enterprise. Multi-volume narratives on national history therefore appeared, such as Jules Michelet's *History of France*, Soloviev's *History of Russia from Ancient Times* and Droysen's *History of Prussian Politics*. Nationalism was manifestly in opposition to the Enlightenment idea of the unity of the human race and its history; it facilitated not so much comparison of the historical experience of various countries, as the development of ideas about a 'Sonderweg' or special mission or path of the very people to which the historian writing about it belonged.

Both of the tendencies mentioned operated simultaneously, creating a cumulative effect, which was not conducive to the development of comparative historical research. The practice that had been developed by the middle of the nineteenth century of writing history by following sources – preferably archival ones – and submitting them to critical examination demanded many years of painstaking studies; this made increasing the geographical scope of research extremely difficult though not impossible, as Ranke's example demonstrates. It is no coincidence that in his article of 1890, discussing what he believed had hindered the comparative method from being more widely used in medieval and modern history, Langlois particularly stressed the fact that only a few scholars had been able to master the history of neighbouring countries as well as that of their own.[29] However, the majority of historians lacked even the stimulus for such extraordinary efforts, since the dominant nationalistic discourse legitimized limiting research interests to the boundaries of one country. If one adds the dominance of political history to this, with its characteristic preoccupation with the course of events and the deeds of great statesmen, then it becomes clear that the historiographical context of the nineteenth century was not conducive to the success of the comparative method among historians.

The historical world view that developed in the nineteenth century acquired the general name of 'historicism' at the beginning of the following century. Germany is commonly seen as the birthplace of this trend in historical thought, but its signs are also evident in other European countries. Leopold von Ranke characterized the essence of historicism very well although he did not use this term: each period, as his famous aphorism put it, 'was immediate to God' and therefore required detailed investigation.[30]

The issue was thus the recognition of the independent meaning and uniqueness of each period and each historical phenomenon. In effect, therefore, evolution, which in the nineteenth century had been a symbol not just of natural science but also of the so-called positive social sciences that were influenced by it, was now questioned. The establishment of historicism as a kind of professional ideology for historians occurred precisely in order to counter a perceived threat that the humanities (*Geisteswissenschaften*) would be penetrated by the alien principles of natural science.

---

[29] Langlois (1890): 260–1.
[30] Cited in Burrow (2009): 461.

The theoretical basis for distinctions between the scientific method and methods of historical research was given in the works of Wilhelm Windelband and Heinrich Rickert, Neo-Kantian philosophers of the Baden School, also known as the Freiburg School after the university at which they taught. Windelband proposed classifying the sciences not by their subject ('nature' or 'spirit') but by method. He called the method of the natural sciences 'nomothetic', that is, literally 'establishing laws' and the method of sciences concerned with culture, including history, 'idiographic' from the Greek 'ἴδιος – *particular, original* – and γράφω – *write*. The idiographic method is focused on a description of the particular characteristics of historical facts, identified within the discipline as significant on the basis of a 'relation to value' (*Wertbeziehung*) procedure. Rickert subsequently developed these proposals. He explained that the fundamental divide between the sciences corresponds to how concepts are developed: since the natural sciences mainly use general concepts, their method is generalizing but historians, who deal with unique phenomena, require a particularizing method. In this, Rickert stressed that this distinction between methods is logical in character and does not depend on the nature of the objects of study. Thus, for example, psychology relates to the generalizing sciences just as physics does, since it uses general concepts.[31]

Rickert identified comparison with the natural sciences; using the example of botany he attempted to demonstrate how the use of comparison reveals the essential from among the existing diversity of natural forms.[32] He did not view this methodological approach as even capable of being used in history, however: from the point of view of an 'idealistic' theory of history as a science of values devoid of any material forms, comparison of individual facts simply did not make sense.

Although Rickert wrote much about the methodology of the natural sciences, his ideas can hardly be said to have influenced the development of physics or biology, but they were clearly not addressed to naturalists either. The Baden School philosophers' aim was to justify the logical independence of history as a science, and their theories attracted much support in the humanities. Additionally, the division of sciences into nomothetical (generalizing) and idiographic (particularizing) drew a 'demarcation line' between history and social sciences such as sociology and anthropology with which they had until recently been grouped. In doing this, the Neo-Kantians essentially legitimized differences that had by then effectively developed in academic aims and practices. The sociologists, whose discipline had been assigned to the nomothetical category, were now able to look for laws governing human society with redoubled energy and historians, drawing on Windelband and Rickert's authority, had every justification for writing in their usual manner, avoiding wide generalizations. The boundary between history and other disciplines concerned with society and asserted by the Baden philosophers to be the boundary between different methods was long considered valid, and it was only in the 1960s and 1970s that some academics began to have doubts about its methodological nature.

Having received powerful support from the Neo-Kantians, historicism as represented by the philosopher and theologian Ernst Troeltsch adopted an openly

---

[31] Rickert (1926): 38, 53–4.
[32] Rickert (1896): 136.

hostile position to the comparative method. In his book *Historicism and Its Problems* (1922), published after the First World War, Troeltsch asserted that by moving away from the focus on humankind and on a universal law of human development one would find relief from an overwhelming dominance of comparison in history. This dominance, in his opinion, constituted a threat of imposing upon us, along with 'an art history of all nations and times', a comparative art along with 'the comparative history of law', a comparative law, etc.[33]

Taking a position of extreme historical individualism, he came out decisively as an opponent of standard 'comparative' concepts like this.

Troeltsch considered the idea that an absolute system of values could be presented as a sum of individual values and that the history of each of these could be studied separately a mistake. Equally mistaken seemed to him the idea that the historical development of humankind should be exhaustively traced in all its aspects, in the belief that each individual value was significant for all human beings. In fact, in his opinion, each cultural sphere contained a vital and cohesive system of values that could be individually understood only in relation to the whole. For him, comparison meant taking a value out of this whole and placing it in various cultural spheres that were alien to it on the basis of a comparison of forms. 'Unlike comparative anatomy or zoology, history is not basically and systematically a comparative discipline', as Troeltsch summed it up.[34]

However, he was prepared to make an exception for one form of comparison, which Wilhelm Dilthey had earlier called 'particularizing comparison':[35] 'Comparison can really help to better understand some peculiarities', wrote Troeltsch, 'and is therefore rightly applicable in the so called humanities'; but in history it always remains only comparison of separate cases, a juxtaposition of formations contacting or struggling with each other, which should never be detached from their common cultural basis.[36]

Thus, although historicism was a serious obstacle for the development of historical comparison (in Germany at least), it was not able to halt it entirely. As it turned out, the only form of historical comparison that was compatible with historicism was particularizing comparison – and it was precisely this form that the great German comparativists of the beginning of the twentieth century, Max Weber and Otto Hintze, chose for their studies.

---

[33] Troeltsch (1922): 190.
[34] Troeltsch (1922): 191.
[35] Quoted in Schieder (1968): 206–7.
[36] Troeltsch (1922): 191.

3

The lessons of Max Weber and Marc Bloch

In the first decades of the twentieth century, historical comparison was a series of individual experiments with few connections between them; moreover, each new author who addressed the topic considered it his or her duty to start anew and explain the advantages of the comparative method to his or her colleagues.

Thus, in France, in the thirty years following the publication of Langlois's 1890 article, only two works devoted to the comparative method in history were published; here I am relying on the observations of Benjamin Kedar, who is responsible for the most detailed overview to date of comparative historical literature published in the twentieth century. The first of these works was the publication in 1907 of the introductory lecture from Gustave Glotz's course on ancient Greek history at the Sorbonne. Like Langlois, Glotz noted with regret that historians rarely use the comparative method, despite its value in revealing 'historical laws' and its contribution to achievements in several disciplines. He called for an abandonment of comparison of great events in favour of careful study of the institutions, customs and legal principles of various societies, the aim of which must be to identify laws regulating social development. Glotz advised comparing societies that were related to each other or were at the same stage of development – Durkheim's influence is noticeable here. As far as filling in gaps in the history of one society using facts known from the history of another was concerned, Glotz advised exercising utmost caution.[1]

The philosopher Henri Berr hailed Glotz's intervention, believing that it had marked out a path for the integration of history and sociology. He welcomed Glotz's advocacy of the comparative method as a means of revealing laws empirically, without *a priori* ideas.[2] It was not surprising when a few years later a lengthy article by Louis Davillé on the theme of comparison in history – in essence an entire treatise – appeared in the *Journal of Historical Synthesis*, published by Berr. In the beginning, Davillé dwelt in detail on the use of the comparative method in the natural and social sciences, liberally citing scholars including Comte, Durkheim, Tarde and Poincaré; the rest of the article was taken up with an analysis of the role of comparison at various stages in the critique of historical sources.[3] There was nothing new in this, however: the use of comparison in various processes for evaluating sources had been described in detail by Ernst Bernheim in the textbook mentioned earlier – characteristically, Davillé does

---

[1] Cited in Kedar (2009b): 3.
[2] See Kedar (2009b): 4.
[3] Davillé (1913–14).

not make reference to him or other German historians. It was customary at the time, however, to call the entirety of methods used to analyse sources the 'critical method' – rather than the comparative method – or simply 'criticism', which was subdivided into 'external' and 'internal'.[4] By the end of the nineteenth century, influenced in part by sociology, the comparative method in history had come to be understood as meaning the comparison of societies or their individual institutions. Langlois, Bernheim, Glotz and other influential scholars of the time understood comparison in history in precisely this sense.

If French historians at the beginning of the twentieth century interpreted the comparative method in the spirit of positivism and even – in Glotz's case – linked it to hopes for the discovery of laws about the development of society, their German counterparts, influenced by the historicism that held sway in Germany, developed a completely different approach to comparative research. A decisive contribution to its formation was made by the outstanding sociologist and historian Max Weber (1864–1920).

Whatever Weber wrote about – from the origin of modern capitalism to world religions, the city or types of legitimate rule – his main interest was in the distinctiveness of Western civilization. Why exactly was it that science, art and industrial capitalism, phenomena that had gone on to acquire universal importance, had developed specifically in the West? This is the question that Weber poses in his articles on the sociology of religion. He saw the key to the problem in a process of rationalization, and therefore tried above all to understand the particular rationality that characterized Western culture. He resorts to comparison in this, contrasting the link between business ethics and religion in Europe and the countries of the East. Weber's view is Eurocentric and he does not conceal this. In a similar fashion, Weber bases his research about the city on the contrast between the cities of medieval Europe and Asian city populations and concluded that only European cities could be called cities in the full sense of the word – that is, urban communities with particular rights.[5]

Thus, the main method that Weber used in his historical and sociological research was a contrasting, particularizing comparison. Additionally, typology played an important part in his constructs. Weber introduces the concept of the 'ideal type', which in his words is a mental image, 'a *utopia* which has been arrived at by the analytical accentuation of certain elements of reality'.[6] (Here and later, the italicization is Weber's.) It is utopia in the sense that 'in its conceptual purity, this mental construct cannot be found anywhere in reality'. 'Historical research', Weber continues, 'faces the task of determining in each individual case, the extent to which this ideal-construct approximates to or diverges from reality'.[7] For Weber, examples of these ideal constructs include the medieval city economy, trade and the abstract model of the capitalist economy.

[4] See Langlois and Seignobos ([1898] 1912): 63–208.
[5] Weber ([1956] 1978), 2: 1226, 1236.
[6] Weber ([1904] 1949): 90.
[7] Weber ([1904] 1949): 90.

Weber deliberately emphasized that ideal types are neither a representation of reality nor some sort of 'model' in the sense of ultimate perfection. Weber's statement that 'the construction of abstract ideal-types recommends itself not as an end but as a *means*'[8] is methodologically important. For Weber, the goal remained comprehension of 'the unique individual character of cultural phenomena',[9] and he therefore considered 'the ideal type . . . as a mental construct for the scrutiny and systematic characterization of individual concrete patterns which are significant in their uniqueness, such as Christianity, capitalism, etc.'.[10]

Otto Hintze (1861–1940) also primarily used the particularizing form of comparison and remained within a Eurocentric perspective. He borrowed the ideal-type theory of forming concepts from Weber and used it actively.

Hintze became interested in the comparative history of European political institutions as early as the end of the nineteenth century. He published several articles on the topic just before the First World War, including 'the Origins of the Modern Ministerial System' (1908) and 'the Commissary and his Significance in General Administrative History' (1910). In the 1920s he worked on a book on comparative institutional history, known in Germany as *Verfassungsgeschichte* (constitutional history), but this was not published and the manuscript was subsequently lost. Nevertheless, articles that he published – including 'The Nature and Spread of Feudalism' (1929) and 'Typology of the Forms of the Estates System in Western Europe' (1930), and 'The Preconditions of Representative Government in the Context of World History' (1931) – exerted a substantial influence on the subsequent development of historical (and sociological) comparison and are still cited today.

In these works, Hintze uses Weber's concept of the ideal type. He examines feudalism in particular as one such ideal-type construction. Using Western European material in an article devoted to this, Hintze starts by identifying the factors determining the phenomenon of feudalism itself as follows:

1) Military – the emergence of a trained, professional military class linked by oath to a ruler and occupying a privileged position;
2) Socio-economic – the formation of a 'landowner and peasant' type of economy, providing this privileged military class with an income in the form of rent;
3) Political – the dominant position of the military nobility locally and its determining influence or even absolute power within the state.[11]

Hintze believed that one could only talk about feudalism in the full sense where all three of these factors were present, as in the successor states of the Carolingian Empire, and not where only one or another of them – or merely their beginnings – were found.[12] Such beginnings, he believes, are found in all times and among many peoples. For example, in antiquity land was distributed as a reward for military service

---

[8] Weber ([1904] 1949): 92.
[9] Weber ([1904] 1949): 101.
[10] Weber ([1904] 1949): 99–100.
[11] Hintze ([1929] 1970): 94–5.
[12] Hintze ([1929] 1970): 95–6.

(a similar arrangement was contained in the laws of Hammurabi in particular), but the particular connection of vassalage and benefice was utterly alien to antiquity.

Comparing the model of Western European feudalism that he proposed with data about socio-economic development and the political arrangement of societies in other parts of the world, Hintze concludes that all the factors noted earlier were found together in only three places: Muscovite Rus'; Islamic countries (primarily Turkey); and Japan.[13] But while acknowledging their typological similarity with feudalism under the Franks, Hintze also notes important special characteristics present in each of these versions of feudalism – in particular, the Russian estate like Arabic *iqta'* but unlike the Frankish fiefdom of his native land had a 'ministerial' rather than a chivalric character.[14]

In Hintze's opinion, identifying versions of feudalism in different countries allows us to understand the essence of the feudalization process as a whole: feudalism, he claims, is not the result of immanent national development; it is generated by 'a global historical conjuncture that occurs only in greater cultural spheres'.[15] That is, apart from the social process – the transition from tribal to state organization – a cultural factor was also operating in all the examples studied; this was the contact between the Franks and the fading Roman empire; the eastern Slavs and Byzantium; the Turks and the Sasanians; and the Japanese and the great Chinese cultures. The main conclusion of his studies is therefore that feudalism was not a universal phenomenon but rather a deviation from a 'normal' path of development.[16]

Hintze also used methods of typification and particularizing comparison when studying the phenomenon of medieval Estates, the prototype of the modern system of representation. Having examined this phenomenon in a worldwide historical perspective, he concluded that it is only inherent in the Christian West. Hintze explained the rise of representative forms of rule by a unique combination of several factors: European feudalism, the influence of Catholic Church through ecumenical councils and theology and characteristics of the emergence of states in Europe.[17]

In a special article Hintze also tried to explain the existence of two basic types of European representative institutions in the Middle Ages and the Early Modern period – the bicameral type, like the English parliament, and the three-chamber type, like the French Estates-General – 'genetically' and geographically: the first type was earlier in origin and arose at the edges of the Carolingian Empire, and the second was formed later and was characteristic primarily of areas at the former nucleus of this empire, France and Western Germany.[18]

The 1920s and the early 1930s, when Hintze published the articles mentioned, marked a period of growth in comparative historical research throughout Europe. Contemporary historians rightly link this surge in interest in historical comparison

---

[13] Hintze ([1929] 1970) 99.
[14] Hintze ([1929] 1970): 110.
[15] Hintze ([1929] 1970): 100.
[16] Hintze ([1929] 1970): 101, 117–18.
[17] Hintze ([1931] 1975).
[18] Hintze ([1930] 1970).

to the influence of the First World War.[19] Indeed, the Great War of 1914–18 starkly demonstrated the interdependence of the world at the time. The threat that extreme nationalism posed to the humane values of civilization, including academia, was equally evident.

The Belgian historian Henri Pirenne (1862–1935), who was deported to Germany from Ghent in 1916 for disobeying the occupying powers observed with sadness that German historians took an active part in propaganda campaigns. After the war, Pirenne became committed to overcoming the narrow boundaries of national history and returning to the worldwide perspective that had dominated from antiquity to the Enlightenment. To achieve this and return history to a proper academic status, free of constraint by the interests of politicians and the military, he believed it was necessary to use the comparative method. This was the leitmotif of the welcoming address entitled 'On the Comparative Method in History', with which Pirenne addressed the audience at the Fifth International Congress of Historical Sciences in Brussels on 9 April 1923. 'By using comparison and only by using comparison', he said, 'we can arrive at scholarly knowledge. We will never achieve that if we confine ourselves to the limits of national history.'[20]

In contrast to Weber, Hintze and Bloch – who will be discussed later – Pirenne did not make a particular contribution to the development of a comparative historical method and his own use of comparison sometimes took the form of superficial analogies.[21] But, nevertheless, as Kedar rightly noted,[22] he was able to attract his colleagues' attention to the comparative method with his speech at the congress and thereby undoubtedly facilitated the development of comparative research. In France, Pirenne's speech about the use of comparison in history drew an immediate response from Berr and the economic historian Henri Sée; in Belgium itself, with the active involvement of Pirenne's follower Alexandre Eck, the Jean Bodin Society of Comparative History of Institutions was founded in 1935.[23]

The First World War did not merely stimulate historians to overcome national frameworks and use the comparative method more actively, but also made very wide historical parallels topical. Tragic experience insistently demanded philosophical reinterpretation of the entire previous course of world history. Oswald Spengler

---

[19] Haupt (2001): 2398.
[20] Cited in Kedar (2009b): 4–5.
[21] Thus, in the book 'Medieval Towns and the Revival of Trade' (1925), Pirenne adduces a parallel with the consequences of the nomad raids on Rus' in the eleventh century: 'The invasion of these barbarians (the Pechenegs – MK) along the shores of the Caspian and the Black Seas brought in their train consequences identical to those which the invasion of Islam in the Mediterranean had had for Western Europe in the eighth century' (Pirenne ([1925] 1969): 53). In both episodes the intrusions severed market ties, the towns emptied and the population turned to agriculture. 'So, in both cases', the historian concludes, 'the same causes produced the same effects. But they did not produce them at the same date. Russia lived by trade at an era when the Carolingian Empire knew only the demesnial régime, and she in turn inaugurated this form of government at the very moment when Western Europe, having found new markets, broke away from it' (Pirenne ([1925] 1969): 54). Pirenne claims to have proved, 'by the example of Russia, the theory that the economy of the Carolingian era was not the result of the internal evolution but must be attributed to the closing of the Mediterranean by Islam' (Pirenne ([1925] 1969): 55).
[22] Kedar (2009b): 5.
[23] For more details, see Kedar (2009b): 5–6, 12.

undertook such an attempt at a radical review of ideas that had developed about the past in his celebrated book *The Decline of the West* (1918–22).

Spengler broke decisively with the usual linear view of history and returned to the models of cyclical development that had existed in antiquity, for example with Polybius, and in the Enlightenment, particularly with Vico, and which had enjoyed renewed popularity at the cusp of the nineteenth and twentieth centuries: a version of cyclical history had been proposed in particular by the Russian philosopher Nikolai Danilevskii. Spengler also tried to break free of the fetters of Eurocentrism: 'Of what significance to us, then', he asks rhetorically, 'are conceptions and purviews that they (philosophers and historians – MK) put before us as universally valid, when in truth their furthest horizon does not extend beyond the intellectual atmosphere of Western Man?'[24] However, he was not properly able to overcome Eurocentrism: for all his erudition, Spengler possessed only a very fragmentary knowledge of the history of non-European peoples.

For Spengler, the real figures in history were cultures, each of which had its own 'spirit' and its own character. He counted eight such cultures in all – Egyptian, Babylonian, Chinese, Indian, Classical, Byzantine-Arabic, Western European and Mayan. Likening cultures to the human body, Spengler believed that each went through exactly the same stages in its development, from conception to its decline and demise. Spengler identified this last stage with civilization. Borrowing the concept of 'homology' from biology (i.e. morphological equivalence as distinct from 'analogy' which denoted similarities in the functions of organs of different origin), he applied the concept to the study of historical phenomena. Spengler thus identified the following 'homologous' entities: ancient sculpture and Western instrumental music; the pyramids of the Egyptian Fourth Dynasty and gothic cathedrals; Indian Buddhism and Roman scepticism; and the ancient Greek Dionysian movement and the Renaissance.[25] From here, he deduced the concept of 'contemporaneity' to describe phenomena or individuals occupying an identical position and having a corresponding significance in their culture, and therefore considered Pythagoras and Descartes; Archimedes and Gauss; and Polykleitos and Bach 'contemporaries'.[26] Spengler found a correspondence between his own era of imperialism and world war and the civilization of ancient Rome, which was set on a path of conquest and on this basis prophesied the inevitable decline of the Western world.[27]

The roaring success of Spengler's book with the general reading public contrasted with its manifest rejection by historians. Thus, Collingwood criticized it for its manifestly positivist character, its naturalistic view of history and its claims to predicting the future, as well as its plain distortion of facts.[28] Lucien Febvre, one of the founders of *Annales* School wrote with undisguised irony about the new 'prophet' – a

---

[24] Spengler ([1918] 1927): 22.
[25] Spengler ([1918] 1927): 111.
[26] Spengler ([1918] 1927): 112.
[27] Spengler ([1918] 1927): 36–40 and Table III at the end of the volume.
[28] Collingwood ([1946] 1961): 181–3.

'crafty and captivating gasbag', who had managed to guess the tastes of the bourgeoisie in a Germany gripped by post-war turmoil.[29]

It might be possible to detect a haughty reaction on the part of professionals, angered by a dilletante's intrusion into their area of expertise, in historians' lack of particular interest in Spengler and the 'morphological' comparative method he proposed. But when the first three volumes of Arnold Toynbee's main work *The Study of History* were published in 1934, which developed some of Spengler's ideas, these also received a critical reaction from a number of his authoritative colleagues although they received a more thorough critique.

A historian of tremendous erudition, Toynbee (1889–1975) undertook a large-scale comparison of all the civilizations that supposedly had ever existed in history, which his original calculations put at twenty-one; later, in the concluding twelfth volume of his work (1961), he reduced their number to thirteen. Toynbee shared with Spengler the idea of stages (genesis, growth, breakdown and collapse) that civilizations go through during their development and also of the naturalistic principle of the 'contemporaneity' of all the societies studied. In trying to substantiate the possibility of comparing civilizations that had long since disappeared with those existing now, Toynbee referred to the biological concept of a species which was stable over several generations. Since there were no more than three links in the chain joining contemporary civilizations to the societies that preceded them (for instance, Minoan-Hellenic-Western or Minoan-Hellenic-Orthodox), Toynbee identified them as one and the same 'species':

> The fact that, in our survey of civilizations, we have found in no case a higher number of successive generations than three means that this species is very young in terms of its own time-scale. Moreover, its absolute age up to date is very short compared with that of the sister species of the primitive societies, which is coeval with man himself and has therefore existed, to take an average estimate, for three hundred thousand years. If by history we meant the whole period of man's life on Earth we should find that the period producing civilizations . . . covers only two per cent of it, one-fiftieth part of the lifetime of mankind. Our civilizations may, then, be granted to be sufficiently contemporaneous with one another for our purpose.[30]

Having made civilizations units of comparative analysis, Toynbee attempted to establish the causes of their origin, growth and collapse. In explaining the genesis of civilizations, he made active use of categories that he proposed of 'challenge and response', which involved a society's response to an unfavourable natural environment (such as a harsh climate or poor soil) and the hostility of neighbours (such as invasions and external pressure). All these 'challenges' were stimuli for the development of a corresponding

---

[29] Febvre (1936): 574–81.
[30] Toynbee ([1946] 1987): 42.

society.³¹ In a similar way, Toynbee introduces the concept of 'withdrawal and return' to explain the mechanism by which civilizations grow.³²

These large-scale comparisons, bold generalizations and effective metaphors did not impress the major historians of the time. Having assessed Toynbee's 'a very fine historical sense', which was shown 'in the detail' of his work,³³ Collingwood criticized the 'main principles' of Toynbee's work, seeing in it 'a restatement of historical positivism'.³⁴ 'His whole scheme', Collingwood observes, 'is really a scheme of pigeon-holes elaborately arranged and labelled, into which ready-made historical facts can be put.'³⁵

In his 1936 review of the first volumes of *The Study of History*, Febvre also noted the carefully numbered civilizations.³⁶ His 'sentence' on this work was even more severe than Collingwood's appraisal. On the subject of Toynbee's discovery of laws such as 'challenge and response' and 'withdrawal and return', Febvre writes, 'And this time we historians say: it is a philosophical formula. . . . We will not discuss it. . . . There is nothing for us, nothing related to our work, our concerns and our methods.'³⁷ Toynbee's comparative method was also unacceptable for Febvre, although he by no means rejected comparison itself; it was simply that the method of comparison that Toynbee had selected did not suit him: Febvre made it clear that he was in favour of comparison in an explicit, focused form that was appropriate for the practical needs of historians but not of comparison that involved abstruse reflection.³⁸

Febvre therefore drew a line between philosophical and professional historical knowledge of the past. In his opinion historical comparison is needed not for deducing abstract 'laws' but for obtaining new knowledge. It seems that it is precisely the completeness of the systems built by Spengler and especially by Toynbee (Collingwood's metaphor of 'pigeon-holes elaborately arranged and labelled' into which 'ready-made historical facts' are fitted is apt), which ultimately made this line of comparison a dead end. The discovery of 'laws' of history in essence makes further empirical research redundant; therefore, historians avoid overly wide generalizing comparisons: as Febvre puts it, this would leave them with 'nothing to live on'.

Historians' attitude to Toynbee's comparative method did not change in subsequent decades. In the mid-1960s, after the publication of the concluding volume of *The Study of History*, Schieder noted that Toynbee, having plucked civilization from the stream of historical time had turned it into 'an almost material object of research' imbued with a certain 'corporality': 'when cultures are turned in this way into compared units', Schieder continued, 'they seem to be sterile objects created in the science laboratory, with which any experiment can be conducted.' They can be compared any way and above all, by a generalizing method.³⁹

---

[31] Toynbee ([1946] 1987): 88–139.
[32] Toynbee ([1946] 1987): 217–40.
[33] Collingwood ([1946] 1961): 164.
[34] Collingwood ([1946] 1961): 161.
[35] Collingwood ([1946] 1961): 163.
[36] Febvre (1936): 591.
[37] Febvre (1936): 594.
[38] Febvre (1936): 598.
[39] Schieder (1968): 214.

A quarter of a century later, at the beginning of the 1990s, referring to Toynbee's famous work in connection with the problems of comparison in history, Peter Burke underlined its inherent reductionism (in order to make a comparison of civilizations possible, each of them was reduced to a small selection of features), and also the lack of a suitable conceptual apparatus for such an ambitious project: the categories Toynbee invented ('challenge and response', 'withdrawal and return', and so on) were inadequate for fulfilling the grandiose task he had set himself.[40]

But let us return to the period between the two world wars when along with the paradigm of particularizing comparison set out in the works of Weber and Hintze and the extremely wide comparisons of cultures and civilizations associated with Spengler and Toynbee, another programme for comparative research in history was proposed: its founder was the great French historian Marc Bloch (1885–1944).

In August 1928, Bloch spoke at the Sixth International Congress of Historical Sciences in Oslo with a paper entitled 'Toward a Comparative History of European Societies', which had been published that year as an article in the *Journal of Historical Synthesis*. This work was to become the most cited text of historical comparison.

Like Pirenne, and Glotz and Langlois before him, Bloch begins his article by praising the comparative method: he calls its 'perfection and general use' 'one of the most pressing needs of present-day historical science'.[41] These constantly repeated appeals to fellow historians from the end of the nineteenth century to use the comparative method are in themselves telling: they are evidence of a demand from a perceptible part of the academic community for a systematic use of comparison in their work, and of a distrust of comparative methods of analysis among the majority of historians. Bloch writes directly about this distrust in the article cited, explaining it by the inclination of his colleagues to see 'comparative history' as part of the philosophy of history or general sociology and something remote from their research practice. He tries to convince them of the reverse – that the comparative method is a convenient 'technical instrument . . . capable of giving positive results'. Bloch is convinced that this method 'can and must penetrate monographic studies. Its future is at stake, and therewith perhaps the future of historical science as a whole'.[42] In his speech and then in the article based on it, Bloch tried 'to clarify . . . the nature and applications of this excellent tool'. He promised to cite 'some examples' illustrating 'the main services which one may rightly expect from the method' and to suggest 'some practical means of facilitating the comparative approach'.[43]

An emphasis on the practical application of the comparative method stands out here; this is what Bloch called the 'historian's craft' in his posthumous book (and testament of sorts), which took this phrase as its title.[44] It is precisely the tone used, that of a workman giving his colleagues practical advice about using a 'handy tool' – the comparative method – and giving convincing examples from his own research

---

[40] Burke (1992): 27.
[41] Bloch ([1928] 1953): 494–5.
[42] Bloch ([1928] 1953): 495.
[43] Bloch ([1928] 1953): 495.
[44] Bloch ([1949] 1954).

experience, that would appear to explain the success of 'Toward a Comparative History' among subsequent generations of historians.

Commentators have often noted the influence of the social sciences, particularly Durkheim's sociology and Antoine Meillet's historical linguistics, on Bloch's development of the comparative method.[45] Indeed, Bloch repeatedly referred to Meillet's works in his article,[46] particularly to his book *the Comparative Method in Historical Linguistics* (1925) whence Bloch said that he borrowed 'a general idea ... of the two forms of the method'.[47] His words about the future of history as a discipline potentially depending on the introduction of the comparative method into specific research directly echo the concluding phrase of Meillet's book.[48]

On close inspection, however, the dependence of the methodology that Bloch developed for historical comparison on linguistics and other humanities and social sciences turns out to be more an aspiration than a reality. As Alette and Boyd Hill showed,[49] Bloch certainly did not follow the linguistic model of comparison proposed by Meillet; in particular, he did not attach particular significance to the principle of a common origin in the societies compared, while Meillet indicated that correspondences between languages must be due to a 'genetic link'.[50]

It is still harder to find traces of Durkheim's influence in 'Toward a Comparative History'. Of course, it is impossible to deny the fact that the works of the master of the French School of Sociology left an impression on Bloch's understanding of social history precisely as the history of societies and not of individuals. But the methods of historical comparison he suggested had nothing in common with Durkheim's methodological instructions: unlike Durkheim, Bloch certainly did not regard comparison as a means of discovering laws about the development of society; the 'concomitant variation' method that Durkheim had recommended also failed to attract his attention. Nevertheless, the impression that Bloch created the comparative method 'from a blank sheet' is deceptive: in fact, as Kedar correctly noted,[51] he developed and generalized proposals and observations that had already been made by a number of historians – Langlois, Davillé, Sée and Pirenne – whose names Bloch lists in a short note to his article.[52]

Bloch's attitude to the social sciences was therefore ambivalent: he gave examples of successes in historical linguistics achieved using the comparative method and readily cited Meillet and the anthropologist James Frazer[53] – but in formulating practical recommendations for using comparison in history, he was led not by any ready-made

---

[45] Hill and Hill (1980); Walker (1980); Burke (1992): 24; Haupt (2001): 2398.
[46] Bloch ([1928] 1953): 507, 515.
[47] Bloch (1928): 16, footnote 1. In the English translation of 1953, the author's notes have been omitted.
[48] Pointing to the necessity of systematic research, including the study of French towns, the fate of the English language in different countries, the languages of the Caucasus and so on, Meillet wrote, 'On these investigations and on the rigor with which they will be conducted depends the future of linguistics.' (Meillet ([1925] 1967): 138).
[49] Hill and Hill (1980): 832–4, 837.
[50] Meillet ([1925] 1967): 24.
[51] Kedar (2009b): 7.
[52] Bloch (1928): 15, note 2.
[53] Bloch ([1928] 1953): 497–8.

theory but primarily by his own research experience and that of his fellow historians; let us now examine what these recommendations of Bloch to future comparativists were.

First, he considered it essential to refine the concept of 'comparative history' itself. In his opinion, there are two essential conditions for comparison in a historical context: 'a certain similarity or analogy between observed phenomena – that is obvious – and a certain dissimilarity between the environments in which they occur'. Explaining the second condition, he gives an example:

> If I study the landholding system of the Limousin region, for instance, I will constantly compare fragments of evidence drawn from the records of this or that *seigneurie*. This is comparison in the common sense of the word, but, nevertheless, I do not think that I engage here in what is, technically speaking, comparative history; for the various objects of my study are all derived from parts of the same society, a society which in its totality forms one large unit.[54] It has become common practice [Bloch continues] to reserve the term "comparative history" almost exclusively for the confrontation of phenomena which have occurred on different sides of the boundary of a state or nation.[55]

However, he considers such an understanding of the term oversimplified: 'Let us therefore use here the notion of a "difference of environment" – a notion which is more flexible and more precise.'[56]

The criterion of a different environment would appear to be the best requirement for selecting objects of historical comparison that has been formulated to date. Bloch's warning against identifying comparison exclusively with comparison of nation states appears 'particularly topical in the light of the polemic which proponents of transnational history and other contemporary research trends are conducting against "comparative history", which they consider obsolete' (see Chapter 5 for more detail).

Following his predecessors,[57] Bloch identifies two forms of historical comparison. One of these is the comparison of two societies so far removed from each other in time and place that similar phenomena found in both cannot be explained by a common influence or origin; it is precisely these comparisons that ethnographers practise (Frazer's famous *Golden Bough* is referenced). Bloch does not deny the usefulness of such a 'comparative method on the grand scale', which is a 'procedure of interpolation of lines of development': using this, one can, in particular, fill in certain gaps in sources, using hypotheses based on analogies; formulate new approaches to research; and explain the vestiges of ancient customs. Nevertheless, Bloch accords decisive preference to another type of comparison: 'that in which the units of comparison are societies that are geographical neighbours and historical contemporaries, constantly influenced by one another'. Bloch's arguments in favour of the advantages of parallel

---

[54] Bloch ([1928] 1953): 496.
[55] Bloch ([1928] 1953): 496.
[56] Bloch ([1928] 1953): 496.
[57] Bloch prefers to cite Meillet, but the same juxtaposition of these forms of comparison is contained in Langlois's 1890 article (Langlois (1890): 260–1), with which he was familiar.

comparison are worth citing in full: 'From the scientific point of view the method with the more restricted outlook appears to be the most promising.... The latter method may arrive at more precise and less hypothetical conclusions, because its classifications can be more rigorous and critical.'[58] A characterization of the cognitive possibilities of this type of comparison, mainly using western and central European material, also formed the main content of the article.

Bloch identified several useful functions of comparing societies close to each other in space and time. First, such comparison allows the discovery of previously unknown phenomena (in contemporary theory of historical comparison this function is generally known as heuristic).[59] Bloch demonstrated the types of discoveries the comparative method allows using the example of the agrarian history of France, which he was studying intensely during the period: having thoroughly studied the well-documented enclosures in the rural economy of England from the sixteenth to early nineteenth centuries, Bloch attempted to find something similar in France and, indeed, discovered processes in Provence in the fifteenth to seventeenth centuries which were in essence similar to the English enclosures but at the same time had a number of specific features. This discovery, which was unexpected for historians of Provence, fundamentally changed notions of the socio-economic history of the region.

Second, comparing neighbouring societies allows the identification in Bloch's words, of the 'transmissions of cultural traits among medieval societies which have hitherto remained somewhat obscure'.[60] As a working hypothesis, Bloch proposed and argued for the probable influence of Visigoth Spain on the Carolingian monarchy both in the formation of the concept of royal power and in the field of canon law.

Another example, which was also taken from Bloch's work, can be added to that which he gave in his 1928 article: in his innovative book *The Royal Touch: Sacred Monarchy and Scrofula in England and France* (1924), Bloch made a thorough study of the rite of healing scrofula, performed by French and English monarchs until the beginning of modernity, and concluded that this rite and the associated representations of a power of healing given by God to the anointed, first developed in France around 1000 CE, after which approximately a century later English kings acquired the same 'miraculous gift', following the Capetians' example.[61]

In general, his book about the 'royal miracle' helps us to understand how Bloch developed the methods of comparative analysis that he recommended to his colleagues in 1928. In his article he intentionally emphasized the important role of comparison in seeking the causes of historical phenomena, and above all in eliminating imaginary causes and fallacious explanations. As an example, Bloch pointed to questions about the origin of representative institutions in Europe such as the *États* in France, the *Cortes* in

---

[58] Bloch ([1928] 1953): 498.
[59] Haupt (2001): 2400; Kocka and Haupt (2009): 3.
[60] Bloch ([1928] 1953): 502.
[61] Bloch ([1924] 1973): 47. Contemporary historians incline towards later dates, believing that the first reliable testimony about the healing of scrofula by a French king, Louis VI, was from the twelfth century and by an English king from 1276 (see Le Goff (1990): 150–3), but Bloch's remaining conclusions are not in doubt and his work itself has long since acquired the status of a classic of historical research.

Spain and the *Parlamenti* in Italy, which could not be understood by staying within the rigid confines of the history of individual regions or even countries. Having become caught up in 'a bewildering maze of local facts', historians risk giving these a significance they do not possess and missing what is most important. 'A general phenomenon', Bloch continues, 'must have equally general causes. Now the phenomenon described as the rise of Estates is certainly a phenomenon which occurs all over Europe.'[62]

Building on Bloch's idea we can say that yet another useful function of comparison lies in the fact that it can be used to help determine the real scale of phenomena studied, and consequently to better understand the causes of their development. In his book about 'healer' kings, Bloch followed this principle precisely, going on to formulate it in his 1928 article. Having described the development of the rite of healing scrofula in France, Bloch does not rush to an explanation of its origin: 'for the moment, this is not something that can be undertaken with a full measure of success. For the royal miracle was just as much English as French, and in any explanatory study of its origins, the two countries must not be treated separately.'[63]

Finally, Bloch considered that the correct understanding of the comparative method presupposes not only a search for similarities but also an explanation of differences; in his words, comparative history 'should analyse and isolate the "originality" of different societies'.[64] The issue, therefore, is the particularizing function of comparison. In his article, Bloch, in particular, revealed the pseudo-similarity of English *villainage* of the thirteenth to fifteenth centuries and French *servage*, showing fundamental differences between the two medieval institutions.

Bloch subsequently continued to ponder the possibilities of the comparative method in history. In 1930, he came up with a project for an entry entitled 'Comparison' for a historical dictionary that was planned at the time; in the same year a text was published in the *Bulletin du Centre international de synthèse* (an appendix to Berr's *Revue de synthèse historique*). This publication remains little known; it certainly merited the attention Kedar gave it,[65] but in essence it is Bloch's last detailed presentation of the problems of historical comparison. In this draft of the dictionary entry, Bloch returned primarily to questions of terminology: in particular, he draws a line between comparison – a mental process which is 'simultaneously essential and banal' – and the 'method used very precisely in the humanities' that it gives rise to – the comparative method.[66] Bloch again stressed the conventional nature of the concept of 'comparative history', noting that by cross-checking documents issued by the same clerical office or simultaneously studying the development of the majority of enterprises in the history of French industry, he is performing a mental process, which in contemporary language is called comparison: 'however not one historian', notes Bloch, 'would speak of comparative history in this regard'.[67] The main focus of the article was a description of the results of using the comparative method. Bloch identified five useful effects

[62] Bloch ([1928] 1953): 505.
[63] Bloch ([1924] 1973): 21.
[64] Bloch ([1924] 1973): 507.
[65] Kedar (2009b): 9, note 23.
[66] Bloch (1930): 32.
[67] Bloch (1930): 34.

that comparison has in history, apologizing to his readers for the rather scholastic character of his enumeration. The first was 'proposals for study' – or as we would now say, 'setting the agenda': if certain phenomena are very evident in one society – because of the condition of sources or for other reasons – and in another social environment they are barely noticeable, even if they play an important role, then comparison will provide a stimulus for detecting them. The second effect was explaining relics through 'extrapolation of curves': here, Bloch cites Frazer and other ethnographers who had compared societies that were very remote from each other. The third effect or useful function of comparison was the study of influence; the fourth was 'filiation', that is, tracing continuity of such practices as techniques in the rural economy and rites. Finally came 'similarities and differences of development' and 'the search for causes'.[68]

In Bloch we therefore see one of the first comparativist historians, who systematically used comparison in his research and strove to develop a rigorous comparative method. Comparison is present in all the monographs Bloch wrote in the mature period of his work. We have already considered *The Royal Touch*. In his next book, ostensibly devoted to the history of one country, *French Rural History: An Essay on Its Basic Characteristics* (1931), Bloch was, again, unable to avoid using comparison. In the introduction, Bloch wrote:

> Unless we first cast our eye over France as whole, we cannot expect to grasp what is singular in the development of the various regions. And what was happening in France can only be properly appreciated when seen in the context of Europe. This is not the question of straining after forced comparisons but of making proper distinctions; we are not engaged in some kind of trick photography, which would produce a fuzzy conventional image, deceptively generalized; what we are looking for are characteristics held in common, which will make whatever is original stand out by contrast. Although the subject treated here is part of our national history, it also impinges on the type of comparative studies I have tried to define elsewhere.[69]

Comparison plays an important role in the last major work to be published in Bloch's lifetime, his book *Feudal Society* (1939–40). Comparing the social institutions of many medieval countries, Bloch highlighted the main features of European feudalism.[70] The general model that was constructed certainly did not obscure regional differences, however: on a mental map of feudal Europe he noted a central nucleus (the region between the Loire and the Rhine) as well as a periphery, where features of the feudal structure were not pronounced or were entirely absent.[71] In a worldwide historical perspective Bloch, like Voltaire, considered feudalism a universal phenomenon; in particular, he believed that Japan had also gone through a feudal stage in its development.[72]

---

[68] Bloch (1930): 38.
[69] Bloch ([1931] 1973): XXIV.
[70] Bloch ([1939–40] 1961), 2: 443–6.
[71] Bloch ([1939–40] 1961), 2: 445–6.
[72] Bloch ([1939–40] 1961), 2: 447.

In general, as we can see from the material cited in this chapter, the interwar period was an important stage in the development of historical comparison. The works of Hintze, Bloch and Toynbee appeared in the 1920s and 1930s and demonstrated the possibilities of various scales and forms of comparison. Furthermore, in Bloch's works a detailed rationale for the comparative method in history was given for the first time, which subsequently gave Haupt grounds to claim that theoretical comparison, developed in detail, had existed as a methodological tool only since the 1930s.[73]

---

[73] Haupt (2001): 2397.

4

The rise of historical comparison in the later twentieth century

The wave of interest in comparative historical research that arose after the end of the First World War reached a peak at the cusp of the 1920s and 1930s and declined soon afterwards. A new growth in historical comparison began only several decades later, at the end of the 1950s.

The time interval between 1945 and this new wave is evidence of the fact that unlike the previous war, the Second World War did not provide an immediate impetus for growth in comparative research in history. Rather, the later wave of comparison was linked with worldwide trends that developed further soon after the end of the war, influenced by its outcome. In contemporary parlance, these trends can be summed up as 'globalization'. The historians of the 1950s and 1960s did not yet use this term, but they well appreciated the link between the growing interest in comparative research and the changes that had occurred in the world around them.

Thus, Sylvia L. Thrupp, the founder of the new journal *Comparative Studies in Society and History* whose establishment in 1958 was itself an important milestone in the history of comparison, wrote in her editorial foreword to the first issue:

> Today there is a revival of interest in the method of comparison, forced on us by the times. Without relinquishing the sense of nationality, we have acquired a sense of humanity. The notion of being ethnocentric has become a matter for reproach. Even scholarship is not free from reproach on this score, for, as many great names have pointed out, how can those who study only their own country tell what is truly unique about it?[1]

Commenting on Thrupp's words, Schieder concluded that recourse to comparative research was 'a symptom of a willingness to overcome national boundaries in history', which had always effectively expressed political interests, as well as academic content – previously within an academic tradition determined by the nation state and now within a more or less universal tradition.[2] He also noted an enormous expansion and proliferation of academic information – 'beyond all national borders'. Although this trend, in Schieder's opinion, could not entirely overcome the national structure of

---

[1] Thrupp (1958): 1.
[2] Schieder (1968): 195–6.

history and historiography, it had nevertheless given rise to powerful changes which were then at their inception.³

Among factors favouring the development of comparative research in the post-war decades, contemporary scholars have identified various effects of globalization (including a growth in international academic contacts that increased the numbers of people studying and working abroad and the complex intertwining of the interests of various states)[4] as well as the process of decolonization, which, as Nancy L. Green put it, intensified demand 'for a less ethnocentric history'.[5]

It was not only the political and economic situation in which academics lived and worked that changed but the academic environment itself: thanks to grants, stipends and guest professorships, it became significantly easier to study history from a comparative perspective (clearly this applies mainly to historians in western Europe and America: this opportunity became available to Soviet academics only in the late 1980s and early 1990s). Moreover, historians had increased contact with other social sciences, in particular sociology and anthropology, where comparative research had already long since been actively practised.[6]

But changes within the discipline of history had a decisive significance for the success of historical comparison. After the Second World War, the stances of political history, which inclined towards a national narrative, were seriously constrained by new trends such as economic and social history which since Bloch's time had shown an interest in a wider comparative perspective. Research themes also changed: as Kaelble notes, the study of historical transformations such as democratization, industrialization and changes in mentality, values and identities was put on the agenda and academics sensed the necessity of comparing the processes associated with these fundamental historical changes.[7]

Indeed, in contrast to previous waves of historical comparison, the growth that began in the 1950s was accompanied by an interest in comparing processes rather than events or institutions. This tendency was first manifested in economic history.

In 1958, Fritz Redlich, a specialist in the history of German and American entrepreneurship, published an article in which he argued in favour of developing comparative historical research; he particularly recommended that historians compare processes rather than facts, and gave several recommendations on this.[8] The programme Redlich advanced for developing 'comparative historiography' (which as Kedar noticed was strikingly reminiscent in several points of Bloch's 1928 article, with which Redlich was apparently not familiar)[9] and the publication of *Comparative Studies in Society and History*, the first number of which came out almost simultaneously with Redlich's article, should be viewed in the context of the renaissance in the comparative movement among American economic historians in the second half of the 1950s.

[3] Schieder (1968): 196.
[4] Kaelble (1999): 7–8.
[5] Green (1990): 1336.
[6] Kaelble (2002): 304.
[7] Kaelble (1999): 9.
[8] Redlich (1958): 380–2.
[9] Kedar (2009b): 14.

A special session which the American Association of Economic History devoted to the problems of comparison at its annual conference in 1957 was in the same vein.[10] Speaking at this forum, Thrupp put an emphasis on 'deliberate intensive comparison' through which she believed it would be possible to solve the main problem of economic history, that of constructing a general theory of economic growth.[11] MIT professor Walt Rostow's 1960 book *Stages of Economic Growth*, which rapidly achieved worldwide renown, was a kind of response to this challenge.

Rostow proposed breaking down the history of each national economy into five stages: traditional society; preconditions for 'take-off'; take-off; a period of maturity; and finally the era of high mass consumption. Rostow designated all past economies where there had been a ceiling to the volume of production per head of population due to the unavailability of modern[12] scientific or technological potential 'traditional economies'. The second stage (preconditions for growth) was achieved in western Europe from the end of the seventeenth century to the beginning of the eighteenth when scientific discoveries began to be converted into new production functions in agriculture and industry. With the Industrial Revolution, which Rostow dates from 1783 to 1802, Britain was the first to succeed in going through the third stage, take-off proper, and the other large countries of Europe, America and Asia followed it with a lag of from half a century (like France or Belgium) to one and a half centuries or more (like China or India). In the twentieth century, the 'leader' changed: from as early as 1901 to 1916, the United States achieved the mass consumption stage.

Rostow does sometimes use comparison in his work; for example, he draws parallels between the economic development of Sweden and Japan in the nineteenth century and Russia and the United States in the twentieth century; he also tries to understand why Britain was the first to reach the stage of unlimited economic growth, comparing its development on the eve of take-off with Holland and France:[13] the comparative method is not the main driver of his research, however. In essence, Rostow compresses several centuries of world history into his model, without being overly concerned about how far individual cases correspond to his rather simple and rigid model. Like runners in a race, according to Rostow's theory, economies pass through exactly the same stages of development, with the 'stragglers' chasing the 'leaders'.

In addition to its obvious reductionism, this model has serious shortcomings: it is clearly focused on western Europe and the United States; the stages of development described by Rostow are clearly inapplicable to Asian and African countries. Contemporary researchers believe that nowhere – not even in Britain – was the Industrial Revolution as fast-paced as Rostow depicted it. We will return to this question in the third part of the book. Finally, Rostow does not offer any point of reference to historians of the pre-industrial era, since he places Chinese dynasties and the civilizations of the Mediterranean in the general category of 'traditional societies' explaining directly to the reader that 'we are, after all, merely clearing the way in order

---

[10] For a review of the discussion that took place, see Heaton (1957).
[11] Thrupp (1957): 555, 567, 570.
[12] For Rostow, the discoveries of Isaac Newton serve as a boundary here: he calls traditional societies 'the pre-Newtonian World': Rostow (1960): 5.
[13] Rostow (1960): 31–5, 63–4, 93–105.

to get to the subject of this book; that is, post-traditional societies'.[14] Nevertheless, thanks to its simplicity and clarity, Rostow's theory of stages of economic development exerted an undoubted influence on various theories of modernization that became widespread in the 1960s and 1970s.

The possibilities for a more fruitful use of comparison in economic history were demonstrated at exactly the same period by Harvard professor Alexander Gerschenkron (1904–78). His book *Economic Backwardness in Historical Perspective* (1962) is a collection of articles, bringing together research published from the beginning of the 1950s. A strength of the approach used by Gerschenkron to the study of the history of industrialization in Europe is its explanation of the features characteristic of countries that have at one time or another gone through this process. In Gerschenkron's words, 'the industrial history of Europe is conceived as a unified and yet graduated pattern'.[15] Thus, in his book there is no hint at all of the oversimplification that was so characteristic of Rostow's approach. Gerschenkron's model proved to be sufficiently flexible to accommodate a variety of empirical material; in this case, he drew a number of novel conclusions.

Gerschenkron was able to show that in relatively underdeveloped countries, industrialization had a number of fundamental differences from Britain, which had assumed the role of the 'pioneer' of the Industrial Revolution: as a rule, these countries demonstrated a higher pace of economic growth; they counted on the most advanced technology and major enterprises, and most importantly, different institutional tools were used to stimulate the development of industry than those used in the 'birthplace' of industrial capitalism. Thus, in France, Germany, Austria, Switzerland and Belgium, the banks played a major role in financing industry and in less developed European countries such as Hungary and Russia, the development of the economy was stimulated by government subsidies.

Drawing on these observations, Gerschenkron subjected several established ideas about European industrialization to revision. In particular, he criticized the thesis of there being certain essential preconditions or prerequisites for this process, which, thanks to Marx, are usually taken to mean an initial accumulation of capital, as was well known from the history of Britain. In fact, as Gerschenkron showed, this famous original accumulation was not a precondition of industrial development in the majority of countries on the European continent. Moreover, what had been a precondition and, in a certain sense the 'cause' (Gerschenkron puts the word in quotation marks – MK) of industrialization in one country was an effect of this process in another.[16]

At the same time, Gerschenkron does not suggest completely rejecting the idea of preconditions to industrialization: it can be used as a heuristic method within the framework of the comparative approach to the problem that he recommends. Gerschenkron believes it is useful to ask how one country or another was able to begin industrialization without having the starting conditions that more advanced countries possessed, and which substitutes for these missing factors were found

---

[14] Rostow (1960): 6.
[15] Gerschenkron (1962): 1.
[16] Gerschenkron (1962): 50.

there.[17] In Gerschenkron's opinion, such research could rid the European model of industrialization of its inherent dogmatism and show the process as being more flexible and allowing significant variation.[18]

In the half-century that has passed since the publication of Gerschenkron's book, many critical observations have, of course, been expressed on the subject of his specific observations on the course of industrialization in certain countries, including Russia.[19] But his approach to the problem itself has stood the test of time. As O'Brien puts it, 'Gerschenkron's typology inspired generations of scholars and survives as the best frame of reference for economic historians concerned to place their research within wider and potentially deeper perspectives that emanate from comparisons across Europe.'[20] The academic longevity of Gerschenkron's work is explained in particular by his masterful use of methods of comparative analysis, which allowed the streamlining of a vast amount of empirical evidence on the one hand, and correction of the original model on the other, making it more realistic.

Gerschenkron can rightly be called one of the most important comparativists of the first post-war decades. Among his works, *Europe in the Russian Mirror* (1970) also merits particular mention in connection with the problem of comparison in history: the book contains the lectures Gerschenkron gave in Cambridge in May 1968. In this, Gerschenkron wanted, in his own words, to show what light studying Russian economic history sheds on several questions occupying researchers of the economic history of the West.[21] One such question is Max Weber's hypothesis about the connection between the Protestant ethic and the spirit of capitalism.

Addressing this issue, Gerschenkron, above all, reminds us that Weber himself presented his famous hypothesis as a proposal for future research but in the subsequent literature, caveats accompanying his thesis were discarded and the hypothesis was accepted as an 'unshakeably established truth'. Gerschenkron attempted to test the plausibility of Weber's idea about the existence of a causal connection between theological doctrine and economic activity with one case example, selecting what he called an 'exceptionally appropriate' case – that of the fate of the Russian merchants from the Old Believers' community.[22]

It is well known that many prominent nineteenth-century entrepreneurs such as the Morozov and Ryabushinsky families were members of the Old Believers' community; however, in Gerschenkron's opinion the superior moral and business qualities of these individuals did not derive from the specifics of the religious doctrine to which they adhered (in terms of dogma, the Old Believers differed very little from official Orthodoxy) but was a consequence of the specific position of this social group, which was persecuted by the authorities.[23] Furthermore, although the contribution of the Old

---

[17] Gerschenkron (1962): 46, 50.
[18] Gerschenkron (1962): 32, 40, 50.
[19] For a discussion of the model of industrial development in Russia proposed by Gerschenkron, taking account of subsequent literature on the issue, see: Gregory (1977), Bovykin (2003), esp. 11–13, 16–18.
[20] O'Brien (2001): 7366.
[21] Gerschenkron (1970): 1.
[22] Gerschenkron (1970): 11.
[23] Gerschenkron (1970): 31, 37.

Believer merchants to the establishment of the textile industry in Russia cannot be denied, as Gerschenkron stresses, these achievements occurred in pre-reform times, while the rapid industrial growth of the end of the nineteenth century was the result of the activities of another generation of entrepreneurs entirely, individuals with a western education who unlike the Old Believers had not experienced distrust of the state and who did not shun contact with foreigners.[24]

Gerschenkron believes that this example is evidence that the social position of a persecuted group was a sufficient stimulus for its members to participate in profitable economic activity and the development of specific qualities, which Weber had considered inherent in the 'capitalist spirit'. Thus, Weber's thesis about the significance of Calvinist doctrine for the development of contemporary capitalism is also subject to doubt.[25]

Developing the attack on Weber's idea, Gerschenkron gives another example from Russian history: he cites a treatise written by the Croatian Jesuit scholar Juraj Križanić while in exile in Siberia in which he advises the Tsar to establish craft guilds like those in Western Europe in Russia, in order to develop trade and foster qualities such as industriousness, honesty and enterprise in Russian merchants and craftsmen. Gerschenkron finds it highly indicative that the list of positive qualities that Križanić – a fervent Catholic who despised Protestants – wanted to see in Russian merchants and craftsmen matched those that Weber considered specifically generated by the puritan spirit. In addition, in Gerschenkron's opinion, an underestimation of the influence of craft guilds on the formation of the puritan ethic and bourgeois rationalism is a serious shortcoming of Weber's idea.[26] Gerschenkron himself agreed fully with the viewpoint of the seventeenth-century economist William Petty, who had believed that 'trade is not fixed to any species of religion as such'.[27]

Of course, Gerschenkron did not bring an end to this famous dispute, and proponents of Weber's idea have much to say in its defence,[28] but in this case it is mainly Gerschenkron's reasoning and the role within it that is devoted to comparison that we are interested in. Specialists in Russian history usually use the European model as a benchmark by which phenomena and processes originating in Russia are compared. In Gerschenkron's work, however, Russian case studies are an effective tool for testing an influential theory.

If economic historians set the tone of comparison in the 1950s and 1960s, then in the 1970s specialists in various issues in social history such as the family, social groups

---

[24] Gerschenkron (1970): 18, 42–3.
[25] Gerschenkron (1970): 45–6.
[26] Gerschenkron (1970): 54, 56, 58–9.
[27] Cited in Gerschenkron (1970): 46.
[28] In particular, it is worth remembering that Weber did not try to establish a direct causal link between Calvinist doctrine and 'the spirit of capitalism'; he wrote only of the 'capitalist form of enterprise' and the 'spirit' in which it is carried out, which 'stand in some sort of adequate relationship to each other, but not in one of necessary interdependence', see Weber ((1905) 2002: 27). Elsewhere in his work he speaks of 'certain correlations between forms of religious belief and practical ethics' ((1905) 2002: 49). The issue is not therefore one of determinism or strict interdependence but of the correspondence of particular forms of religious experience (in the Weberian sense of 'ideal types') to certain forms of economic behaviour. In such an interpretation, Weber's famous thesis is more than able to withstand criticism.

and strata, social movements, education and urbanism took the baton from them. By Kaelble's calculations, between two and five books and articles on comparative social history were published every year in the 1970s in Europe; 'production' increased in the 1980s to fifteen publications a year on average, and 'records' of sorts were set in 1988 and 1994, with forty and twenty works, respectively, being published. In the United States in the same period (1970–95), publications on this theme were at an average level of ten per year.[29]

Thus although comparative research continues to make up only a small proportion of works on history overall, interest in comparison undoubtedly grew towards the end of the twentieth century when compared to the pre-war period, when individual enthusiasts such as Bloch and Pirenne tried to convince their colleagues of the advantages of the comparative method. Today, dozens of scholars around the world make systematic use of comparison in their research. Geographically, the United States and Germany currently stand out as two centres where comparative historical research is most developed.

For a long period, specialists in European history were dominant among comparativist historians working in the United States, while 'Americanists' failed to show particular interest in comparison. As mentioned, the main focus of Gerschenkron's study was European industrialization from the nineteenth to the early twentieth century, and the special field of Thrupp, also an economic historian, was craft and trade in medieval England.

Robert Palmer – historian of the French Revolution and author of the two-volume *Age of the Democratic Revolution, 1760-1800* (1959–64) in which he showed the struggle between the forces of democracy and aristocracy in one of the key periods in the history of western civilization using material from countries in western and central Europe as well as the United States[30] – was also not an Americanist. In the literature, this book is sometimes given as a model of comparative historical research.[31] Carl Degler's viewpoint appears more reasonable, however; he rightly notes that comparison does not play a great role in the work of Palmer, who did not seek to identify common features or differences in the countries he studied, but simply traces the fate of an idea that interests him across national borders.[32] Assessing Palmer's work from today's standpoint, it must be acknowledged that he did not make any particular contribution to the development of historical comparison, but he can nevertheless be regarded as providing a prototype for contemporary research approaches such as globalization and transnational history.

Meanwhile, the need to make sense of the United States' national past using comparative analysis was felt ever more strongly among both historians and the wider public. A response to this growing demand was the publication of a collection of articles entitled *The Comparative Approach to American History* in 1968, edited by C. Vann Woodward. The collection grew out of a series of broadcasts by the Voice of

---

[29] Kaelble (1999): 153 and diagram on p. 54.
[30] Palmer (1959–1964).
[31] See, for example Schieder (1968): 212.
[32] Degler (1968): 426–7.

America radio station, which were given by invited experts on a wide range of aspects of the history of the United States over a number of years.

As Degler noted in his review of the book, the unusual origin of the collection was reflected in its contents: in particular, the authors of the articles do not show a common understanding of the essence of comparative history. Furthermore, in Degler's opinion, many of the contributors do not use comparison at all or use it in relation to secondary subjects; in this, characteristically, the most consistently comparative approach is used not by the Americanists, who make up the majority of the authors, but by several specialists in the history of other countries such as Peter Gay, Robin W. Winks and Palmer.[33]

However, one article written by an Americanist deserves mention precisely because of its successful use of comparison: David A. Shannon asks why, unlike in other countries, a politically influential Marxist party and strong socialist movement failed to develop in the United States. Comparison enabled Shannon to see an issue that had previously gone unnoticed and also to identify a way of understanding it. In particular, parallels with countries where Marxists had had a great influence allowed him to avoid false explanations – or local pseudo-causes as Bloch would have put it. Shannon rightly avoids trusting the popular account, according to which the lack of success of the socialist movement in the United States is explained by factors such as mistaken tactical decisions, instances of betrayal and corruption in its ranks. 'No one would seriously submit', he writes, 'that American socialists were more inept or venal than British, Japanese, Swedish, Russian, or Australian Marxists, all of whom have enjoyed far greater success.'[34] Therefore, one must seek an explanation for the differences between the American socialist movement and those in Japan or Sweden, Shannon rightly concludes, not in the specifics of the movement as such but in the features of the respective societies as a whole. Developing this line of argument, Shannon enumerates a number of factors which in his opinion negatively influenced the fate of the socialist idea in the United States, including the specific nature of the political structure (the two-party system and the institution of the presidency); the pace of economic growth; and the heterogeneity of American society, which entails the working classes identifying themselves primarily with a certain religious or ethnic group such as Irish Catholics or Puerto Ricans and not with the working class.[35]

It is also worth noting the successful comparison of American imperialism with the similar policies of other great powers in Robin Winks' article,[36] and Peter Gay's characterization of the American Enlightenment as part of the wider Enlightenment and of the newly formed United States after the Declaration of Independence as a 'laboratory for Enlightenment ideas'.[37]

The appeal of Vann Woodward and his colleagues to carry out comparative research on American history had an influence on the next generation of scholars. A quarter of a century later, Carl Guarneri recalled the impression that the collection made on

---

[33] Degler (1968): 428.
[34] Shannon (1968): 242.
[35] Shannon (1968): 242–7.
[36] Winks (1968): 253–70.
[37] Gay (1968): 35, 42.

him in his student years: 'Rereading it today', he wrote in 1995, 'we can find much in its promoting a comparative agenda that would not only test American claims of national uniqueness but set United States history in an international frame of reference.'[38]

However, the development of comparative historical research in the United States did not occur as quickly as the proponents of the approach would have liked. Analysing the state of comparative history in America in 1980, Fredrickson established with regret the fragmentation of the field and the rarity of similar work: 'Comparative history', he wrote, 'does not really exist yet as an established field within history or even as a well-defined method of studying history.'[39] Grew assessed the state of affairs in American historiography equally critically: in his article 'The Comparative Weakness of American History' (1985), whose title speaks for itself, he linked the extremely limited influence of Americanists on history worldwide with the weak interest in comparison among Americanists as an academic community.[40] By Grew's calculations material on American topics in *Comparative Studies in Society and History*, the journal he edited, comprised less than ten per cent of the total number of articles published in it in since 1958.[41]

Attempting to explain the relatively weak interest of the Americanists in comparison on an international scale in the 1970s and 1980s, Guarneri pointed to the growth in those years of the 'new social history', which consumed the energy of a new generation of researchers and directed their efforts to the study of topics such as the family, gender, ethnic minorities and private life.[42]

Other appraisals were given, however. Thus, Peter Kolchin began his article with the phrase, 'comparative history is now in fashion'. In support of his claim, he referred to the 1978 session of the American Historical Association, which was especially devoted to this theme, and also the October and December 1980 issues of the *American Historical Review*.[43] One can add to this list the materials of discussion about comparative history that were published in the same journal at the beginning of 1982, when Kolchin's article was already in print.[44] As for the various opinions expressed in the literature about the state of comparative history, Kolchin noted reasonably that these appraisals depended on an understanding of what 'comparative history' meant – and that there was no consensus about this term among researchers.[45]

Indeed, Fredrickson, for example, drew a sharp distinction between 'comparative history in the full sense', by which he meant 'a relatively small but significant body of scholarship which has *as its main objective* the systematic comparison of some process or institution in two or more societies', and 'the limited use of the generalized "comparative perspective"'[46] (emphasis added by Fredrickson – MK). Furthermore, he asserted that '[u]nless comparative history becomes a distinct field or recognized

---

[38] Guarneri (1995): 553.
[39] Fredrickson ([1980] 2000): 24.
[40] Grew (1985): 89.
[41] Grew (1985): 88.
[42] Guarneri (1995): 552–3, 559, 560.
[43] Kolchin (1982): 64.
[44] Comparative History (1982).
[45] Kolchin (1982): 64.
[46] Fredrickson ([1980] 2000): 23.

subdiscipline within history, in the manner of comparative sociology, politics, or literature, it is unlikely that it will become a major trend within the profession'.[47] One can therefore agree with Kolchin that Fredrickson's pessimistic evaluation of everything that had been done by American historians in the field of comparison was partly a consequence of an overly narrow understanding of comparative history.[48] Kolchin himself was certainly not inclined to contrast comparativist historians with other historians:

> the comparative historian does overtly what other historians do too, for virtually all historical statements are implicitly comparative. . . . Because most of historical judgements are implicitly comparative, what we term comparative history constitutes the effort to do explicitly, rigorously, and thoroughly what most historians do most of the time.[49]

It is unsurprising that with such a wide interpretation of the key concept, Kolchin assessed the achievements of historical comparison in America far more positively than several of his colleagues. In particular, he claimed that 'a comparative consciousness is now widespread among American historians', which was already a sign of progress in and of itself, and 'explicit comparison has yielded positive results in a number of areas'.[50]

It was the theme of slavery and race relations that the Americanists studied comparatively with the greatest success.[51] Thus, in *Neither Black nor White: Slavery and Race Relations in Brazil and the United States* (1971), for which he was awarded the Pulitzer Prize, Degler identified differences in the position of the black population in the two countries and attempted to explain these through features of demographic, economic and cultural development in each society. In a series of works published during the 1980s and 1990s, Fredrickson compared race relations in the United States and South Africa in the twentieth century.[52] Kolchin's book *Unfree Labor* (1987), in which slavery in the southern states of America and Russian serfdom up to 1861 are examined in parallel also attracted a wide response (this work will be examined in detail in the third part of the book).

The emergence and development of systems of social insurance and social security was another topic of comparative research by American historians (Americanists as well as specialists in western European history) at the end of the twentieth century. Thus, having examined maternal and child welfare policy in the United States and France at the cusp of the nineteenth and twentieth centuries, Alisa Klaus identified significant differences which she believed were explained by features of culture and ideology in each of these countries. She observed that at the beginning of the twentieth

---

[47] Fredrickson ([1980] 2000): 36.
[48] Kolchin (1982): 78.
[49] Kolchin (1982): 65.
[50] Kolchin (1982): 77, 78.
[51] For overviews of the literature on this topic, see Fredrickson ([1980] 2000): 30–4; Kolchin (1982): 69–74; and Fredrickson (1995): 593–8.
[52] See Fredrickson (1981), Fredrickson (1995a) and Fredrickson (2000).

century, the French government – which, given conditions of threatened war, was concerned about a fall in the country's birth rate – was the driver of this policy; in the United States, though, the initiative came from women's independent organizations and the ideological basis for measures to protect the health of women and children were formed by racial and eugenic arguments such as those about the dying out of 'indigenous' (white) Americans due to the higher birth rate of recent immigrants.[53]

A gender-based approach also characterizes another piece of comparative historical research on a closely related theme – Pedersen's *Family, Dependence and the Origins of the Welfare State: Britain and France, 1914-1945* (1993). As Pedersen notes, British social policy was guided by a 'male breadwinner logic'; the labour market was organized around the earnings of the 'head of the family', and social programmes supported the 'right' of working men to support their wives and children even during a temporary break in employment or when leaving work. In France on the other hand, social welfare measures were characterized by a 'parental logic': parents were helped to bear the expenses of bringing up children, who were regarded as a national asset; resources were redistributed from childless families to families with children. Instead of a guarantee of the 'right' of men to support their families, therefore, French policy was aimed at countering a reduction in the birth rate and on building the nation in the context of constant military and economic competition with a more densely populated Germany.[54]

Peter Baldwin approached the question of the origin of the welfare state in Europe differently. Unlike Klaus and Pedersen, he was not interested in the features of social policy in one country or another, but by factors facilitating the development of the 'welfare state' in western Europe as a whole. Since this was a general European phenomenon, it was important to take into account not only the internal development of individual states but also their influence on one another and direct borrowings. Therefore, Baldwin did not use parallel and contrastive comparison like Klaus and Pedersen, but methods of mapping reminiscent of those that Bloch had used in *Feudal Society* and Hintze had also employed. Nevertheless, Baldwin's *Politics of Social Solidarity: Class Bases of the European Welfare State, 1875-1975* (1990) is a valuable piece of empirical research, based on vast factual evidence: Baldwin examined thirty-four archives and collections of documents of government agencies, political parties and trade unions in Denmark, Sweden, France, Britain and Germany.

Baldwin traced the establishment of the welfare state over the course of a century – from the first experiments in policies of solidarity in Denmark and Sweden at the end of the nineteenth century to social welfare reforms in European countries in the 1970s. His attention was focused primarily on the social basis of a policy of collective solidarity: Which political parties initiated the adoption of laws about social insurance and old-age pensions? Which social classes' interests did they serve? Baldwin ultimately concluded that there was no real basis for ideas widely held in academia about a connection between this programme and the labour movement and workers' representation; in fact, social solidarity policies in both Scandinavian countries,

---

[53] For a review of Klaus's book, see Fredrickson (1995b): 601.
[54] Pedersen (1993).

Germany and France were supported not only by workers but also by centrist and even right-wing parties.[55]

Baldwin also used comparison successfully in his subsequent major works. In *Contagion and the State in Europe, 1830-1930* (1999), which concerns the interface between the history of medicine and the history of political institutions, he tried to determine what dictated the choice of one type of preventative measure or another (from quarantine to sanitation and prevention) that different countries used in countering infectious diseases in the nineteenth century and early twentieth century. In some cases, geography was the decisive factor and in others, economic interests. The theme was continued in a monograph *Disease and Democracy: The Industrial World Faces AIDS* (2005). Baldwin's reputation as a modern comparativist was consolidated by his book *The Narcissism of Minor Differences: How America and Europe Are Alike* (2009) in which using vast statistical evidence, he shows convincingly that according to most parameters, the population of America at the beginning of the twenty-first century matched average European indicators and that differences between the Swedes, for example, and the Portuguese are much greater than those between Europe as a whole and north America.

Haupt observed that historical comparison has developed unevenly: in France, despite Bloch's well-known appeals, its success was hindered by an orientation towards monographic works and a sceptical attitude to the theory; in Britain it was limited by the dominance of national history and a dissociation from the social sciences; in Italy it was impeded by the regional orientation of local historiography.[56] For similar reasons, Spain, Portugal and eastern Europe remained on the sidelines of comparative historical research until the end of the 1980s. More favourable conditions for the development of comparison developed in the historiography of West Germany, Switzerland, Austria and the Scandinavian countries.[57]

The growth of interest in comparative analysis in post-war West German historiography was brought about by a range of factors. The national catastrophe into which Hitler's regime had plunged the country demanded a historical explanation. Many historians regarded Nazism as a deviation from the main route along which other civilized countries were travelling; thus, a theory of a German 'special path' (*Sonderweg*) in the period up to 1933 emerged. Proponents of this theory pointed to a number of features distinguishing the fate of the country in the nineteenth century from England, France and the West in general, including the late development of a nation state; a lack of development of parliamentarianism; and the dominance of anti-liberal and militaristic elements in the political culture. In the end, a nation that lagged behind in every respect embarked on a road that led it to National Socialism. In response, opponents stressed the role of factors exerting a direct influence on the events of the 1920s and 1930s (primarily the repercussions of the First World War, which Germany had lost) and focused on the idealization of the West implicit in the

---

[55] Baldwin (1990).
[56] For more details about the development of comparative historical research in post-war France, see Haupt (1996); in Great Britain: Crossick (1996); and in Italy: Salvati (1996).
[57] Haupt (2001): 2399–2400.

theory about a German 'special path'.[58] But whatever the arguments of each side, this debate about the origins of the catastrophe that befell the Germans in the twentieth century undoubtedly facilitated the development of historical comparison in West Germany.

In addition, German historicism, which had a negative attitude towards the comparative method and had resisted the influence of the social sciences, lost ground significantly after 1945. A new methodology of historical research was developed which took account of the gains of sociology, political science and economics. In this context, a re-evaluation of the role of comparison in history also took place.

In the 1960s, Theodor Schieder (1908–84), one of the most influential German historians of the time, proposed a typology of the emergence of nation states in Europe in the nineteenth century[59] and also formed a number of principles of comparative historical research.[60] And in 1972 Hans-Ulrich Wehler, a student of Schieder's and founder of the Bielefeld School of historical social science (*historische Sozialwissenschaft*) called comparison the 'royal road' (*Königsweg*) of historical research, which allows one to 'test the validity of very general or very specialized hypotheses'.[61]

From the 1970s to the 1990s, a powerful comparative social history 'industry' developed in West Germany. The numerous topics of comparative analysis included German and British trade unions in the nineteenth century; German and American workers in the iron and steel industries between the 1860s and 1930s; lawyers and individuals from other professions in various countries; the labour movement in nineteenth-century Europe; European liberalism; and the welfare state.[62] It is appropriate to supplement this general picture with a few sketches of prominent modern German comparativists.

In the 1970s, Jürgen Kocka (b. 1941) studied the social position of office workers in America and Germany in the nineteenth and twentieth centuries; in the second half of the 1980s he took part in a large collective research project devoted to the European bourgeoisie of the nineteenth century. From 1993 to 1997, Kocka was director of the Department of Comparative Social History at the Free University of Berlin and in 1998 he became director of the Centre of the Comparative History of Europe at the same university (from 2004, the Berlin College of Comparative History of Europe) and held this office until his retirement in 2009.[63] Kocka is the author of many reviews and seminal articles (some written with Haupt) on the challenges of comparison in history, which have been published in journals and collections in several languages.[64] These articles, which have in large part defined the modern paradigm of historical comparison, are cited frequently in this book.

---

[58] For an overview of the debates about *Sonderweg*, see Kocka (1988) and Kocka (1999).
[59] Schieder (1966).
[60] Schieder (1968).
[61] Cited in Kocka (1996): 48–9.
[62] For an overview, see Kocka (1993, 1996).
[63] See Kocka's page on the website of the Free University of Berlin: http://www.geschkult.fu-berlin.de/e/fmi/mitglieder/Emeriti_Professorinnen_und_Professoren_im_Ruhestand/jkocka.html (accessed 26 November 2019).
[64] See Haupt and Kocka (1996b); Kocka (1993); Kocka (2003); Kocka and Haupt (2009); for an overview of Kocka's theoretical works on historical comparison, see Kedar (2009b): 23–6.

Kocka's colleague and co-author Heinz-Gerhard Haupt (b. 1943) has taught at many German universities and the European University Institute in Florence. He has worked on the comparative history of trade and guilds in the nineteenth century and also consumerism, violence and terrorism in nineteenth- and twentieth-century Europe. Along with Kocka, Haupt is one of the most authoritative theorists of historical comparison; in particular, he is the author of the 'Comparative History' entry in the *International Encyclopedia of the Social and Behavioral Sciences*.[65]

This overview is completed by Hartmut Kaelble (b. 1940), professor at Humboldt University in Berlin and leading specialist on the comparative history of Europe in the nineteenth to the twentieth century. In his book *Social Mobility and Equality of Opportunity in the Nineteenth to Twentieth Centuries* (1983), he made a long-term comparison of the chances of members of various social groups in Germany (office workers, teachers, businessmen and others) of obtaining an education and achieving a successful career with those in similar conditions in other countries – in particular in the United States and France. As a result, Kaelble identified general tendencies in the growth of social mobility in Europe and individual characteristics of the development of German society between 1850 and 1960.[66] Kaelble went on to examine issues of stratification and social inequality in various European countries in the nineteenth to the twentieth century, and also the establishment of a European identity.[67] In addition, Kaelble wrote the only book of its kind on the methodology of historical comparison, which was conceived as an introduction to the comparative study of social history in the nineteenth and twentieth centuries.[68]

Surveying the journey that historical comparison has travelled since Bloch's memorable 1928 article, it is impossible not to see definite progress. To date, dozens of books and hundreds of articles have been published in which historical comparison is the main research method. The comparative perspective has become a usual and perhaps even essential link that conference organizers use to give a semblance of coherence to diverse presentations by participants from different countries and regions. There is no shortage of seminal articles or thematic edited collections (in the last fifteen years alone there have been at least three collections on issues in comparative history).[69] But despite the quantitative growth in comparative historical research, when contemporary comparativists assess the state of their field, they are not inclined to euphoria; their speeches contain uneasy and even pessimistic notes.

Like their predecessors a hundred years ago, today's comparativist historians constantly emphasize that they are part of an insignificant minority: 'Historians are notoriously resistant to comparisons,' writes Peter Baldwin. 'Despite nods in the direction of comparison, the profession remains organized by national field. Historical

---

[65] Haupt (2001).
[66] Kaelble (1983).
[67] See the list of Kaelble's publications on the website of Humboldt University in Berlin: https://www.geschichte.hu-berlin.de/bereiche-und-lehrstuehle/kaelble (accessed 26 November 2019).
[68] Kaelble (1999).
[69] Cohen and O'Connor (2004); Haupt and Kocka (2009); and Kedar (2009a).

methodology emphasizes the uniqueness of its subjects, explaining their development by presenting a narrative of their evolution.'[70]

Cohen seconds Baldwin: 'Despite paeans to the method and conference sessions devoted to its propagation, comparative history has remained a marginal affair in the United States,' Cohen observes with sadness. 'Unlike gender history or new cultural history, it is neither fashionable nor, until recently, a matter for controversy.'[71]

Kocka was the most thorough in his attempts to explain the reason for historians having a sceptical attitude towards comparison, and the consequent marginal position of comparative history. He identified three features of comparison that complicate its use in historical research since they create 'a certain tension between the comparative approach and the classical tradition of history as a discipline'.[72] First, the more subjects that are compared, the stronger researchers' dependence on secondary literature, and the further they are from original sources; meanwhile, proximity to sources and a command of the languages in which they are written are major tenets of modern academic history. Second, comparison entails identifying the objects being compared and isolating them from each other – but this itself destroys the continuity of the process being studied and the link between phenomena, and the narrative thread is thus broken. All these are after all classical elements of history as a discipline. Third, says Kocka, since comparing objects from every angle is not possible, it is vital to select a point of view, issue or question in relation to which they are compared; this, however, implies decontextualization, and therefore attention to context, another principle that is important for history, suffers.[73]

Many of the claims above are debatable. Above all, the notion of historians' deeply rooted distrust or even resistance to comparison seems strange if one remembers that as has been mentioned repeatedly comparison in history has existed since the times of Herodotus. It is difficult to believe in the marginality of comparative history when reading reviews and numerous bibliographies that are mindful of comparison.[74] The fact that comparisons can be undertaken in different ways – systematically or chaotically; in a well thought out or random manner; effectively or fruitlessly – is another matter. In this sense, exponents of 'refined' comparison such as Bloch, Hintze, Gerschenkron and, today, Kocka, Baldwin and certain other scholars, of course, belong to a select minority.

A parallel with source analysis emerges here: all historians use sources, but not all historians choose studying documents and preparing them for publication as their academic specialism. In addition, not all countries have what the Germans call *Quellenkunde* and what in Russian is called *istochnikovedenie* (the field of study relating to sources) in their historiographical traditions. Tellingly, there is no exact equivalent for this term in English. Nevertheless, no one has so far complained that source analysis has gone out of fashion or occupies a marginal position in history. Similar complaints

---

[70] Baldwin (2004): 1.
[71] Cohen (2004): 57.
[72] Kocka (2003): 41.
[73] Kocka (2003): 41–2.
[74] See such bibliographies in Kaelble (1999): 161–79; Cohen and O'Connor (2004): 181–97; and Haupt and Kocka (2009): 276–90.

from comparativists on the one hand reveal their sizeable ambitions and on the other are evidence of the lack of a clear common idea about what so-called 'comparative history' consists of: a particular method, a research trend, or maybe as Fredrickson believed (see earlier, p. 46), a separate subdiscipline of history. This important question on which specialists are not yet agreed will be considered in detail in the second part of the book where we will consider specific difficulties of comparative historical works such as the problem of access to primary sources and potential dependence on existing historiography.

Those representing new research approaches, such as the history of cultural transfers, transnational and global history and others, have also contributed to contemporary debates around historical comparison. They have criticized what they see as the obsolete paradigm of comparative history and proposed their own approaches which are designed to replace it. These new challenges to historical comparison, which emerged at the turn of the twentieth and twenty-first centuries will be the subject of the next chapter.

5

New challenges

Cultural transfers, *histoire croiseé*, transnational history and criticism of traditional comparison

A new research trend known as the history of transfers developed among a small circle of French historians of German literature and culture in the mid-1980s; it related to the history of cultural borrowings. The new approach was signalled in an article by Michel Espagne and Michael Werner about the reception of German philosophy in France from the eighteenth to the nineteenth century, which was published in the influential historical journal *Annales* in 1987. Espagne and Werner's edited collection *Transfers: Intercultural Relations in the Franco-German Space* was then published in 1988. Later, however, Espagne and Werner went their separate ways. Espagne continued to fly the flag of the history of transfers, while Werner founded a different but closely related approach, *histoire croisée*, with the political scientist Bénédicte Zimmermann. Representatives of both trends were critical of historical comparison, at least in the form in which it had been widely known in the later decades of the twentieth century.

In an article entitled 'On the Limits of Comparison in Cultural History' (1994), Espagne pointed to a number of limitations that national historiography puts on the method although he did not dispute the usefulness of comparison in general. Above all, he believed that 'comparison requires closed cultural spaces, in order to then be able to look beyond the particular features of the objects using abstract categories'.[1] Espagne points out that the existence of a link (*tertium comparationis*) between the items compared is an essential foundation of the comparative process[2] but in the case of comparisons between nations there is a serious risk of this 'mediation' leading to the projection of a strictly national point of view. Historians are obliged to use concepts such as 'intellectuals', 'politicians', 'teachers' and 'the European bourgeoisie of the nineteenth century' which Espagne is convinced are not so much research tools as new ideological shackles. Deciding against using these overly wide categories, however, often means that there is nothing left to compare. By way of example, Espagne cites research conducted in the 1980s on duels in France, Germany and England, which

---

[1] Espagne (1994): 112.
[2] For more detail on *tertium comparationis* (literally, the third element of comparison), see Part II, Chapter 9.

as he put it 'showed nothing other than an incompatibility of value systems and heterogeneous codes'.[3]

Espagne emphasizes that the fundamental problem is the position of the observer; in research on the European education system written in Germany a central place would be given to the concept of *Bildung* – education in a metaphysical sense – while French or English academics might not mention the concept at all.

Another criticism that Espagne levelled at comparison also merits attention: in his words, comparison compares synchronic 'constellations' without taking sufficient account of the chronological sequence of their interactions.[4] Explaining this idea, he notes that comparisons are usually focused on 'points of culture that are perceived as parallel phenomena because of semantic similarities. But these points themselves are rooted in development that has stretched back over decades and even centuries'.[5] If one were to attempt to compare libraries or the role of the church in France and Germany, Espagne continues, an impressive list of structural differences would immediately be produced. However, in and of themselves these differences explain nothing 'since the places they occupy in their respective national spheres are not in any way symmetrical'.[6]

Espagne concluded his article on a conciliatory note: he believed that the appeal to carry out comparative research could lead to positive results if it was understood as a 'systematic expansion of the field beyond the limits of national differences (*clivages*)'. But comparison as a method should never be understood uncritically, and Espagne considers the theory of cultural transfers a 'contribution to the methodological correction of comparison in cultural history'.[7]

A number of Espagne's observations can be regarded as useful cautions that are relevant for both comparativists and historians in general; this is true of his words about the dependence of observers (i.e. researchers) on their national culture or academic tradition and of his reminder about the deceptiveness of the semantic proximity of concepts in different languages. But as Paulmann rightly notes, some of Espagne's reproaches are part of the self-criticism by comparativists who fully recognize that the subject of comparative research is artificially constructed.[8] Moreover, Espagne's claim that comparisons are always made from a national point of view and that a comparative history that does not rely on the concept of the nation is impossible to imagine[9] is incorrect: there are some contemporary works in which regions rather than nation states are compared.[10] Therefore, one cannot but agree with Paulmann that Espagne's criticism is not a criticism of comparison as a whole, although it is not difficult to produce examples of unsuccessful comparative research.[11] But the main argument that Paulmann advances against Espagne's idea is that studying cultural transfers as Espagne

---

[3] Espagne (1994): 113.
[4] Espagne (1994): 113.
[5] Espagne (1994): 113.
[6] Espagne (1994): 113.
[7] Espagne (1994): 121.
[8] Paulmann (1998): 671.
[9] Espagne (1994): 120.
[10] See, for example, a comparison of the American South and the Italian Mezzogiorno: Dal Lago and Halpern (2002).
[11] Paulmann (1998): 671.

does makes no sense without comparison: 'As a historian, it is essential to compare in order to understand what is actually happening during intercultural transfer,' he writes: one must compare 'the position of the object of study in the old context and the new; the social origin of intermediaries and stakeholders in one country or another; terms in one language or another; and finally, the interpretation of the phenomenon in the culture from which it originates with that which it acquires after being incorporated into another culture'.[12]

This is also true of the ambitious project of *histoire croisée* which Michael Werner and Bénédicte Zimmermann presented to the academic community as an approach that was new and promising in a methodological sense and free from the shortcomings of both comparison and the history of transfers. A drive to transcend the limits of comparative history is perceptible in their seminal article, which in the most recent, English version is entitled, 'Beyond Comparison: *histoire croisée* and the Challenge of Reflexivity' (2006).

Werner and Zimmermann enumerate five problems they believe comparison inevitably confronts. The first problem, which Espagne wrote about in the article mentioned earlier, is the position of the observer which should ideally be neutral and equidistant from the objects of study; in practice, however, scholars are always involved in the field of observation in one way or another.

The second difficulty that Werner and Zimmermann note is selecting the scale of comparison:

'Whether situated . . . at the level of the region, nation-state, or the civilization, none of these scales is absolutely univocal and generalizable. They are all historically constituted and situated', Werner and Zimmermann emphasize, 'filled with specific content and thus are difficult to transpose to different frameworks.'[13]

In other words, every region is different from any other. As the authors point out, yet more difficulties arise when one tries to use the concept of civilization, which developed in particular historical conditions, as a general basis for comparison.

The third problem is linked to the previous one and relates to defining the objects of comparison, which is never a neutral process. Even when objects are clear and simple to define (e.g. the unemployed, students or kinship links), schemes of analysis will differ not merely because of differences in the scale of comparison but also because of the features of one academic discipline or another and the research traditions that are relevant to the researcher. 'To avoid the trap of presuming naturalness of the objects', the authors recommend, 'it is necessary to pay attention to their historicity, as well as to the traces left by such historicity on their characteristics and their contemporary usages.'[14]

The fourth problem is the conflict between synchronic and diachronic logic: as Werner and Zimmermann note, the comparative approach presupposes synchronicity or at least a pause in the flow of time. Even if comparativists study processes of transformation and compare events in time, it is essential to fix, or 'freeze', the object.

---

[12] Paulmann (1998): 683.
[13] Werner and Zimmermann (2006): 34.
[14] Werner and Zimmermann (2006): 34.

It can be difficult for researchers to explain why one element has either implicitly or explicitly been emphasized at the expense of another in their comparative schemes. 'The result', Werner and Zimmermann say, 'is a search for balance that in practice turns out to be tenuous and unstable.'[15]

Finally, a fifth problem relates to cases where the objects of comparison interact: since objects and practices are transformed as a result of contact, this demands that researchers rethink their conceptual frameworks and analytical tools.

The last problem Werner and Zimmermann identified is by no means new, and comparativists learned to deal with it long ago. The works of Bloch (*The Royal Touch*); Gerschenkron (*Economic Backwardness in Historical Perspective*); and Baldwin (*The Politics of Social Solidarity*) and a series of other pieces of research are excellent examples of successful comparative study of societies in contact with each other. The other problems listed constitute real difficulties, but they are problems that all historians face rather than comparative historians alone. Issues such as the position of the observer, the 'historicity' of objects studied, the conditional nature of categories of analysis, or the temporal complexities of processes are not particular to comparison: they apply to history as a whole.

Which new research methods do the creators of *histoire croiseé* therefore propose? What makes them believe that the approach they recommend will prove to be more effective than previous ones?

As the name of the approach itself makes apparent, a metaphor of crossroads lies at the basis of *histoire croisée*, which is understood as a meeting and interaction of individuals, practices, objects and points of view.[16] When it comes to selecting from the range of academic tools, Werner and Zimmermann particularly recommend paradigmatic induction, the historicization of categories of analysis and reflection, which presupposes adjusting the principles of research according to how it is conducted.[17] This is reminiscent of a recipe that lists the ingredients of a new dish – but as the saying goes, the proof of the pudding is in the eating: only research practice is capable of confirming the advantages of the approach proposed. Meanwhile, as Kaelble rightly reminds us, neither *histoire croisée* nor similar approaches can currently boast an abundance of empirical work; neither are there examples of model research that have received international recognition and been widely translated.[18]

Indeed, in the nearly twenty years that have passed since the first mention of *histoire croisée*, other than a few seminal articles by Werner and Zimmermann only two collections on the subject have been published.[19] In this context, attempts by proponents of the approach to present it as a new stage, superseding comparison which is supposedly obsolete,[20] appear manifestly premature.

---

[15] Werner and Zimmermann (2006): 35.
[16] Werner and Zimmermann (2006): 31, 37–44.
[17] Werner and Zimmermann (2006): 44–50.
[18] Kaelble (2009): 37.
[19] Zimmermann, Didry and Wagner (1999); Werner and Zimmermann (2004).
[20] The title of a 2004 collection is *De comparaison à l'histoire croisée*, that is, *From Comparison to Histoire Croisée*.

Histoire croisée, like transfer history, reflects an important tendency in contemporary historiography that has become widespread since the end of the twentieth century thanks to a wave of globalization and manifests itself in a drive to go beyond the limits of nation states and national points of view and in increased attention to points of commonality, intersection and interaction. Approaches similar to *histoire croisée* have developed under different names in various countries. Thus in Germany Shalini Randeria, an ethnographer specializing in India and Sebastian Conrad, a historian of Japan, have put forward a project of 'divided history' (*geteilte Geschichte*); in English, they use the terms 'a shared history' and 'entangled histories' to convey this concept.[21]

The project, based on a history divided into several societies – or 'entangled' histories – originates from a post-colonial perspective, which takes into account the link between the centre and its former colonies. The creators of this project also take issue with comparison: in Randeria's words, '[s]tandard comparisons in modern historiography, sociology, and political science are based on a conceptual nationalism that treats European metropole societies as if each one of them developed *sui generis* and compares them to one another'.[22]

In the context of ideas about modernization, European societies are compared with non-European societies in terms of shortcomings and backwardness, which is attributed to non-Europeans. Randeria believes that such a comparative approach not only ignores the relationships between European societies but worse is incapable of placing the development of European ideas and institutions in a transnational and imperial context. Instead, Randeria proposes the perspective of 'entangled histories' of Western and non-western societies which in her opinion helps to overcome the 'methodological nationalism' and Eurocentrism characteristic of the social sciences and to see in colonialism not an external factor, but a component of European modernity.[23]

However, Randeria's proposal to replace comparison of western societies and the rest of the world with the concept of entanglement[24] would appear hasty and insufficiently justified. As in the case of transfer history and *histoire* croisée, the blame for the unsuccessful use of comparison is transferred from individual researchers to the method as a whole. But, of course, comparison is not the cause of nationalism, Eurocentrism or other faults from which contemporary historiography has been unable to extricate itself. Clearly, comparison has always been a part of historians' work, but its forms and the reasons for using it have changed as history itself has developed. It would therefore seem that the only constructive conclusion that can be drawn from the criticism of comparison made by proponents of these contemporary approaches (which in many ways are justified) is that methods of comparison need to be improved. Dispensing with comparison or replacing it with something else, as some suggest, is simply not possible but adapting comparative analysis to history's current tasks and taking account of experience, including failures and criticism, is something that not only can but must be done.

---

[21] See Conrad (2009): 53–4, 58 and Randeria (2009): 77–81, 86.
[22] Randeria (2009): 79.
[23] Randeria (2009): 80.
[24] Randeria (2009): 80.

Neither transfer history, nor *histoire croisée* nor entangled histories have acquired general recognition in contemporary historiography; transnational history, which is the most amorphous of all such approaches in a methodological sense, has recently been making a successful claim for the role of a collective concept uniting the diverse approaches that transcend national limits.

Transnational history was first mentioned three decades ago: back in 1991, while criticizing the idea of American Exceptionalism, which he believed was continuing to have a negative influence on historiography in the United States, Ian Tyrrell put forward a 'new transnational history' project.[25] In passing, he noted that comparative history does not necessarily run counter to national exceptionalism, since there is 'the tendency to compare whole countries and to take for granted the primacy of the national unit of analysis'.[26] However, replying later to criticism levelled at his article, Tyrrell stressed that he by no means intended a rejection of comparative history but that he simply considered it essential to distinguish it from the question of national differences; he also remarked that comparative analysis was perfectly capable of being combined with transnational analysis.[27]

Since then, transnational history has acquired a great many adherents; a commonly agreed definition of the approach is still lacking, however. As a discussion in *the American Historical Review* has shown, the boundaries of the concept of 'transnational history' remain blurred; it overlaps with another popular term – 'global history', but unlike the latter it does not necessarily encompass the entire world, instead describes the connections between regions, for example.[28] As Sven Beckert understands it, transnational history is 'an approach to history that focuses on a whole range of connections that transcend politically bounded territories and connect various parts of the world to one another'.[29]

Evidently, the idea of intersecting boundaries forms the core sense of the new approach: since, in Akira Iriye's words, '[t]ransnational history may be defined as the study of movements and forces that cut across national boundaries'.[30] Meanwhile, the 'methodological pluralism' characteristic of the approach is constantly emphasized: in Beckert's opinion, 'transnational history is not bound to any particular methodological approach'; it is a 'way of seeing'.[31] This is mentioned by Sebastian Conrad and Jürgen Osterhammel in their edited collection about the German Empire from 1871 to 1914 in a transnational dimension. The concept 'transnational' concerns 'a paradigmatic approach, which does not have either an elaborated theory or particular research methods behind it'; the concept focuses on links and situations that cross national boundaries.[32]

---

[25] Tyrell (1991a): 1033, 1038, 1044.
[26] Tyrell (1991a): 1035.
[27] Tyrell (1991b): 1069–70.
[28] AHR Conversation (2006): 1442–3, 1446.
[29] AHR Conversation (2006): 1446.
[30] Iriye (2004): 213.
[31] AHR Conversation (2006): 1454, 1459.
[32] Conrad and Osterhammel (2004): 14.

Clearly, the elasticity of transnational history and the fact that it does not have its own methodology facilitates its use as an umbrella concept, drawing together a whole series of closely related approaches. Thus, in one of his articles, Kocka regards *histoire croisée* and 'entangled histories' as varieties of the transnational approach.[33] In a number of joint publications, Kocka and Haupt insist on the fundamental compatibility of comparative and transnational history,[34] and of comparison and the study of 'entanglements' in history,[35] and appeal for 'better combining of comparative and entangled history'.[36]

While these assessments appear generally correct, an important qualification is necessary: unlike *histoire croisée*, 'entangled', transnational and similar histories, comparison is neither an old nor a new historical approach. And if comparative analysis is, indeed, compatible with very diverse approaches and adapts to them, this is not because those using various approaches show 'goodwill' and a readiness for mutual dialogue. The reason is far simpler: as an intrinsic part of historical knowledge there is comparison in virtually everything historians do. Contemporary discussions about the various versions of transnational history therefore bring us back to the fundamental question of the nature of historical comparison, which we will consider in the second part of the book.

---

[33] Kocka (2003): 43.
[34] See their 2009 edited collection: Haupt and Kocka (2009).
[35] Haupt and Kocka (2004): 33.
[36] Kocka and Haupt (2009): 21.

6

Comparative historical sociology

The story of historical comparison in the twentieth century would not be complete without mentioning comparative historical sociology which had its heyday from the 1960s to 1990s, primarily in America.

There were excellent examples of historical sociology in Max Weber's work at the beginning of the twentieth century, but the genre was then long forgotten; even Norbert Elias's major work *The Civilizing Process*, which was published on the eve of the Second World War and was subsequently recognized as a classic of sociology, went virtually unnoticed at the time. Historical sociology enjoyed a revival in America in the first post-war decades. The leaders of its 'second wave' – Barrington Moore Jr. (1913–2005), Reinhard Bendix (1916–91), Charles Tilly (1929–2008) and Theda Skocpol (b. 1947) – succeeded in making historical sociology an influential trend in sociology. From the very beginning, its hallmark – the trend's calling card as it were – was the comparative method, which was used actively by these academics.

Moore's *Social Origins of Dictatorship and Democracy* (1966), in which he attempted to clarify the political role of the rural classes, that is, the landed aristocracy and the peasants, during the transition from an agrarian to an industrial society, became widely known. The book bears the obvious stamp of the Marxist tradition: Moore deduces a kind of class formula for the origins of bourgeois democracy as well as those of fascist and communist dictatorships. This, however, is not the key to the book's success: Moore's research impresses, above all, with its scale (the stories of six countries – England, France, the United States, China, Japan and India – are traced over several centuries, with frequent digressions into the history of Russia and Germany); the boldness of historical parallels; and the originality of its conclusions. Other merits of the book include attention to context, richness of detail and Moore's excellent knowledge of a wide range of literature in several languages, including Russian.

Moore identifies three basic routes to modernization for traditional agrarian societies. Of the countries he studied, Britain, France and the United States took the first route – that of democracy. Moore considers the following to be essential historical conditions for democratic development:[1]

---

[1] Moore (1966): 430–1.

1. Maintenance of a balance of powers that allows the avoidance of too great an intensification of monarchical power and too great a dependence on the landed aristocracy.
2. A shift to a commercial rural economy.
3. A weakening of the landowning nobility.
4. Averting the creation of a coalition between the aristocracy and the bourgeoisie directed against the peasants and workers.
5. A revolutionary break with the past.

Moore notes that individual countries exhibit significant variations within this general trajectory of development. Thus, in England agrarian relations were fundamentally transformed during the lengthy process of enclosure and the puritan revolution in the middle of the seventeenth century curbed the growth of absolutism, but in France, where the socio-economic situation was substantially different at the end of the Ancien Régime, the power of the landed aristocracy was destroyed as a result of the revolution in 1789. Moore's notion that the French Revolution was a partial substitute for, or historical alternative to, the development of the commercial rural economy observed in England is interesting.[2] Furthermore, Moore suggests that if it had not been for the revolution, a merging of the nobility and the bourgeoisie could have led to a conservative modernization from above, as happened in Germany and Japan.[3]

Ultimately, Moore accords the decisive role in his analysis of societal transformations to the balance of class powers. Following Marxist thought, he acknowledges the historical role of the bourgeoisie in the development of parliamentary democracy: 'No bourgeois, no democracy', he states.[4] As for the traditional agricultural classes – the landlords and the peasants – for the sake of democracy they must either change or disappear. But if the bourgeoisie is weak, and the landed aristocracy and the peasantry continue to exist in the new era, a fork in the road appears between two different, non-democratic routes. A reactionary alliance between the landowners and the bourgeoisie, as in Germany and Japan, leads to fascism. Noting a whole series of differences between these regimes,[5] Moore emphasizes very important similarities between Asian and European (German) fascism: both Japan and Germany were late to industrialize and in both countries regimes that combined internal repression with external expansion arose; in both cases, the social basis was a coalition between an industrial elite and the traditional ruling classes in the countryside. Right-wing radicalism developed in both countries due to the petit bourgeoisie's and the peasants' fears of capitalism.[6]

Finally, a third path which leads to communist dictatorship becomes possible where, as in Russia and China, the bourgeoisie is very weak (so much so that the landed aristocracy did not even attempt to make an alliance with it), but where at the same time in the countryside, which was almost untouched by commercialization, peasant communities persisted that had no institutional connections with the higher classes,

[2] Moore (1966): 106.
[3] Moore (1966): 109.
[4] Moore (1966): 418.
[5] Moore (1966): 302–5.
[6] Moore (1966): 305.

and therefore regarded relations with them purely as exploitation. The large agrarian bureaucracies (in Moore's terminology) that existed in these absolute monarchies were another factor that facilitated the unleashing of peasant revolutions.[7]

Of course, such an ambitious and large-scale work could not avoid attracting numerous critical comments. The critics, however – among them both historians and sociologists – were unanimous in recognizing the innovative nature of Moore's book. Thus, in his review ironically entitled *The News from Everywhere*, Lawrence Stone noted many shortcomings in Moore's work including an exaggeration of the degree of landlords' adoption of commercial principles and the speed and violent nature of the disappearance of peasant smallholders in England; a complete disregard for the demographic factor in history; and inattention to the role of ideology in revolution. At the same time, he praised Moore for his 'sophisticated awareness of the complexities of social change', applying the comparative method on a large scale, thorough use of the academic literature and a number of valuable observations. 'A flawed masterpiece' – that was Stone's final judgement. 'Moore's book is nonetheless a pioneer study', wrote Stone, 'remarkably perceptive in its understanding of social and political developments. It is an excellent introduction to the problem of the role of rural society in the creation of the modern world. Challenging, provocative, and irritating, it is a book which forces its readers to think, often in new ways.'[8]

As the sociologist James Mahoney showed recently, having analysed contemporary researchers' observations on the issues of the origins of democracy and authoritarianism, some of Moore's key hypotheses – in particular, that a strong and independent position of the bourgeoisie facilitates the establishment of democracy but its alliance as a junior partner with the landed aristocracy, directed against the peasantry leads to dictatorship – were not borne out by empirical evidence from precisely those countries that he studied (England, Germany, the United States and Japan). Meanwhile, these hypotheses were unexpectedly confirmed as applicable to several countries that remained outside Moore's purview (Austria, Switzerland, Argentina and others).[9] In general, Mahoney believes that Moore's book deservedly takes pride of place in 'the annals of comparative historical research', since Moore's fundamental contribution was not putting an end to the discussion of the sources of dictatorship and democracy, but inspiring subsequent development of hypotheses on a scale that exceeds almost any other work in contemporary social science.[10]

Reinhard Bendix, a colleague and almost exact contemporary of Moore, who had emigrated from Nazi Germany to the United States at the end of the 1930s, used comparison equally actively in his works in the 1960s and 1970s, but in a different, neo-Weberian style. In their chronological and geographical scope, some of Bendix's works are perhaps even wider than *Social Origins of Dictatorship and Democracy*. Thus, in *Kings or People: Power and the Mandate to Rule* (1978), Bendix traces the changes in types of government from medieval monarchies to twentieth-century states using

---

[7] Moore (1966): 477–8.
[8] Stone (1967): 34.
[9] Mahoney (2003): 139–45.
[10] Mahoney (2003): 138.

material from England, France, Germany, Japan and Russia, and in the concluding chapter he touches on the Chinese revolution and modern Arab countries.

In defining the tasks of his research in the introduction to his book, Bendix stresses that unlike numerous works on economics, sociology and psychology that focus on the search for hidden forces governing human behaviour, what interests him are entities that are more accessible to direct observation. By studying the roots of current political and cultural institutions in the distant past, he strives to liberate public consciousness from a stereotypical notion of a contrast between tradition and modernity.[11] An important role in Bendix's project is assigned to comparative analysis, which is intended to 'sharpen our understanding of the contexts in which more detailed causal inferences can be drawn'.[12] Nonetheless, comparative research should not be regarded as a substitute for analysis of cause and effect, because dealing as it does with only a few cases, it cannot identify variables (i.e. the function of causal analysis).

Thus, Bendix uses the comparative method in an entirely different way from Moore: he does not try to search for the causes of historical phenomena and events, does not formulate hypotheses, and following the Weberian tradition of particularizing comparison, accords particular significance to context and strives 'to preserve a sense of historical particularity while comparing different countries'.[13] Bendix's preferred comparative method is contrast: thus, he contrasts Russian autocracy and Prussian absolutism; French and English monarchy at the beginning of the modern era and the Reformation in both countries; and revolutions and the position of the peasants in Russia and China.[14]

However, despite the richness of the material cited in the book, which is gathered from the existing literature and Bendix's solid erudition, the scholarly value of his work provokes serious doubts: the issues and the polemic against his predecessors are not clearly set out; new observations and conclusions are lacking. Bendix's voluminous tome rather resembles a textbook, of particular use to those students interested in Weber's theory of legitimate power, but academic historians are likely to be disappointed by the colourful mosaic formed of well-known facts and lengthy quotations from the works of authoritative scholars.

A complete contrast to Bendix's work is a book by Moore's student Theda Skocpol, which was published almost simultaneously: her *States and Social Revolutions* (1979), which has become one of the most famous but also one of the most contentious works of comparative historical sociology. In this book, based on comparative analysis of the French Revolution, the Russian Revolution of 1917 and the 1911 Chinese Revolution, an attempt is made to explain the general reasons why social revolutions against existing regimes succeed. Skocpol solves the problem she sets, in her words, by the inductive route, consistently employing methods of comparison described by Mill in his *System of Logic* – the method of agreement and method of difference. Underlining common features of the French, Russian and Chinese revolutions (usually seen as being different

[11] Bendix (1978): 14.
[12] Bendix (1978): 15.
[13] Bendix (1978): 15.
[14] Bendix (1978): 239–40, 321–3, 583–5.

in type), Skocpol reinforces her arguments with counterexamples from the history of countries where social revolutions in similar circumstances either did not occur (as in Japan in the Meiji period) or were unsuccessful (as in Germany in 1848).

Eventually, Skocpol comes to the conclusion that sufficient causes for the revolutionary situations in France in 1789; Russia in 1917; and China in 1911 were

1. The administrative and military collapse of state organizations, which were under strong external pressure from more developed countries; and
2. The existing agrarian sociopolitical structures, which facilitated widespread peasant uprisings against landowners.[15]

To a historian's eye, much in Skocpol's book seems strange and even inadmissible. This starts with the fact that of the three languages of the countries she studies, she knows only French; original sources are not cited at all, and she uses secondary sources from monographs written mainly in her native English. The chapters devoted to Russian history are striking for their oversimplification and abundance of stock phrases, and the eulogies to the victorious Bolsheviks are strongly reminiscent of Soviet textbooks. One would need to possess a genuinely boundless faith in the power of induction and Mill's canons to count on using them to draw convincing conclusions from such a highly questionable empirical basis.

Skocpol's book drew serious criticism even from other sociologists. In particular, it was observed that in using the rules of induction formulated by Mill, Skocpol had ignored Mill's own clear instructions that having been developed for the natural sciences, these rules were not applicable to the study of social phenomena[16] (see earlier, p. 14 for Mill's cautions on this). Michael Burawoy notes regarding this that Skocpol was able to develop an influential theory of revolutions thanks to her 'macrosociological imagination that *overrode* Mill's methods at crucial points'[17] (emphasis added by Burawoy – MK). In other words, contrary to Skocpol's assertions, her theory is certainly not the result of induction and does not derive directly from the facts she adduced.

Burawoy rightly points out that in attempting to follow Mill's methods, Skocpol entirely excludes the possibility of the influence of previous revolutions on subsequent ones (after all, the method of agreement assumes a comparison between phenomena that are independent of each other); however, as Skocpol herself mentions in her work, Chinese revolutionaries consciously imitated the Bolsheviks and for a period received advice and assistance from them.[18] Finally, it is impossible to disagree with Burawoy that assumptions made by Skocpol 'are tantamount to freezing world history for three centuries from 1640 to 1947, in the sense that throughout this period revolutions are of a single kind and have the same causes'.[19] Indeed, the events of 1789, 1911 and 1917,

---

[15] Skocpol (1979): 154.
[16] See John Goldthorpe's article, which summarizes the critical remarks previously directed at Skocpol by Elizabeth Nichols and Stanley Lieberson: Goldthorpe (2006): 395.
[17] Buravoy (1989): 763.
[18] Buravoy (1989): 769–70.
[19] Buravoy (1989): 769.

taken out of their historical context as represented by Skocpol, look like abstract logical variables.

Despite being widely known, Skocpol's book can hardly be considered the calling card of contemporary historical sociology: clearly Victoria Bonnell is right in cautioning against underestimating the heterogeneity existing within this research approach.[20] In particular, far from all historical sociologists share Skocpol's satisfaction with secondary sources. Bonnell cites a series of works, including her own and those of Charles Tilly, in which a large amount of empirical evidence is collected and analysed.[21] Some historical sociologists are genuine polyglots like Moore, who used literature in French, German and Russian as well as in his native English in his book on the social roots of democracy and dictatorship. Methods of comparison also vary: the use of induction and Mill's canons has by no means been the rule in historical sociology.

Nevertheless, certain features inherent in Skocpol's work are characteristic of all or most historical sociologists, who attempt to enrich social theory using historical comparison, to dispute previous conceptual models and to propose new ones. Causal analysis is also far more widespread among them than among historians. Finally, several of Skocpol's colleagues who belong to the second wave of historical sociology also show a lack of historical context and sense of zeitgeist. This is true, in particular, of one of Tilly's last works, *Coercion, Capital, and European States AD 990-1992* (1992), in which the effect of two factors – military force and economic resources (capital) – on the formation of states in Europe is studied. All other factors and the diverse interrelations are excluded for ease of analysis; there is virtually no historical context, and the narrative skips from one century or era to another like the gauge on a scientific instrument. Time in Tilly's book is also a physical and not a historical value, which changes evenly, so that each subsequent century is distinguished from the previous one only by number: in particular, the number of sovereign states or other independent political entities diminishes steadily.[22]

As can be seen, sociologists' comparative historical research differs substantially, in both aims and results, from similar work by historians; these differences will be examined in detail in Chapter 8. Nevertheless, despite the clear presence of a disciplinary boundary, familiarity with sociological comparison can be useful for historians.

First, sociologists have long been providing their colleagues in other disciplines with academic terminology (obvious examples are the Weberian buzzwords such as 'charisma' and 'legitimacy', which have become very widely used). Second, however debatable the elaborations of historical sociologists may be, they are capable of providing a conceptual framework for historians' research. Thus, Weber's famous thesis of the Protestant ethic has become a starting point for a number of comparative historical works, including Gerschenkron's essay, which was discussed in Chapter 4. Likewise, specialists in European political history would be hard-pressed to do without Tilly's concept of the correlation between military and economic factors

---

[20] Bonnell (1980): 158.
[21] Bonnell (1980): 172 and note 53.
[22] Tilly (1992).

in the formation of states in modernity. Third, since the problems of the comparative method have been elaborated in far greater detail within sociology than in history, consulting the relevant methodological works[23] can be useful for comparativist historians. Finally, there is value in reading the best works of comparative historical sociology if for no other reason than, as Stone put it of Moore's book, they compel us to think in a new way.

---

[23] See, for example, Ragin (1987), Mahoney and Rueschemeyer (2003), Sica (2006), and Mahoney and Thelen (2015).

Part II

Historical comparison in search of a method

7

Does method exist?

As shown in the first part of this book, comparison has always been part of history. However, history as an academic field began to address the use of the comparative method in research only at the end of the nineteenth century, having been influenced by natural and social sciences that already applied this method widely.

Initially, the comparative method was typically considered to be uniform and applicable to all forms of scholarship. Disagreements over the comparative method related to how fruitfully it could be applied in academic history. Charles-Victor Langlois, while expressing high hopes for the comparative method in an 1890 article (as did his colleagues Gustave Glotz and, later, Louis Davillé), also wrote a textbook with Charles Seignobos entitled *Introduction to the Study of History* (1898), in which he expressed doubts about the feasibility of using the method in historical research. Ernst Bernheim and a number of other German scholars also shared these doubts (see Part I, Chapters 2 and 3).

Subsequently, however, the idea arose that historians required a particular form of the comparative method for their work. Russian historian Nikolai Kareev had already clearly expressed this thought in 1913: mindful of the neo-Kantian division of sciences into the nomothetic and idiographic disciplines, he wrote that the 'comparative study of historical facts is a bridge linking history and sociology. It can serve both the objectives of historical (idiographic) knowledge and the purposes of sociological (nomothetic) knowledge'.[1] Kareev indicated that in 'general historical methodologies... the question of using the comparative method for idiographic purposes remains underdeveloped'.[2]

As mentioned earlier, in an article entitled 'Toward Comparative History of European Societies' (1928), Marc Bloch readily cited linguist Antoine Meillet and anthropologist James George Frazer. Bloch did not borrow their techniques of comparison, however, nor did he borrow any techniques developed by other social scientists. Instead, using examples from his own work, he attempted to demonstrate to his fellow historians the heuristic potential of the comparative method and 'some practical means' of facilitating it.[3]

The development of the comparative historical method continued in the 1960s. In particular, based on descriptions of five distinct functions of comparison, Theodor Schieder identified corresponding forms of the comparative method that were relevant

---

[1] Kareev ([1913] 2010): 193.
[2] Kareev ([1913] 2010): 187, note 1.
[3] Bloch ([1928] 1953): 495.

to history: paradigmatic, analogical, generalizing, particularizing and synthetic.[4] These forms of comparison are given here in the order in which they appeared within academic history. Paradigmatic comparison (i.e. the inference of historical facts from general concepts) and comparison by analogy, as Schieder noted, were already known to historians during the Enlightenment. Generalizing and particularizing comparison, whose nature is clear from their names, have been used since the nineteenth century. Finally, Schieder links synthetic comparison to the development of a typology of historical phenomena and generalizing concepts and sees examples of its use in Max Weber's concept of 'ideal types' and in the works of Otto Hintze and other twentieth-century historians.[5]

However, because of the ambiguity of Schieder's terminology, it is unclear whether he was referring to forms of a single method or the coexistence of different methods. The plural is used in the title of the article concerned ('The Possibilities and Limitations of Comparative Methods in Historical Science'), while in the text Schieder mainly uses 'method' in the singular.[6] But in the conclusion, 'methods' appears again in the plural.[7] Moreover, two of these methods, 'particularizing' and 'generalizing', are mentioned directly.[8]

The historian William H. Sewell based his thinking about the comparative method in history on Bloch's work, and primarily on his classic 1928 article. In Sewell's opinion, the many and varied useful functions of comparison that Bloch noted all have a common logic – that of hypothesis testing.[9] However, in one respect, Sewell was prepared to take issue with his eminent predecessor: he did not agree with Bloch's preference for comparing neighbouring societies, contemporaneous with each other. Sewell believed that comparing social systems that were remote from each other in time and space – such as Germany and Japan as a part of a global analysis of industrialization, for example – could be no less fruitful.[10] Furthermore, Sewell found it necessary to specify the limitations of the potential of the comparative method, which Bloch had not done. Sewell described the most important limitation thus: '*The comparative method is a method, a set of rules which can be methodically and systematically applied in gathering and using evidence to test explanatory hypotheses. It does not supply us with explanations to be subjected to test: this is a task for the historical imagination*'[11] (highlighted in Sewell – MK)

In Sewell's work the clarification of various meanings of the term 'comparative history' stands out: the comparative method, which is the main focus of the article, is just one such meaning. 'Comparative history' can also be understood as meaning comparative perspective – that is, the consideration of historical problems in a wider context, going beyond specific circumstances of time and place. Comparative

[4] Schieder (1968): 217.
[5] Schieder (1968): 199–202, 206–12.
[6] Schieder (1968): 197, 199, 201, 202, 206, 210, 212.
[7] Schieder (1968): 216–17.
[8] Schieder (1968): 218.
[9] Sewell (1967): 209.
[10] Sewell (1967): 215.
[11] Sewell (1967): 217.

perspective does not have the limitations inherent in the comparative method, and it cannot therefore be reduced to a set of simple rules. However, Sewell emphasizes that the majority of historians do not understand 'comparative history' as a method or perspective, but as a kind of subject matter, that is, research that systematically applies comparisons of two or more societies and presents its results in comparative form. Nevertheless, Sewell recommends not restricting the term to such a limited usage, underlining the value of the comparative method and the comparative perspective for all historians.[12]

Bloch's classic article remained a source of inspiration for scholars interested in historical comparison; however, with time, the confidence of historians in the existence of a particular comparative method began to disappear. The year 1980 was crucial in this respect.

In their article, 'Marc Bloch and Comparative History' (1980), Alette and Boyd Hill showed that in practice, Bloch certainly did not follow the linguistic models of comparison that, in his words, were borrowed from Antoine Meillet and which he recommended to his fellow historians.[13] This would appear to be true: the similarly ambivalent relationship that Bloch, one of the most influential historians of the twentieth century, had to the social sciences and the humanities has already been discussed above (see Part I, Chapter 3). But the Hills did not stop at merely establishing this fact: underlining the lack of 'specificity and consistency' in Bloch's assertions about the methodology of comparative history they noticed that because of his enormous influence on all subsequent historiography, the 'flaws' in Bloch's reasoning about the value of linguistic models were reproduced in the work of his followers. Thus, the methodological tradition that had developed the required critical revision.[14] As an example of this influence, the Hills cited Sylvia Thrupp's editor's preface to the first issue of *Comparative Studies in Society and History* (1958) and the article by Sewell cited earlier about Bloch and the logic of comparative history (1967). As the Hills correctly noted, neither of these works contained a clear definition of the comparative method in history.[15]

In a subsequent discussion, Sewell and Thrupp published a response defending the founding father of the comparative historical method against what they regarded as an unjustified attack. Sewell acknowledged the Hills' convincing conclusion that Bloch did not follow the rules of linguistics in his comparative historical research and that his analogy between comparative history and historical linguistics was based on a mistaken understanding which could only lead to error. However, Sewell strongly rejected the Hills' idea that comparative linguistics can in principle serve as a model for comparative history. In Sewell's opinion, 'a strict application of linguistic methods to comparative history is impossible because social structures differ in character from linguistic structures'.[16] Additionally, in responding to the critique, Sewell claims that in spite of Bloch's characteristic 'lack of rigor as a theorist ... he elaborated *in practice*

---

[12] Sewell (1967): 218.
[13] Hill and Hill (1980): 832–4.
[14] Hill and Hill (1980): 837–8.
[15] Hill and Hill (1980): 838, 840.
[16] Sewell and Thrupp (1980): 848.

a comparative method that was consistent, coherent, and appropriate to the subject-matter of history'.[17] Referring to his own 1967 article, Sewell argued that a common logic of hypothesis testing ran through comparative history as Bloch practised it, and for that reason his practice of comparison could be used to formulate methodological rules, which Bloch himself had expressed only partially and imperfectly in his theoretical work.[18]

In her turn, Thrupp considered the Hills' article 'myth-making' and pointed out a number of passages in Bloch's work that they had misunderstood. In her opinion, the weakness of the Hills' thesis about Bloch's mistaken methodology, perpetuated by his 'disciples' after his death, becomes clear in the context of the diversification of comparative methods in all disciplines. In addition, according to Thrupp, many scholars with whom she had long been acquainted shared several of Bloch's views about method without being familiar with his work.[19] It must be said, however, that she was willing to acknowledge one mistake on Bloch's part: in her opinion, Bloch needlessly adhered to the term 'comparative history', which, in Thrupp's words, is 'just about as silly as the term "comparative religion"'.[20]

The attempt to explain the underdevelopment of the comparative method in history with the assertion that historians did not understand or were unable to use the more advanced methodology of comparative linguistics undoubtedly seemed oversimplified and rather unconvincing. However, the defenders of Bloch's legacy, in their turn, could not give a clear answer to the Hills' question about what the comparative method in history actually consists of – such a method, as Sewell's commentary showed, had not yet been created.

In the same October 1980 volume of the *American Historical Review* where the Hills' article and Sewell and Thrupp's reaction appeared, an article by Raymond Grew was published in which he claimed directly that there is no comparative method in history. In the introduction to this book, I have already presented this radical assertion by Grew, who for many years had headed *Comparative Studies in Society and History*, the leading journal on comparative research. It is appropriate to analyse his reasoning in more detail at this point.

Grew maintains that the comparative method in history does not exist. 'The "comparative method"', he writes, 'is a phrase as redolent of the nineteenth century as "the historical method" with which it was once nearly synonymous. For historians, at least, the idea of comparison still needs to be demystified.'[21] In his opinion, 'historical comparison is no more attached to a single method than is the discipline of history itself'.[22]

Concerning the frequently cited distinction between 'method of agreement' and 'method of difference' proposed by Mill, Grew notices that this distinction is a contribution to logic as a discipline, but one that gives scope for different views of

---

[17] Sewell and Thrupp (1980): 850.
[18] Sewell and Thrupp (1980): 850
[19] Sewell and Thrupp (1980): 853.
[20] Sewell and Thrupp (1980): 852.
[21] Grew (1980): 776.
[22] Grew (1980): 776.

comparison depending on whether scholars are studying new questions, defining problems, constructing general models or testing hypotheses. The criteria for selecting items for comparison, as well as criteria for testing internal logic or the relevance of data used in comparative research, are fundamentally no different from those that apply in any social analysis. 'There are not even general rules', claims Grew, 'except for those of logic, and they apply differently according to one's purpose.'[23]

But if historical comparison is not a method, then what is it? It must be acknowledged that Grew's answer to this question is by no means certain: 'To call for comparison is to call for a kind of attitude – open, questioning, searching – and to suggest some practices that may nourish it, to ask historians to think in terms of problems and dare to define these problems independently, and to assert that even the narrowest research should be conceived in terms of the larger quests of many scholars in many fields. To call for comparison, however, says almost nothing about how to do any of this well,' he concludes.[24]

Grew's article could be called a 'manifesto of methodological anarchism', in relation to historical comparison: it offers no rules of comparison and makes no distinction between comparative and any other type of historical research. If in Sewell's above-mentioned 1967 article a wider 'comparative perspective' figured alongside the 'comparative method' – that is, a limited set of rules – then for Grew, this vague 'perspective' replaced method.

However, Grew adds the further proviso that acknowledging that comparison does not involve a particular method does not negate the importance of methodology. In Grew's words behavioural, quantitative, inductive and deductive methods, and formal models and theories of change can all be applied in comparative research.[25] This 'methodological advice' however, is of little help to practitioners of historical comparison, who need specific recommendations for their work rather than simply general words of encouragement.[26]

Grew's article has exerted a noticeable influence on historiography, especially American historiography. Several historians (such as Peter Kolchin and Deborah Cohen) supported his opinion about the 'comparative method',[27] and this term subsequently became used far more rarely in academic literature. The question of how best to clarify the nature of historical comparison persists to this day. Various definitions and descriptions have been proposed, sometimes even in extremely poetic forms: the title of George M. Fredrickson's recent book *The Comparative Imagination*

---

[23] Grew (1980): 776.
[24] Grew (1980): 776.
[25] Grew (1980): 777.
[26] Commenting on his essay twenty-five years later, Grew noted with satisfaction that there had been a significant increase in the volume of comparative historical research published. In doing so, however, he maintained his earlier thesis about the absence of a comparative method in history. In his words, 'Efficacious comparison still seems to me to rest on a cast of mind. More than from any particular method, theory, or topic, comparison flourishes from an imaginative openness to discovery, from an ability to recognize when assumptions need to be challenged, from a willingness to probe expectations unmet, and from the capacity to move across established conceptual boundaries. [. . .] But historical comparison in itself is neither theory nor a method' (Grew (2006): 118, 125, 131).
[27] Kolchin (1982): 75; Cohen (2004): 59.

pleased many.²⁸ More often than not, however, as an alternative to 'comparative method', the vaguer term 'approach' has been used.

The historian Thomas Welskopp wrote in 1995 that the 'comparative approach is not a method but a perspective (*Betrachtungsweise*) that determines a distinctly comparative research strategy when formulating questions'.²⁹ Heinz-Gerhard Haupt and Jürgen Kocka arrived at a similar opinion at the same time: in their words, historical comparison 'is not method in a strict sense, but is more like perspective, technique, approach'.³⁰ They consistently used this same term – 'comparative approach' – in their joint essays in the 2000s.³¹

However, there cannot be said to be a consensus – far less a strict terminology – in contemporary comparative studies: many authors use both 'comparative method' and 'comparative approach' interchangeably in their work, sometimes on the same page, clearly considering them synonymous terms.³² Moreover, the entirely amorphous concept of 'comparative history', a concept Thrupp and Grew long since recommended abandoning, is still in common use.³³

Accordingly, there has been a tendency in historical comparative studies from the end of the twentieth century to replace the term 'comparative method', now recognized as far too strict and constraining, with freer but also more indistinct categories, with the buzzword 'approach' the most prominent of these. No one has tried to accurately characterize this notion, but as indicated earlier, it can be inferred that the term 'comparative approach' is understood to mean a certain 'perspective' or set of techniques (Haupt and Kocka) as well as a 'means of considering problems' (Welskopp). In fact, both 'open and inquisitive attitude' (Grew) and 'comparative imagination' (Frederickson) are close to this understanding of 'approach'.

In order to clarify the concept, it is important to note that in a recent article by Kocka and Haupt, the term 'approach' designates not only historical comparison but also the techniques applied in contemporary research trends, such as the history of transfers³⁴ and transnational and cross-cultural history (*histoire croisée* and entangled histories)³⁵ (see Part I, Chapter 5). Consequently, in contemporary historiography 'approaches' are associated with tendencies or trends, which differ from each other in features such as the attitudes to the world, choice of the scale and subject matter of research and writing style rather than in working methods in the strict sense of the word.³⁶

In view of a rather noticeable though not explicitly articulated tendency in current academic discourse to contrast 'methods' and 'approaches', one can attempt to summarize existing observations and present these as categories of two 'ideal types' (in the Weberian sense). This allows us to understand which of the two more accurately

---

[28] Fredrickson (2000).
[29] Welskopp (1995): 343.
[30] Haupt and Kocka (1996): 12.
[31] Haupt and Kocka (2004): 25, 26, 28; Kocka and Haupt (2009): 8, 13, 20.
[32] Fredrickson (1995b): 599; Kaelble (1999): 11; Miller (2004): 116.
[33] Sewell and Thrupp (1980): 852; Grew (1980): 764, 777.
[34] A history of cultural, conceptual and technological borrowings, influences and exchanges.– MK
[35] Kocka (2003): 39–44; Kocka and Haupt (2009): 1, 6, 8, 13, 20, 21.
[36] These and the subsequent observations are based, in part, on my study of such contemporary trends as historical anthropology, micro-history, new cultural history and so on; see Krom (2010a).

reflects historical comparison – the strict 'method' or the vaguer 'approach'. In this case, the benchmark for 'method' will be quantitative (statistical) methods, which are also used in history, and the description of contemporary 'approaches' will be based on the author's familiarity with such trends as historical anthropology, micro-history, history of everyday life (*Alltagsgeschichte*) and new cultural history.

The resulting picture is shown in Table 1.

As can be seen, historians intuitively distinguish between methods and approaches with good reason (using other words such as 'perspective', 'attitude' and 'imagination', instead of 'approach' at times). These are, indeed, academic research tools belonging to different categories. Method is primarily aimed at gathering and processing material: it is impersonal (the individual who actually invented regression or the interview method is not significant); free from ideology; not susceptible to academic fashion; and resistant to the influence of time. Approach, on the other hand, is very changeable and ideologically charged: it bears the imprint of its creator's personality and brings originality to the research. Above all, 'approach' constitutes a set of ideas and values rather than particular methodological techniques.

Let us now look at which of these two categories proves to be closer to historical comparison. According to criteria such as ideological bias, stability over time and connection with academic trends (characteristics 3–5 in Table 1), comparison is a method. Its origins are lost in the mists of time, but even if its existence is dated to the early decades of the twentieth century, when its systematic development began thanks to the efforts of Max Weber, Otto Hintze and Bloch, the comparative method is approaching its centenary. Several distinct approaches and trends have come and gone during this period. It would be a mistake to conclude from the length of time it has existed that historical comparison has ideological biases. Scholars with entirely different political beliefs and academic views – conservatives and liberals, Marxists and anti-Marxists, and feminists – have successfully employed the comparative method.

Does comparison typically show the influence of the author's personality? Clearly, *The Royal Touch*, Bloch's masterpiece, was dissimilar to Alexander Gerschenkron's *Economic Backwardness in Historical Perspective*, another outstanding achievement

Table 1 Differences between Methods and Approaches Used in Historical Research

№	Characteristic	Method	Approach
1	Potential for use (ease of describing and replicating)	Simple to describe as a sequential operation and to replicate	Difficult to describe and replicate
2	Influence of the scholar's personality (the author's style)	Impersonality, anonymity	Clear expression of the author's style
3	Ideological bias	Freedom from any ideology or world view	Connected to distinct political and academic world views
4	Stability over time, longevity	Exhibits longevity; slightly susceptible to academic fashion	Susceptible to academic fashion; changes with successive generations of scholars
5	Connection to academic trends	Not connected to any academic trend	A synonym for academic trend

of comparative research. But each of these books uses other research tools than comparison and each has its own authorial intent. Techniques of comparison naturally recur: to give a personal example, I became convinced of the heuristic possibilities of comparison in my own research experience even before reading of this function of the comparative method in Bloch's work.

But there is one characteristic of a 'real' method to which comparison does not seem to conform: an unambiguous and exhaustive description of procedures that historians should complete in order to compare various events, developments or processes simply does not exist.

As there are no hard rules about comparison (although since Bloch's time a good many useful recommendations related to various aspects of historical comparison have been proposed), comparativists are not immune to mistakes or simple bad luck. 'Comparative history is a tremendously uncertain business,' Cohen noted on this topic.[37] Certainly, comparative research must be designed afresh for every specific situation; a simple reproduction of past experience is not useful or effective. But does this mean that critics who have completely denied the existence of the comparative method in history are correct?

It is important to state that in Table 1, 'method' represented quantitative (statistical) methods, but other methods usually known as 'qualitative' exist in the social sciences, which also exist in history; these include source criticism, prosopography, the interview method (oral history) and others. No historian is likely to question the existence of the methodology of source criticism, but it would be stretching matters to maintain that only one method of studying sources exists; rather, it is more accurate to speak of methods (or methodological techniques) in the plural. Source criticism theory cannot be expressed in a few single rules; it requires whole books – and as we know, many such books have been written since Langlois and Seignobos's time. And, of course, all practising historians are fully aware that no manual on source studies can replace individual trial and error. The historian's craft – this metaphor, which Bloch brought to prominence, aptly encapsulates the specific character of the profession – is very much determined by the individual scholar's talent and experience and the majority of 'methods' (statistical formulae aside) are in reality simple sets of 'good examples' carried over from the academic practice of previous years.

Consequently, I believe that there is just as much basis to speak about the methodology of historical comparison as about that of source criticism. Taking into account the proliferation of more changeable and short-lived research practices in the contemporary humanities, which are usually referred to as 'approaches', there appears to be sense in reserving the term 'method' for the long-established and better developed basic methods of analysis, of which comparison is one.

The basic tools of historical research comprise the recording of eyewitness narratives (now known as 'interview'), the critical analysis of preserved evidence (i.e. source criticism) and the comparison of the fates of different peoples (comparative studies), all of which were practised in classical historiography, although naturally the ancients did not reflect particularly on these methods or give them any kind of special name. As

---

[37] Cohen (2004): 60.

historical scholarship progressed in the modern age, from the end of the seventeenth century to the end of the nineteenth century, source criticism and auxiliary historical disciplines were elaborated in more detail. As indicated earlier, the methodology of historical comparison began to develop in the first third of the twentieth century – a process that continues to this day. Oral history (the interview method) is more recent still, tracing its origins from the late 1940s.

The answer to the question posed in the title of this chapter would appear to be that a single, comparative historical method – meaning a set of procedures that must be carried out in a specified order – does not, of course, exist. But the methodology of historical comparison has been successfully developing for a hundred years, thanks to the efforts of many distinguished scholars, and many valuable insights have been accumulated within this store of collective experience.

In this respect, the cumulative effect of historical scholarship is very important. Benjamin Kedar has rightly highlighted the lack of emphasis on the accumulation of past research experience in historical comparative studies in the last century: historians have repeatedly presented certain principles of comparison, unaware that similar ideas had already been expressed by one of their predecessors[38] (this fact appears to be an elegant argument in favour of a thesis about the proximity of historical comparison to method, rather than to approach: see the second characteristic in Table 1).

In the following chapters, we will become acquainted with useful observations and recommendations accumulated by several generations of historians who have practised comparison in their work.

---

[38] Kedar (2009b): 26.

8

The functions of comparison and its specifics in historical research

Historians, unlike both sociologists and political scientists, are conspicuous for never having shown particular interest in the logical bases of comparison. When they do reflect on methodology – which they are less given to doing than social scientists – historians prefer to speak about the tasks or useful functions of comparative analysis in the study of the past.

In his day Bloch, one of the founders of modern comparative studies in history, took just such a position. In an article originally written as an entry for *Vocabulaire historique* ('Historical Dictionary') (1930), Bloch quoted the standard definition of the term 'comparison' as the comparing of two or more objects with the aim of establishing similarities and differences between them. Bloch observed

> that comparison understood in such a way is inherent to almost every experience goes without saying. It is important... to be able to establish how this intellectual operation, at the same time both necessary and banal, could give birth in the humanities to a method with a very precise application – the comparative method. In other words, what will be of special interest to us is the definition of historical comparison.[1]

Half a century later, Grew, who had as we know denied the existence of a special comparative method in history, nevertheless reasoned the same way as Bloch in one respect: Grew underlined that the rules of logic (including Mill's canons) did not determine the choice of the types of comparison: the type of comparison applied depended on scholars' aims.[2]

Consequently, historians who consider comparison to be a standard logical operation focus their efforts primarily on determining which research goals can be achieved with the comparative method. The foundations of the contemporary understanding of the useful functions of historical comparison were set out in Bloch's 1928 article. Schieder, Sewell and Kaelble later expanded on his notable contribution to the question of what constitutes the comparative method in history.[3] Today, a larger-

---

[1] Bloch (1930): 32.
[2] Grew (1980): 776.
[3] Schieder (1968): 217; Sewell (1967): 209–11; Kaelble (1999): 48–92.

scale description of the aims that comparison can help achieve in historical research can be found in the works of Kocka and Haupt.[4]

It is mainly the tasks and functions of comparison that define the details of how it is applied in any discipline, including history. One can, moreover, notice important academic shifts by observing how the way in which these tasks are formulated changes over time.

In his article 'Toward a Comparative History of European Societies', Bloch began by enumerating the useful functions of comparison, demonstrating how these functions could assist scholars in discovering previously unknown phenomena. Bloch cited an example from his own research practice, namely the discovery that agrarian reform in Provence was similar to the English enclosure process.[5] In the entry for *Vocabulaire historique* ('Historical Dictionary'), Bloch called this effect of comparison 'propositions for further research'.[6] Contemporary German historians aptly name the function first mentioned by Bloch 'heuristic'. This function, alongside the example cited by Bloch, continues to be the most prominent useful ability of historical comparison.

I can affirm from my own research experience that the heuristic function is a genuinely effective way of transferring academic knowledge and formulating new questions. I will confine myself to one example: until recently, it was thought that the phenomenon of patronage and clientelism – relationships of informal protection – did not exist in Russia before Peter the Great's time. However, familiarity with the extensive literature on patronage in Europe in the sixteenth to the eighteenth century enabled me to develop a programme for researching this issue in the Russian context. It became clear that the sources that should be consulted in order to find traces of the phenomenon lay in private correspondence and that aspects of the subject that merited particular attention included the language of patronage and its social functions. We now know that patron–client relations permeated sixteenth- to seventeenth-century Muscovy just as it did other societies in the early modern age (although naturally this phenomenon exhibited its own particular qualities in Russia).[7]

A different function of comparison, which Bloch noticed and demonstrated brilliantly in *The Royal Touch*, is identifying the directions of borrowings and influences. Contemporary comparativists devote little attention to this use of comparison; this may be because the theme has recently become the subject of a particular trend, that is, the history of transfers. However, I consider the lack of attention to this function an oversight. If we want to see a cumulative effect in the development of the methodology of comparative analysis, then not a single useful observation that is based on research practice should be forgotten. As far as different kinds of transfers are concerned, comparison plays a key role in revealing the sources of borrowing and evaluating its effectiveness. In particular, this function of comparison is illustrated by recent work

---

[4] Haupt (2001): 2400–1; Kocka (2003): 40–1; Kocka and Haupt (2009): 3–5.
[5] Bloch ([1928] 1953): 499–501.
[6] Bloch (1930): 36.
[7] Krom (2009).

on the use of foreign standards during reforms in both the Russian army and Russia's judicial and administrative system in the seventeenth and eighteenth centuries.[8]

Another important function of comparison in historical research is its power to explain or elucidate; German scholars describe this as 'analytical function'.[9]

Historians have long understood 'explanation' first and foremost to be a search for the causes of the phenomena they study, which relies heavily on comparison. Thus, Langlois wrote in 1890: 'If historical science does not consist solely in the critical enumeration of past phenomena, but rather in examination of the laws which regulate the succession of such phenomena, clearly its chief agent must be the comparison of such phenomena as run parallel in different nations; for there are no surer means of knowing the *conditions* and *causes* of a particular fact than to compare it with analogous facts'[10] (emphasis added by Langlois – MK).

Bloch also recommended carefully familiarizing oneself with 'related phenomena', as 'they can be helpful in the discovery of causes'. In his opinion, 'in the exhilarating, never-ending search for causes, the comparative method may again render invaluable service. It may lead historians to track down real causes, and, to begin with a more modest but undeniable advantage, it may guide them away from kinds of research which would lead only to a dead end'.[11]

Characteristically, however, Bloch did not explain how to use the comparative method to reach 'true causes' in either his 1928 article or his later works. Instead, he convincingly demonstrated the important role of comparison in determining the true scale of the phenomena studied and in eliminating local – and, therefore, often false – causes.[12] We notice that the role of comparison here is *negative*: the issue is what Sewell, having analysed Bloch's works, called the 'logic of hypothesis testing'.[13] It is, in fact, sufficient to show just one case analogous to that being studied which does not fit with the explanation suggested previously, in order to reject that explanation as untenable. However, as Sewell correctly noted (his judgement on this was mentioned in the previous chapter), the ability of the comparative method in this respect is limited: it is not able to provide new explanations to replace those that have been rejected.

Bloch reflected on the issue of causality in history until the end of his life. Many will probably remember the lines that abruptly ended his final book, *The Historian's Craft*, and which have become a kind of academic testament: 'in history, as elsewhere, the causes cannot be assumed. They must be sought.'[14] Subsequent generations of historians, as though at his behest, have diligently continued this search for causes. However, faith in our ability to find the 'true causes' of phenomena and events has weakened considerably, as has the hope that this aim can be achieved using comparison.

---

[8] See the articles of Oleg Kurbatov, Dmitrii Serov and Galina Babkova in the edited collection, Krom and Pimenova (2013): 231–89.
[9] Kaelble (1999): 49 et seq.; Kocka (2003): 40–1; and Kocka and Haupt (2009): 4.
[10] Langlois (1890): 259.
[11] Bloch ([1928] 1953): 504.
[12] Bloch ([1928] 1953): 505, 506.
[13] Sewell (1967): 208–10.
[14] Bloch ([1949] 1954): 197.

A turning point in historians' attitude to causal analysis has occurred during the last decade. It is noteworthy that along with hypothesis testing, Kaelble's book (1999) and Haupt (2001) and Kocka's (2003) articles on the analytical function of comparison included the determination of causes.[15] However, Haupt and Kocka's most recent summary of developments in comparison and its future prospects, in the preface to their 2009 edited collection, does not refer to causal analysis. They now mention the 'contribution of comparison to the explanation of historical phenomena', including the critique of false interpretations, hypothesis testing and generalizations.[16]

American comparativists have recently expressed interesting thoughts on the problem of causality in history. Cohen called this problem 'the thorniest' of all those which comparative history raises.[17] She uses her book on the plight of disabled veterans of the First World War in Britain and Germany as an example of the difficulties connected to the search for causes in comparative research. Cohen tried to answer the question of why German veterans, who received a relatively good pension and the best social welfare provision in Europe, appeared inclined to turn against the Weimar Republic. During the same time period, successive British governments did not pay special attention to veterans, who nevertheless remained loyal subjects. Cohen concluded that the decisive factor in the differing reactions of German and British veterans was the relationship of each society to its veterans, as well as the veterans' own opinions of their fellow citizens. Other important differences between the two countries in the 1920s and 1930s, such as the different outcomes of the war for Germany and Britain, and the possibilities of what could be achieved through extra-parliamentary action, were considered context rather than explanation.[18]

However, reflecting on her research some years after the publication of her book, Cohen mentioned that although her research had followed long-established principles, the results of her attempted causal analysis could hardly be considered entirely satisfactory. 'And how do historians, who are, after all, not white-coated rationalists operating in a laboratory', she asked rhetorically, 'disentangle one factor from the other? If we demonstrate that Protestantism was not necessary for the development of capitalism in country A, have we necessarily diminished its significance in country B?' The essence of the problem, as Cohen correctly underlines, is in the *interplay* of different factors that often escape from view in many comparative studies.[19]

It is difficult to disagree with another of Cohen's comments, namely, that every comparativist, in trying to explain the existence of differences, encounters the problem of separating cause from context.[20] In practice, however, explanations that historians offer are more often than not mainly contextual, that is, situational, and not causal. In other words, factors that may be recognized by scholars as crucial in a given historical situation are not strictly 'causes' in a scientific sense, that is, there are no grounds on which to argue that a particular factor will invariably lead to exactly these consequences.

[15] Kaelble (1999): 49; Haupt (2001): 2400–1; Kocka (2003): 40–1.
[16] Kocka and Haupt (2009): 4.
[17] Cohen (2004): 62.
[18] Cohen (2001).
[19] Cohen (2004): 62, 64.
[20] Cohen (2004): 63.

The problem does not change fundamentally even if the number of countries compared increases from two, as in Cohen's book, to, for example, five, as in Peter Baldwin's research on the class bases of the European welfare state mentioned earlier (see Part I, Chapter 4). Interpreting events is difficult in any case, taking into account many factors and local peculiarities, and can in no way be reduced to a single cause.[21]

In the same collection in which the essay by Cohen cited earlier was published, Baldwin also focused on the noticeable recent decline of interest shown by historians in establishing causal connections. Baldwin is inclined to explain this tendency by more than the linguistic turn or a priority of cultural history alone: 'Causality has come to be seen as part of a fixation on monocausal, reductionist, or at least overly parsimonious explanations rooted in an older and increasingly outmoded social-scientific paradigm.' Baldwin observes that history, and particularly cultural history, is much more interested in the question of 'what', rather than the question of 'why', paying more attention to complexity than causal connections.[22]

Thus, as the priorities of historical scholarship change, the aims that scholars try to achieve through comparison also change. If a century ago the basic goal of the comparative method was considered to be the search for causes of phenomena, then it would now appear that this task has largely dropped off the agenda of comparative studies and been replaced by other intellectual goals. Judging by articles in which Kocka and Haupt have reviewed and looked beyond the current state of historical comparison, the most important functions of comparison in history today are heuristic, descriptive, analytic and paradigmatic.[23] We will now turn from the heuristic and the analytic to the two remaining functions.

The term 'descriptive function' is, in fact, rather unfortunate: it obscures rather than elucidates this effect of comparison. What it denotes is the illumination of particular cases and the revelation of their individual nature. It is therefore more appropriate to use 'contrasting comparison', a term utilized by Haupt.[24] The name of the relevant logical operation – in this case, 'particularization', and 'particularizing comparison' – can also be used.

Max Weber and Otto Hintze considered this the main function of comparison (see Part I, Chapter 3). Bloch also saw one of the tasks of comparative history as being the 'clarification of differences' and showing the 'originality' of different types of society.[25] Demonstrating the potential of this method to solve such problems, Bloch conducted a comparative analysis of two forms of medieval personal subordination that were outwardly extremely similar – French serfdom and English villeinage – and established significant differences between them.[26]

---

[21] See the final conclusions in Baldwin's book: Baldwin (1990): 288–99.
[22] Baldwin (2004): 18. In confirmation of Baldwin's keen observation about the attention of contemporary historians to the problem of complexity, one may refer to the recent article by Giovanni Levi, one of the 'founding fathers' of micro-history, see Levi (2012).
[23] Kocka and Haupt (2009): 3–5.
[24] Haupt (2001): 2400.
[25] Bloch ([1928] 1953): 507.
[26] Bloch ([1928] 1953): 507–10.

Subsequently, historians have resorted to comparison time and again in order to discover the specific nature of phenomena. Kocka and Haupt have presented several useful instances: for example, the relatively early appearance of the labour movement in Germany as an independent force merits attention only in the context of the history of labour movements in other countries, particularly in England and the United States. The unusually influential position, cohesion and important historical role of the German-educated middle class is also apparent only in comparison with other European societies.[27]

In my research practice, I have used the particularizing (contrasting) function of comparison to eliminate what Bloch called 'pseudo-similarities'.[28] Until recently, Russian historians gave little thought to using the term 'regency' to describe the rule of Princess Olga in place of her young son Sviatoslav; Elena Glinskaya in place of the young Ivan IV; or Sophia in place of her stepbrothers Ivan and Peter. The use of this conventional European term in this case maintains the illusion of regency, as though referring to the institution of transferring power to a temporary ruler for the period of the monarch's minority which developed in western Europe around the fourteenth century. However, on closer inspection it seemed that before Peter the Great, there was neither the appropriate terminology nor the legal basis for determining the full authority of the regent in Russia, in contrast to what had been established in the West. What had appeared to historians of Russia to be regency, turned out on examination to be a different institution, namely, co-rule. The institution of regency did not, in fact, arise in Russia; my assumption is that this is because it was incompatible with the autocracy that developed in the sixteenth and seventeenth centuries.[29]

Kocka and Haupt named the final purpose or useful function of comparison that they outlined as 'paradigmatic'. This rather vague term signifies the capacity of comparison to make what is familiar and self-evident in history strange and unfamiliar and what appears to be an exceptional case just one of many versions of development. Kocka grasps the essence of this effect of comparison with a term employed in one of his previous articles: the German word, *Verfremdung* ('making strange').[30]

But even this most complete contemporary classification of the functions of historical comparison that Kocka and Haupt present is not exhaustive. If the absence within it of a task such as the search for causes can be considered a reflection of the tendency towards objectivity characteristic of contemporary historiography, then other omissions are apparently due to the authors' individual preferences. This applies in particular to the role of comparison in analysing the various influences and borrowings alluded to earlier, and also to the capacity – which had already been mentioned by figures in the eighteenth-century Enlightenment – of the comparative method to fill in gaps in our factual knowledge using judgements by analogy. Johann Gustav Droysen recommended this use of comparison in the nineteenth century,[31] and

---

[27] Kocka and Haupt (2009): 3.
[28] Bloch ([1928] 1953): 507.
[29] Krom (2010b, 2011).
[30] Kocka (2003): 41.
[31] Droysen (1937): 159–60.

it was also mentioned by Bloch (who referred to the work of ethnographers)[32] as well as Schieder,[33] but contemporary comparativists appear to eschew such uses of analogy.

Additionally, it is important to remember comparison's indispensable function as a determinant of the true scale of the phenomenon studied. For example, until recently, historians regarded the early modern state as a predominantly western European phenomenon.[34] The inclusion of Polish and Scandinavian material in the seven-volume series on the origins of the modern state that was published in the 1990s did not result in a revision of the existing model, and the eastern periphery of Europe remained unexamined (this project by European historians is discussed in more detail in Part III, Chapter 12). Meanwhile, as the latest research indicates, both the Muscovite tsardom and the Ottoman Empire of the sixteenth to the seventeenth century exhibited the main features of an early modern state.[35] Expanding the geographical scope of the model thus substantially changes its description.

Finally, it should be remembered that the terms and generalizing concepts historians use also implicitly involve comparison. As we will see in the third part of the book, established categories such as 'absolutism' or 'feudalism' have recently undergone revision, and it was comparison that served as the main tool of the critique.

Defining the purposes and scope, or functions, is a necessary initial stage in the development of any method. As is apparent from what has been set out previously, only the first steps in this direction have been taken in historical comparative studies. While the heuristic, analytic (hypothesis testing) and particularizing (contrasting) functions of comparison have been described in sufficient detail and specific scenarios for their use in historical research have been suggested, other possibilities for this method, including typological analysis and modelling, have not been developed in detail.

However, despite the incomplete nature of existing descriptions of the purposes and functions of comparison in historical research, these descriptions are still of undeniable interest to historians, both in a methodological respect – as valuable guidelines for scholars practising historical comparison – and in a historiographical sense as a basis for understanding the specific nature of historical comparison.

The question of how comparison in history differs from comparison in the social sciences was raised long ago: contrasting the purposes of history and sociology, Kareev wrote in 1913 that 'it is necessary in a comparative study to distinguish between the comparative historical and comparative sociological parts: both are used for comparison of historical (or ethnographic) facts, but the historian is interested in merely facts between which one can establish a genetic connection, and the sociologist is primarily interested in facts that can provide evidence in every example of the same cause leading to the same consequence'.[36] But the methodological barrier erected by Neo-Kantians between so-called 'idiographical' and 'nomothetic' disciplines turned

---

[32] Bloch (1930): 36–7.
[33] Schieder (1968): 202, 217.
[34] Strayer (1970): VI, 12, 53; Genet (1990b): 261–2, 279; Genet (1997): 6, 8.
[35] On Muscovy as an early modern state see Kivelson (1997): 636, 641, 663; Krom (2018): 16–18, 233–8. For a comparison of the Ottoman Empire and early modern Europe, see Abou-El-Haj (1991); Barkey (1994): 229–42; and Goffman (2002): 1–20.
[36] Kareev ([1913] 2010): 192.

out to be illusory. By the middle of the twentieth century, prominent social scientists began to doubt both their ability to reveal certain 'laws' about the structure of society and the existence of fundamental differences between their disciplines and history.

In 1963, the anthropologist Edward Evan Evans-Pritchard questioned what his colleagues had managed to achieve using the comparative method since the publication of Montesquieu's *Spirit of the Laws* more than two hundred years earlier. Evans-Pritchard appraised the results of the contribution of this method in anthropology with extreme scepticism, stating that there was 'certainly little which could be acclaimed as laws commensurable with those which in the natural sciences have been reached in the two centuries'.[37] Two years earlier, in a lecture entitled 'Anthropology and History' at the University of Manchester, Evans-Pritchard had stated that it is very difficult to draw a clear boundary between the disciplines of anthropology and history. He claimed that differences observed in the approaches of anthropologists and historians arose because of factors such as the differing materials of their research and a rather different descriptive style. In his opinion, 'social anthropology and history are both branches of social science, or social studies'.[38]

Sociologists acknowledged a similar notion in the 1970s and 1980s. Thus, Anthony Giddens argued in 1979 that 'logical, and even methodological, differences simply do not exist between social sciences and history if they are properly understood'.[39] His colleague Jean-Claude Passeron demonstrated that sociology, like history, represents a form of natural reasoning. Historian Antoine Prost noted on this point that historians do not diverge from natural reasoning and suggested that the difference between the two disciplines lay in the stricter and more all-encompassing application of natural reasoning within sociology, as compared to history.[40]

Based on the current understanding of the common nature of social knowledge, one should reject the earlier hypothesis (in particular as expressed by Kareev a century ago, see p. 86) about the existence of various comparative methods such as 'comparative historical' and 'comparative sociological'. There is one comparative method which has a general character spanning all disciplines but adapts according to the conventions of each in terms of basic principles, tasks and priorities. However, one must not underestimate existing disciplinary boundaries: as shown earlier (see Part I, Chapter 6), not only does sociologists' comparative historical research differ noticeably from the work of historians who practise comparison but at times sociologists' work is also completely inadmissible to historians.

The only attempt to highlight the specific nature of comparative studies as opposed to the comparative analysis applied in various social sciences of which I am aware was made by Kaelble. Admittedly, this attempt was not entirely successful. The

---

[37] Evans-Pritchard (1963): 25.
[38] Evans-Pritchard (1961): 18.
[39] Cited in Abrams (1980): 14. Abrams, commenting on this observation of Giddens, called it much too optimistic, believing that history and sociology still had far to go in developing a common language in which to express a clearly visible common logic of explanation (Abrams 1980). Nevertheless, elsewhere in his article Abrams says that history and sociology are in essence 'the same enterprise' (Abrams 1980: 5).
[40] Prost (1996): 206.

characteristic traits of historical comparison that Kaelble noted included a particular treatment of space (more pronounced among historians than among sociologists and anthropologists attempting to learn general rules of human behaviour) and time (for historians, time fragments into many periods); an attention to the context, language and concepts of a period; and a particular attitude towards sources.[41] In fairness, it should be noted that these observations relate not to historical comparison per se but to the specific nature of history as a discipline and to those most basic attitudes and orientations of historians that set history apart from other social sciences. If we are interested in the specifics of comparative analysis in history, we can obtain valuable insights by balancing the judgements of historians on the functions of comparison with sociologists' views on the same matter, as analysed earlier.

Let us, for example, examine the most well-known classification of the types of comparison in historical sociology, proposed by Theda Skocpol and Margaret Somers in 1980. They divide all comparative historical research into categories:

1) parallel demonstration of theory;
2) contrast-oriented comparative studies; and
3) macro-analytical, or macro-causal, analysis.

As an example of the first type, Skocpol and Somers examine Shmuel Eisenstadt's book, *Political Systems of Empire* (1963); for the second type they refer to the works of Reinhard Bendix; and for the third, to Barrington Moore Jr.'s classic *Social Roots of Democracy and Dictatorship* (1966), as well as Skocpol's monograph *States and Social Revolutions* (1979).[42] Naturally, Skocpol and Somers also encounter transitional or mixed types of comparison. For example, in their opinion, Perry Anderson's *Lineages of the Absolute State* (1974) combines both the approaches of 'parallel demonstrations of theory' (in this case Marxist) and the highlighting of contrasts between different versions of the same model of development.[43]

This classification clearly reflects Skocpol and Somers's scholarly interests as well as their style of thinking: these include prioritizing theory, an enthusiasm for causal analysis and a predilection for a clear-cut formal and logical schema. Notably, the heuristic function – detecting previously unknown past phenomena and formulating new questions in relation to these – is very important to historians but clearly not a high priority for sociologists. Conversely, developing theories, which is very significant for sociologists, remains alien to the majority of historians, including comparativists.

Consequently, although the division of sciences into idiographic and nomothetic has long since fallen out of favour, history continues to a greater extent than sociology to be an empirical discipline and as previously, historians are wary of excessively bold generalizations. As Baldwin puts it, 'comparison does not necessarily mean generalization. Indeed, in the hands of historians, it should never do so.'[44] In Baldwin's

---

[41] Kaelble (1999): 97–113.
[42] Skocpol and Somers (1980): 175–87.
[43] Skocpol and Somers (1980): 187–8.
[44] Baldwin (2004): 11.

opinion, testing 'the validity of generalizations formulated by the harder social sciences [is] one of the most common operations of comparative history'.[45]

One can also hypothesize that the focus on searching for causes, so typical of the comparative historical sociology of the 1960s and 1980s, was an attempt to achieve the ideal of 'strict scientific rigour', as Émile Durkheim had understood it, which involved following the methods of the natural sciences. As shown in this chapter, present-day historians have become disillusioned with the capabilities of causal analysis and have ceased to set such tasks in their comparative scholarship.

However, one cannot fail to notice that the agendas of comparativist historians and historical sociologists overlap on several points: tasks such as profiling (contrasting comparison) of cases and hypothesis testing are considered a high priority for comparative research in both disciplines. Moreover, we should not forget that the logical basis of comparison is identical, whatever the purposes of comparative research. Therefore, the sociologist Charles Tilly's 1984 proposition for classifying the types of comparison according to formal criteria (such as the quantity of events studied – one or many – and the homogeneity or heterogeneity of given phenomena) is suitable for describing historians' comparative research as well as the research of historical sociologists (for whom the classification was developed).

This typology includes particularizing, universalizing, variation-finding and, finally, encompassing comparison.[46] Examples of all four types that Tilly describes are drawn from the books of his sociologist colleagues (Bendix, Skocpol, Moor and Stein Rokkan, respectively), but had he wished, Tilly could also have cited works by historians. Notably, an important 1965 article by Schieder, of which Tilly was apparently unaware, listed five forms of the comparative method in history: paradigmatic, analogous, generalizing, particularizing and synthetic.[47] The similarity between the two scholars' classifications is manifest. One must make the proviso that for reasons mentioned earlier, historians are far more willing to use contrasting, or particularizing, comparison than generalizing comparison. Nevertheless, despite the diverse forms and specific methods of comparison arising from the particular nature of each discipline – as well as the preferences of scholars who are currently shaping comparison – the general scientific method retains its cohesion.

[45] Baldwin (2004): 11.
[46] Tilly (1984): 81–2. Belgian philosopher Anton van den Braembussche also developed his classification of comparative methods in history, having combined the versions of Tilly and Skocpol and Somers: Braembussche (1989); however, the proposed typology did not receive wide circulation.
[47] Schieder (1968): 217.

9

Selection of objects for comparison and types of historical comparison

The selection of objects for comparison in comparative studies is considered a difficult and demanding process: disputes over what within history can be compared and what can never be compared have been continuing for more than a century.

Thus, Langlois considered that comparing primitive societies was simple, but complex comparison in the organized societies of the modern age, on the contrary, was very difficult, if even possible: 'it would be useless to compare the present institutions of China with those of France, or of England – even of England under the Georges – with those of France under the Bourbons; they have nothing in common,' he argued.[1] Interestingly, he formed a similar opinion inspired by the theories of natural science:

> we may profitably compare the lower types of vegetable and animal kingdoms, but it is manifestly impossible and absurd to compare the organs of a man and those of an oak with a view to discovering their respective genealogies. Only analogous things can be compared, having real purpose, and in the history of modern nations all the analogies are most remote, for they are beings with peculiar and marked personalities, and have long been such.[2]

Instead, he confidently recommended comparing England and France in the Middle Ages, seeing this instance as 'the ideal condition for an easy and legitimate application of the comparative method'. In that era, almost all of the elements of the history of both countries were symmetrical: they had common origins to a certain degree and had come into contact with each other repeatedly over many centuries.[3]

As we know, Bloch maintained a similar point of view on the issue of selecting objects for comparison, with his preference for neighbouring societies: since this parallel comparison could be more strictly controlled, it meant that Bloch anticipated more exact conclusions.[4] He did not completely reject 'long-range comparison' but

---

[1] Langlois (1890): 260.
[2] Langlois (1890): 260.
[3] Langlois (1890): 261.
[4] Bloch ([1928] 1953): 498.

treated it critically, and judging by examples he quoted, considered this device more appropriate for ethnographers than for historians.⁵

However, Bloch's arguments did not subsequently convince Sewell, who can be said to have 'rehabilitated' the comparison of societies distant from each other.⁶ Furthermore, Sewell significantly deepened the understanding of the issue of units of comparison, having emphasized, first, that they depend on which explanatory hypothesis one is trying to test using comparison. Second, he emphasized that these units do not necessarily need to be geographical in nature (such as villages and regions), because the comparison pertains to different *social systems*, from the family to entire civilizations.⁷ Sewell's idea that there is no value in applying a comparative framework if no explanation is required for the problem also merits attention.⁸

At the very end of the twentieth century, Marcel Detienne, a historian of ancient Greece, expressed an opinion that was in direct contrast to that which had prevailed in Langlois and Bloch's time and which even now has many adherents among historians: he called upon his colleagues 'to compare the incomparable' (*comparer l'incomparable*), believing that only juxtaposing societies that are very distant from each other in time and space (a common practice in anthropology) can be a genuinely fruitful method of comparison.⁹ However, for the moment, there are few historians ready to follow this advice.

Scholars currently tend to consider that the comparability of historical phenomena is not established *a priori*, but is determined in each specific instance depending on how questions are formulated in the research.¹⁰ Thus historians have come, albeit belatedly, to appreciate a principle that has already been long understood by specialists in other disciplines who successfully apply the comparative method. In the words of biologist Georgii Liubarskii, '*uniformity (isomorphism) of objects is the result of the work of the scientific apparatus, and not the attribute of reality.* [. . .] The scientific method (in particular, the comparative method) makes real objects compatible, comparable, available for further study' (highlighted in Liubarskii – MK).¹¹ Accordingly, if certain historians were to accuse others of comparing phenomena that had nothing in common with each other, this would merely indicate that the critics believed that the authors of the research could not draw convincing conclusions from the comparison they conducted. One should not, however, deduce from this that the objects concerned bear no relation to one another: by altering the research design and reformulating the problem, their juxtaposition may be entirely effective. The historian Michael Confino was thus critical of Kolchin's *Unfree Labor* (1987), in which Kolchin compared American slavery and Russian serfdom up to its abolition in 1861. In Confino's opinion, the differences between these phenomena were excessively great in comparison to their

---

⁵ Bloch (1930): 37.
⁶ Sewell (1967): 215.
⁷ Sewell (1967): 213.
⁸ Sewell (1967): 214.
⁹ Detienne ([2000] 2008).
¹⁰ Kaelble (1999): 138; Haupt and Kocka (2004): 27.
¹¹ Liubarskii (2000): 11, 12.

similarities.¹² However, as will be shown in the third part of this book, not all feedback on Kolchin's monograph was as negative. Historians from different specialties showed great interest in the book, suggesting that its successes were greater than its failures. Whatever the evaluation of Kolchin's work, it could not in itself resolve the question of the comparability of the enforced labour systems that Kolchin studied.

From a methodological point of view, asserting scholars' freedom of choice in selecting objects for comparison brings great uncertainty, which in practice poses considerable difficulties for comparativists. Thus, Kaelble cautions colleagues against comparing institutions that, despite having the same name, had entirely different purposes in different societies. A particular example was that of German universities in the nineteenth century, which were schools of higher education, while French universities were, instead, institutions for conducting exams (*Prüfungsbüros*). Kaelble points out that one must bear in mind that one institution can have different functions in different societies. For example, the choice of cities such as Paris, London, Dublin, Bonn, Bern and the Hague for the comparative study of European capitals after the Second World War is extremely problematic: the capital cities of Switzerland, Holland and, until 1990, West Germany functioned as the main political centres of these countries, while London, Paris and Dublin acted as converging points for cultural and economic life.¹³

In my view, the first of Kaelble's examples is more convincing than the second. In any case, this does not mean that certain objects are by their nature incomparable; the issue is the manner and material necessary to construct effective comparative research. Unfortunately, there are evidently not enough practical recommendations on this topic in the existing literature. For instance, Haupt and Kocka write that 'the objects of comparison must show a minimum similarity so as to allow comparison, which of course always means that they can be studied with regard to their differences'.¹⁴ But how should one understand this 'minimum similarity' that is necessary in order for comparison to be possible? I was unable to identify the answer to this question within historical scholarship and therefore turned, instead, to a book by the biologist Liubarskii, which throws light on the problem of comparison in history from the point of view of his discipline, which possesses the most developed morphology at the present time.

As Liubarskii puts it, there are three universal criteria of similarity (homology) in total:

1) distinctive quality: if two phenomena have a common characteristic trait, they are similar, or homologous;
2) location: if two phenomena occupy the same place within a more general phenomenon, then there is similarity between them; and
3) criterion of range: if one can organize a continuous series of transitions between two phenomena, then these phenomena are similar to each other.

---

[12] Confino (1990); Confino (2009): 101–10.
[13] Kaelble (1999): 139.
[14] Haupt and Kocka (2004): 27.

Since the third criterion depends on the first two (similarity between any two members of a series is established by the criteria of quality or location), then it is precisely these two that form the basis of comparison.[15]

However, fundamental arguments arise, as a rule, not over the existence of similarities between historical phenomena (scholars usually grapple with this intuitively), but about the academic significance of these similarities and their priority in relation to other possible lines of comparison. Thus, the American slavery of the first half of the nineteenth century can be compared with slavery in another era (antiquity, for example), in other countries (e.g. in Latin America), or if, as Kolchin does, one considers slavery a variety of unfree labour, then with Russian serfdom or other forms of personal subordination. But if a scholar is interested in the question of the economic effectiveness of slave-holding plantations, then the contrasted unit of comparison must be farming landowners who used the work of hired labourers during the same period. Consequently, the *comparative range* in which the phenomenon studied is embedded depends entirely on the problem set by the scholar.

But whatever the goal of the research, the success of the comparative operation depends on having a 'third item' (*tertium comparationis*) in addition to the units of comparison. This 'third item' acts as a more general and generic concept in relation to the objects compared. Consequently, in comparative research, correct design assumes a particular – hierarchical – relationship between the central problem of study and the cases compared, which demonstrate its manifestations in different contexts.[16] Obviously, the units of comparison along with the 'third item' linked to them must belong to the same categories, for instance, social phenomena, structures and processes, or political institutions.[17]

We return now to the question of the selection of objects of comparison: What is the optimum number of these? There are no definitive recommendations on this, since the answer depends entirely on the aims of the particular research.

More often than not, comparison of any type of phenomenon spans two or more countries. Since Bloch's time, comparison of neighbouring and contemporaneous societies has commonly been called *parallel* comparison. This differs from comparison of communities separated in time and space, which contemporary academic literature suggests calling 'cross-comparison' or 'cross-cultural' comparison.[18] *The Royal Touch* and several of Bloch's other works are excellent examples of parallel comparison – for instance, of the political and social institutions of medieval England and France. The section dedicated to Japanese feudalism in Bloch's book, *Feudal Society*, can also be considered an example of cross-cultural comparison.

---

[15] Liubarskii (2000): 16.
[16] On the notion of *tertium comparationis*, see Welskopp (1995): 343, 345; Kocka and Haupt (2009): 14.
[17] 'Processes can be compared only with processes, and structures only with structures. One cannot compare processes with structures,' Miroslav Hroch said in his 2012 lecture at the European University Institute: Miroslav Hroch, 'Comparing National Movements in Nineteenth-Century Europe', lecture given at the Summer School on Comparative and Transnational History of Europe, European University Institute, Florence, 11 September 2012.
[18] For more about these terms, see Kedar (2009b): 2 and note 8.

Parallel, and especially paired, comparison predominates contemporary historical comparative scholarship. Examples include Alisa Klaus's and Susan Pederson's monographs on the gender aspects of social politics in the United States and France in the nineteenth and twentieth centuries, and in Great Britain and France from 1914 to 1945; Cohen's book about the plight of disabled veterans of the First World War in Germany and Great Britain;[19] Christiane Eisenberg's research on the English and German labour movements from the nineteenth to the early twentieth century;[20] and many others. Cross-cultural comparisons are less common: examples are Kolchin's book on American slavery and Russian peasantry[21] and the works of George Fredrickson about race relations and ideologies in the United States and South Africa.[22]

If the number of objects to be compared is limited to two or three, scholars benefit from the opportunity to engage with rich source materials originating from all of the countries or regions studied, taking the relevant context into account. But serious limitations also exist: as a rule, the problems that interest scholars and which play the role of 'third item' in comparative research do not fit into those few countries that are on individual scholars' radar. For this reason, parallel comparison lacks the potential for any kind of complete generalization about a given phenomenon or for speaking about the reasons that it developed (one otherwise risks being taken prisoner by what Bloch called 'local false causes') or its patterns of development. This type of comparison is best suited to the task of illuminating individual cases and discovering specific behaviours associated with a particular process or the formation of a particular institution in a certain country or region.

But if historians aim to study a certain phenomenon in full – to construct a model of it and show specific regional characteristics or versions as Bloch did in *Feudal Society* – then the number of units of comparison naturally increases. In this case, however, new difficulties arise: as Kocka and Haupt write, 'the more comparative cases are included, the smaller the opportunity to adhere to the sources and the greater one's dependence on secondary literature.'[23] Of course, there are happy exceptions: I have already referred to Baldwin's book on the class bases of the European welfare state (1990) in which he examined dozens of archives in five countries. It is not always possible to replicate his example, however, so these difficulties undoubtedly persist. This problem is familiar to many comparativists for whom it is necessary to overcome language barriers, find comparable materials and adapt to the particular national historiographies of different countries. Several historians have shared practical advice with colleagues about how to overcome numerous difficulties: we will consider their recommendations in the next chapter.

But comparative research can also be constructed around one object. This kind of comparison, which Kocka usefully called 'asymmetrical'[24] suggests that the chosen theme is developed based on information derived from one country, while comparative

---

[19] Cohen (2001).
[20] Eisenberg (1989).
[21] Kolchin (1987).
[22] Fredrickson (1995a); Fredrickson (2000).
[23] Kocka and Haupt (2009): 13.
[24] Kocka (1999): 48–9; Kocka and Haupt (2009): 5–6.

data are used to highlight various aspects of a particular issue and show it from an unexpected perspective. In other words, the objects of comparison remain in the background in this case, serving merely as a backdrop for the main line of research. Given this, one can agree with Kocka and Haupt's opinion that the asymmetrical type of comparison is reduced and incomplete. This form of comparison also involves a serious risk of idealizing the image of the 'other' against whose backdrop the peculiarities of, for example, Germany's historical path or the 'exceptionalism' of America or some other country are emphasized.[25]

Interestingly, in both German and Russian historiography, the mythologized 'West' has often played the role of the 'partner' for comparison. Michael Confino correctly drew attention to the nebulousness and inconsistency of this strange figure of the 'West', against which Russia is usually contrasted in domestic discourse.[26]

But for all the possible risks associated with asymmetrical comparison, it possesses a number of undeniable advantages. The great heuristic potential of this type of comparative analysis should be mentioned: it opens up practically unlimited opportunities for transferring academic knowledge from one field to another; raising new issues; and formulating questions that require study. The comparative perspective is the main route to renewing the agenda in any national historiography.

Moreover, unlike parallel, cross-cultural or typological comparison, asymmetrical comparison is less time-consuming in that it does not require the expansion of the empirical basis of research. The heuristic or the 'making strange' effect is achieved not through additional sources, but through a new reading of existing facts in the light of other historical experience, related to another place and time.

We have so far mainly discussed the comparison of phenomena that occurred simultaneously (synchronically) in different countries. But historians often need to resort to diachronic comparison while studying any kind of process, given that processes often develop unevenly. A classic example is Alexander Gerschenkron's work on European industrialization and the phenomenon of relative backwardness (see Part I, Chapter 4). The same type of comparative research features in Miroslav Hroch's book on national revival in Europe in the nineteenth century,[27] which will be examined in further detail in the third part of this book.

Thus, as is undoubtedly apparent, each type of comparison has its own advantages and limitations. When planning comparative research it is therefore important to determine which type will be most suitable for achieving the aims proposed. For example, if one wishes to confirm or challenge a thesis about the uniqueness of any type of phenomenon, asymmetrical comparison is very suitable: it is sufficient simply to place what is being studied in a comparative context. Parallel comparison is effective if one needs to demonstrate the specific behaviour involved in a certain process or the functioning of an institution in different societies. To achieve the ambitious goals of modelling or constructing a typology of, for example, national movements or the formation of nation states, one will need to compare dozens of separate cases, and

[25] Kocka (1999): 49; Kocka and Haupt (2009): 5.
[26] Confino (2009): 93–6.
[27] Hroch (1985).

even then, one will almost inevitably face criticism from specialists studying the same process within the countries concerned.

A few more words are needed on the *level* of comparison: as we already know, comparison of civilizations in the spirit of Spengler or Toynbee, as well as the global comparisons carried out by a number of sociologists, was not recognized as valid by historians. Until now, historical comparison has predominantly remained at a nation-state level, although the choice of states as units of comparison has not been immune to recent sharp criticism from new trends of research such as the history of transfers and '*histoire croisée*' (see Part I, Chapter 5). In fairness though, it must be said that it is not the states themselves that are usually compared, but the processes or the phenomena that take place within them. To put it another way, in this case national borders mark different social environments (one should remember that it is precisely the criterion of different *environments* that Bloch considered the basis for choosing objects for comparison).[28]

There have recently been an increasing number of appeals to carry out comparison 'at a middle range'. In expressing this opinion, Grew and Baldwin apparently meant this as a middle level of abstraction, retaining the historical context and offering explanations, but not universal laws.[29] But Nancy Green, for example, understands this term in a spatial sense, that is, as levels below the state, such as regions, cities and types of industry; in particular, Green refers to the work in which she compared women's clothing factories in Paris and New York.[30]

But in general, the scale of the objects being compared, along with their spatial characteristics, do not appear fundamentally important from a methodological point of view: the type of comparison and its useful functions do not change according to whether scholars compare a process or phenomena in several cities, regions or countries. We will continue to examine this problem in the next chapter.

---

[28] Bloch ([1928] 1953): 496.
[29] Grew (1980): 773; Baldwin (1990): 39; and Baldwin (2004): 15–16.
[30] Green (2004): 46, 48.

10

Recommendations for newcomers to historical comparison

In the preceding chapters we considered the most frequently discussed questions of historical comparison: whether a comparative method exists; what the useful functions of comparison in history are; and how one selects objects for comparison. A few important methodological problems remain that scholars new to historical comparison should be aware of before commencing their research. In this chapter, I will attempt to summarize the recommendations on this topic in the existing literature, adding several of my own observations.

Main Recommendation: *From the very outset, one must clearly specify the aim of the research and formulate the issue that can be solved or elucidated using comparison.* This may appear self-explanatory, but in research practice it is not uncommon for the lack of a clear aim to make comparison ineffective.

At academic conferences and in edited collections, one often encounters a simple juxtaposition of a number of similar cases rather than comparison as a research operation. As Green puts it, 'the unifying comparative vision is provided by conference commentators or the book's introductory chapter', but, nevertheless, 'specialists tend toward monologue rather than dialogue'.[1]

Consequently, it is only when comparison is built into a study as an integral part that it can be a genuinely useful tool for academic analysis.

Another important condition for meaningful comparative operations was articulated well by Haupt and Kocka: 'one cannot compare phenomena in their multilayered totality. Rather, we select aspects. Comparison requires selection, abstraction, detaching of the case from its context.'[2] In other words, one can only compare 'in certain regards'.[3] From this condition it follows that complex systems, such as societies or states as a whole, cannot serve as objects of comparison. One sometimes encounters parallels between countries in writing on current affairs (e.g. between post-Soviet Russia and Weimar Germany): one can regard these parallels as metaphors, but they lack serious academic value.

Nevertheless, the absence of a fully developed method of historical comparison occasionally leads to attempts to compare entire societies and states of different eras.

---

[1] Green (2004): 48.
[2] Haupt and Kocka (2004): 25.
[3] Kocka and Haupt (2009): 14.

In a series of presentations and articles published in the 1990s, the historian Sergei Kashtanov thus drew parallels between the Rus of the fourteenth to the sixteenth century and the Frankish polity in the seventh to the ninth century (the Merovingian and Carolingian period),[4] and between Ivan III and Charles Martel.[5] Kashtanov traced similarities between these societies, separated by an interval of 600 to 800 years, in the development of monastic landholdings and immunities; the establishment of the beneficiary or land tenure systems; the serfdom of the peasants; and the level of material and spiritual culture. 'The Russian state established by the late fifteenth to the sixteenth century', he claimed, 'had, in general, the same social base as the empire of Charlemagne.'[6] However, this bold conclusion has an 'impressionistic' character, which is not founded on a systematic comparison of the polities concerned. The parallel between the Russian peasantry in the fifteenth and sixteenth centuries and French serfs appears a very stretched interpretation. Moreover, large sixteenth-century cities like Moscow, Novgorod or Pskov, with tens of thousands of residents, did not exist in the Carolingian Empire – to say nothing of radical differences in the military and political spheres such as the use of artillery; the establishment of a rifle force; the organization of the system of central government departments; and the convening of the first assemblies of the land under Ivan the Terrible.

Apparently sensing several inconsistencies in his own work, Kashtanov noted that 'the paradox lies in the fact that the Russian state in the fifteenth and sixteenth centuries, being closer to the Carolingian Empire in terms of social relations, had a different historic perspective from that monarchy (Carolingian Empire – MK): not one of disintegration, but one of consolidation and a transition towards absolutism'.[7] But this 'paradox' was primarily a consequence of the inappropriate choice of era with which to compare Muscovite Rus, and second, of the attempt to compare *all* aspects of the life of the society concerned at one stroke: from the harvesting capacity and form of landholdings to political structure and literary culture. Meanwhile, this type of multistaged, diachronic comparison that Kashtanov resorted to supposes that the objects compared are societies undergoing the same phase *of the same process*. As far as Russia in the second half of the fifteenth century and the sixteenth century is concerned, this was the process of modern-state building. Indeed, such features of the modern state as the delegation of the judicial and administrative power of the monarch to his advisers and authorized officials; the bureaucracy of the administrative staff apparatus; and the emergence of representative institutions of a parliamentary type characteristic of western and central European kingdoms in the thirteenth to the fifteenth century were found in the Muscovite tsardom of the sixteenth century.[8]

Naturally, one should take into account not only the general features of the process described but also its specific nature in a region. But so long as the problem we are interested in has not been formulated and the scholar continues to adhere to a holistic approach in history (in Kashtanov's case, this approach was clearly inspired by a

---

[4] Kashtanov ([1992] 2015).
[5] Kashtanov (1999).
[6] Kashtanov ([1992] 2015): 444.
[7] Kashtanov ([1992] 2015): 444.
[8] See more in Krom (2018).

Marxist model of socio-economic formations), the study of the local features of some kind of Europe-wide process appears impossible: the comparative method simply does not work.

I see the benefit of the unanticipated and speculative parallels that Kashtanov draws between Ivan III and Charles Martel, and Ivan IV and Charlemagne, as resting in the 'making strange' effect, because his comparison emphasizes the archaic nature of social relationships in Muscovite Rus. However, similarities are found between the European states of the late Middle Ages and the early modern age and a number of other aspects of Russian life at the end of the fifteenth to the sixteenth century.

A holistic approach is a serious impediment to comparative research, regardless of the level or scale at which phenomena are studied: countries, regions and even small towns or other local communities cannot easily be compared if one attempts to study them in their entirety and every detail. It is therefore not fruitful to regard units of comparison as physical entities – large or small. It is more productive to compare the various contexts in which the processes, trends or phenomena that historians study occur.

Thus, a further recommendation that can be given to scholars who are starting to use historical comparison is that *in order to be successful, comparison should be limited and focused on one kind of process, phenomenon or institution*. It should also be restated that as discussed in the previous chapter, the central problem scholars select (such as the course of a certain process or the evolution of an institution) should be a 'third item' (*tertium comparationis*), providing a line of comparison linking the individual cases compared, which themselves belong in logical terms to the same category.

The recommendations mentioned here relate mainly to the design of comparative research, and reflect aspirations for making the procedure of comparison conscious and controlled to the greatest extent possible. (It is no accident that Durkheim called the comparative method 'indirectly experimental'.)[9] But having set the research goal, defined the issue requiring study, selected cases to illustrate the problem and meticulously considered the logic of the comparison, scholars who widely use historical comparison inevitably encounter a number of practical difficulties. Apart from the complexity of overcoming language barriers or gaining access to foreign archives, let us consider in more depth the frequently discussed problem of scholars' reliance on original sources in the comparative research process and their potential dependence on the existing academic literature.

This issue has long attracted the attention of comparativists. Reflecting on methods of comparative study in history in 1923 the historian Nikolai Rozhkov wrote that 'it is enough if a person undertaking comparative historical synthesis is a specialist in the history of one country and is informed about the most important phenomena of historical literature in the history of others'.[10] Nevertheless, Rozhkov considered it important for a scholar working on a comparative monograph to be familiar with the main sources available on the history of different countries, since this is necessary if one is to have a critical attitude towards the conclusions of others. Rozhkov acknowledged

---

[9] Durkheim ([1895] 1966): 125.
[10] Rozhkov (1919–1926), VI: 5.

that a familiarity – albeit not an exhaustive one – with many sources on the history of the West, ancient civilizations, the Middle Ages and the modern age had been the means by which he himself had resolved contentious issues.[11]

In the present day, Haupt and Kocka believe that the isolation from sources and context characteristic of comparative history, as well as the dependence on secondary literature that is growing with the increase in the number of comparative cases, contradicts the 'basic principles of the historical profession'. Consequently, according to Haupt and Kocka, unlike social scientists, comparativist historians try to limit the scope of comparison to two or three objects.[12]

Fredrickson also advised his colleagues that if they wanted their work to be respected and useful to historians in all topics using comparison, they must limit themselves to no more than two cases.[13]

However, as shown in previous chapters, the choice and quantity of objects of comparison are determined by the aim of the research: a number of problems simply cannot be solved with only two or three cases. Successful examples of comparative research that use many units of comparison can be found in Gerschenkron's classic works, and, in contemporary historiography, in Baldwin's monographs. Therefore, neither Haupt and Kocka's nor Fredrickson's suggestions can be taken as dogma. Furthermore, the same problem of the choice between primary sources and information gleaned second-hand from monographs or articles on a particular theme does not depend on the quantity of objects compared: this secondary information can be relevant, even if scholars have only two cases in their field of vision.

Citing his own experience of the study of race relations in two countries, the United States and South Africa, Fredrickson notably expressed the opinion that 'good comparative history' does not necessarily imply time-consuming archival research or work with primary sources in every case. 'If the topic is broad, and the secondary literature voluminous and of high quality', he maintained, 'there is no reason not to rely heavily upon it.'[14] He also approvingly cited Fritz Redlich, a scholar of the older generation who had argued that the monographs of earlier historians are the fundamental sources for comparative historiography, and that it is necessary to consult archives in order to fill in the gaps in our understanding and ascertain whether the authors of the monographs also saw the aspects of the problem that interest us. Redlich summed up the credo of comparativists aphoristically: 'while traditional monographic historiography begins its work in archives, comparative historiography ends it there.'[15]

However, Fredrickson recognized that some types of comparative history can and should be based on sources, although not necessarily those found in archives. This applies in particular to intellectual history; one example of this is Fredrickson's book about the ideology of black liberation movements in the United States and South Africa (*Black Liberation*, 1995),[16] which was specifically written on the basis of original texts

---

[11] Rozhkov (1919–1926), VI: 5.
[12] Haupt and Kocka (2004): 25, 26; Kocka and Haupt (2009): 13, 15.
[13] Fredrickson (2000): 11.
[14] Fredrickson (2000): 11.
[15] Redlich (1958): 386.
[16] Fredrickson (1995a).

echoing protest discourse. In Fredrickson's opinion, the history of ideas and ideologies, unlike the history of institutions, does not require large-scale 'excavations' and can be studied in the comparative vein without the support of monographic literature. Furthermore, primary sources can be prescribed as the basis of comparative social history on a local level: if comparing, for example, two cities or two organizations, then it is entirely feasible to conduct serious archival research on each case.[17]

Fredrickson's recommendation that scholars establish direct contact with historians specializing in the study of the country that is being compared with their own country merits attention: this contact allows historians to stay abreast of new trends in the corresponding historiography.[18]

Without doubt, the ideas presented here are not universal prescriptions, suitable for all situations in which scholars using historical comparison may find themselves. Elaboration of the principles of historical comparative research began relatively recently and to date only a small proportion of the lessons learned have assumed the form if not of rules, then at least of valuable recommendations. The third and final part of this book aims to demonstrate the diversity of subject matter in contemporary historical comparison, and to reinforce some of the general principles of comparative analysis formulated in this methodological section with specific examples.

---

[17] Fredrickson (2000): 12.
[18] Fredrickson (2000): 12.

Part III

Themes of comparative historical research

As Hartmut Kaelble remarked, the success of historical comparison is largely due to a 'flexibility of topic' (*thematische Flexibilität*): initially it dealt only with the history of the state, institutions, social structures and economic development; later its use widened significantly, coming to take in the history of culture, symbols, rituals, gender relations, ideas, events (revolutions in particular) and biographies.[1] This broadening of scope established its usefulness.

The focus in Part III of this book will be on the most successful examples of comparative analysis within various fields and approaches of contemporary historical research.

---

[1] Kaelble (2002): 304.

11

Comparison in economic history

Since its rise in the 1950s, a number of features have characterized comparative research in economic history. First, it is always directly linked to the problems of economic theory itself; Sylvia Thrupp wrote explicitly about this in 1957[1] as do today's proponents of economic comparison. Thus, in the introduction to their edited collection *The New Comparative Economic History* (2007), Hatton, O'Rourke and Taylor remark that this approach is guided by questions posed by economists. These questions include the sources of economic growth; the significance of institutions; and the influence of globalization. Dispelling any remaining doubt about the orientation of the new subdiscipline, the authors emphasize further that it is 'motivated by current debates among academic economists and policymakers rather than following agendas set by historians'.[2]

Second, economic historians have always actively used quantitative methods and the proponents of the 'new comparative economic history' are continuing this cliometric tradition.[3] However, comparative economic history at the beginning of the twenty-first century differs from the classical models of half a century ago.

Above all, the scale of comparison is now global. Comparisons on the nation-state level, which dominated entirely in Rostow and Gerschenkron's day, do not suit current economists who now also study areas beyond western Europe and the United States; Japan, Latin America and the rest of the world are now included within their research.[4] The chronological framework has also widened: economic historians now work in eras lasting several centuries and even millennia. This is illustrated by Angus Maddison's *Contours of the World Economy 1-2030 AD: Essays in Macro-Economic History* (2007). The book is a treasure trove of statistical information about the economies of various eras and is not in a strict sense comparative; Maddison does not emphasize comparison of regions or continents but their mutual influence and the book therefore lies within the global history movement. But the global approach is fully compatible with the comparative method, as Kenneth Pomeranz successfully demonstrated in his research, which we will consider later.

This increased scale has been accompanied by a radical change in research perspective. In its time, Rostow's theory of the stages of economic growth (see Part I,

---

[1] Thrupp (1957).
[2] Hatton, O'Rourke and Taylor (2007): 2.
[3] Hatton, O'Rourke and Taylor (2007): 1–2.
[4] Hatton, O'Rourke and Taylor (2007): 2, 4–5.

Chapter 4) gave an impetus to comparative historical research which itself later led to the discrediting of the theory,[5] so that now as Patrick O'Brien put it, all that now remains of Rostow's idea is its familiar terminology of 'take-off', 'maturity' and so on.[6] This is not merely because some of the tenets of the theory did not withstand empirical scrutiny but because a number of its inherent characteristics such as Eurocentrism, linearity and the invariable order of the stages – which were very much in tune with the modernization theory of the 1950s and 1960s – proved methodologically inadmissible for the next generation of researchers.

While Britain's leadership of the Industrial Revolution seemed natural and self-evident to Rostow and the scholars of his generation, in the global perspective that prevails today it requires explanation. In, *The Great Divergence: China, Europe, and the Making of the Modern World Economy* (2000), Kenneth Pomeranz explores why an economic spurt occurred in the western Europe of the nineteenth century rather than elsewhere in the world.

Unlike his predecessors, Pomeranz does not ascribe Britain's success to endogenous factors. He contrasts the thesis of British and more widely European exclusivity with his own observations (he specializes in Chinese history) and those of a number of other modern researchers, which showed remarkable similarities in many respects between the economic development of western Europe and eastern Asia by the middle of the eighteenth century. 'Far from being unique, then', writes Pomeranz, 'the most developed parts of western Europe seemed to have shared crucial economic features – commercialization, commodification of goods, land and labor, market-driven growth, and adjustment by households of both fertility and labor allocation to economic trends – with other densely populated core areas in Eurasia.'[7] (Pomeranz primarily has in mind the Yangtze valley in China – MK).

The concept that Pomeranz introduced of two-way, or reciprocal, comparison also merits attention from a methodological point of view; according to this when two societies are compared, neither is taken as the model or norm, but, instead, each is perceived by the other as a 'deviation'.[8] In addition, Pomeranz rightly criticizes the habit – associated with Eurocentric notions of industrialization – of taking modern nation states as units of comparison, whereby Britain is compared with China or India. Pomeranz believes with good reason that in terms of their size, population and internal diversity, China and India are comparable with Europe as a whole rather than with individual European countries; a particular area within one of these two subcontinents, in and of itself comparable with Britain or the Netherlands, becomes lost in average indicators which include the Asian equivalents of areas such as the Balkans, southern Italy and Poland. Pomeranz encapsulates this by saying that 'unless state policy is the center of the story being told, the nation is not a unit that travels very well.'[9]

Thus, having compared the most developed regions of western Europe and eastern Asia in the pre-industrial period, Pomeranz concludes that none of them would have

---

[5] Kocka and Haupt (2009): 7.
[6] O'Brien (2001): 7366.
[7] Pomeranz (2000): 107.
[8] Pomeranz (2000): 8–9.
[9] Pomeranz (2000): 7.

been able to break out of the economic cul-de-sac caused by various limitations – primarily environmental in nature, such as a shortage of land – through their own resources. The Industrial Revolution therefore strikes Pomeranz not as a routine stage of development but as a rare leap and a break with the previous stagnant position. Pomeranz is inclined to explain the fact that Britain in particular was able to make this leap by external or chance causes such as its large coal deposits and the fact that it was able to import agricultural products, precious metals and other essential resources from its colonies.

Another economic historian, Gregory Clark, gave a different explanation of the same issue. In his book *A Farewell to Alms* (2007) he gave a detailed description of the Malthusian trap; this involves limitations that constrained economic development for many centuries when due to the state of technological development at the time, population growth inevitably led to a fall in people's living standards. The British Industrial Revolution, which allowed an escape from this 'trap' strikes Clark as a largely mysterious event. Nevertheless, unlike Pomeranz, he does not explain it with external or chance circumstances. Clark emphasizes the smooth, evolutionary nature of development, noting a stable if small year-on-year economic growth in England from 1600 to 1760 and from 1780 to 1860.[10] As for Pomeranz's comparativist arguments and his pointing to the existence of land, labour and capital markets in Japan and China around 1800, Clark considers these preconditions completely insufficient for accelerated economic growth. Clark turns to highly convincing diachronic comparison, demonstrating (in line with Adam Smith's theory) that in England in 1300, market institutions and, consequently, economic stimuli were even more favourable than in 2000 although they did not produce the same effect in the Middle Ages as they do today.[11]

Clark believes that cultural factors such as way of life and level of education played a crucial part in Britain's economic success. Japan and China lagged behind Britain by 1800 on these indicators.[12] In attempting to explain British society's dynamism and its inclination towards innovation, Clark also highlights demographic features: the birth rate in rich British families as well as the level of downward mobility was significantly higher than among the Chinese or Japanese elites. In Britain the mores and culture of the middle class correspondingly penetrated far more deeply into the lower levels of the social hierarchy. 'Thus we may speculate', Clark concludes, 'that England's advantage lay in the rapid cultural, and potentially also genetic, diffusion of the values of economically successful throughout society in the years 1200 – 1800.'[13]

British economic historian Robert Allen recently commented on these issues. While acknowledging institutional, cultural and geographical differences, he believes that the immediate causes of economic inequality between countries are technical changes, globalization and economic policy. Furthermore, as he saw it, the Industrial Revolution was the result of the first phase of globalization, which began at the end of

---

[10] Clark (2007): 231–2.
[11] Clark (2007): 147–8 and table 8.1.
[12] Clark (2007): 262–6.
[13] Clark (2007): 271.

the fifteenth century with the Age of Discovery. Clark sees the origin of the subsequent Great Divergence in this 'first globalization'.[14]

The level of workers' wages in real terms plays an important part in Allen's explanatory model: if this is low, the stimulus for technical innovation disappears and with it the stimulus for economic growth. Therefore, Allen believes that the Industrial Revolution not only caused high wages but was also a consequence of these.[15] For the same reason the inventions that brought profit in Britain proved ineffective in poor countries.

Using the example of the Indian textile industry, which could not withstand competition from British looms, Allen convincingly demonstrates that the flip side of European industrialization was the de-industrialization of ancient textile mills in Asia. In the mid-twentieth century the problem of the Asian economy was conceived in terms of the modernization of 'traditional societies'. In actual fact, though, tradition was irrelevant here: 'Underdevelopment', Allen rightly notes, 'was the product of 19th-century globalization and Western industrial development.'[16]

As analysis of the discussion in this chapter about the causes of the British 'economic miracle' of the nineteenth century and the sources of the Great Divergence between the East and the West shows, comparative economic history has certain features that distinguish it from other themes in contemporary historical comparison. What particularly stands out is the global scale and wide chronological framework of the research, which is in line with the 'huge comparisons' that Charles Tilly enjoined his fellow sociologists to use. Its similarity to historical sociology is seen in the use of comparison to explain the causes of the processes studied.

Meanwhile, judging by the complaints of comparativists such as Baldwin and Cohen mentioned earlier, researchers in social and cultural history have been disappointed by the possibilities of comparison for establishing causal links (see Part II, Chapter 8). In addition, the leading figures in contemporary historical comparison, Kocka, Haupt and Fredrickson, strongly recommend limiting the objects of comparison to two or three cases (see p. 100).

This specificity of comparative economic history appears to be explained by the close link between it and economic theory and the scholars' focus on the problems and methods of economics.

---

[14] Allen (2011): 16.
[15] Allen (2011): 13.
[16] Allen (2011): 61.

12

Comparison in political history

As the oldest form of historical writing, political history has long been an area of comparative research. Thus as far back as 1890 Langlois drew attention to numerous resemblances between the administrations of the English and French medieval monarchies – the *curiae regis* of the Plantagenets and the Capetian kings; the exchequer in England and the *chambre des comptes* in France; the English courts of the King's Bench and of Common Pleas and the French *parlement*; English sheriffs on the one hand and French bailiffs and seneschals on the other – and so forth.[1] Since then, the political institutions of the two countries have often been the subject of comparative analysis.

As mentioned earlier, Bloch devoted his most famous book to contrasting several rites and beliefs that existed in the English and French courts. However, in the way in which he formulated the issue and his chosen approach, which was reminiscent of anthropological research, his *Royal Touch* (1924) differed significantly from the conventional institutional history of the time – including comparative institutional history. Typical examples of this are the interwar publications of Hintze, Charles Petit-Dutaillis and Heinrich Mitteis.

Petit-Dutaillis's monograph *The Feudal Monarchy in France and England, from the Tenth to the Thirteenth Century* was swiftly acknowledged by specialists and was translated into several languages soon after its publication in 1933. In justifying the order of the presentation he had chosen for his narrative, in which the history of the French monarchy 'was presented . . . on the same scale as the history of the English monarchy', Petit-Dutaillis pointed to the close links between the two countries during much of the period he described, when following the conquest in 1066 English kings were of Norman and Angevin origin, spoke French and spent much of their time in France.[2] Using the current terminology, it could be said that Petit-Dutaillis proposed one of the early experiments of what is now known as *histoire croisée* or *entangled histories*. Unlike the proponents of these current trends, however, Petit-Dutaillis made comparison an important part of his work.

He readily turned to contrast, underlining a weak romanization of Britain, in contrast to Gaul for example,[3] and subsequently the early development of a tax system in England and the resulting large financial opportunities of the English kings

---

[1] Langlois (1890): 261.
[2] Petit-Dutaillis ([1933] 1936): 372.
[3] Petit-Dutaillis ([1933] 1936): 38.

compared to their French counterparts. Petit-Dutaillis also noted similarities in several institutions, however. Thus, contrary to historiographical tradition he sees the English 'parliament' of the thirteenth century not as a prototype for the legislature that exists today but as an expanded *curia regis*, like the French institution of the same name and period.[4] He also notices instances of borrowing. In particular, he shows how Philip Augustus introduced the institution of the bailiff into local administration in France, following the model of Anglo-Norman institutions. As a whole, thanks to comparison, Petit-Dutaillis was able, in his words, to shed 'a little more light on the history of the two peoples'.[5]

Mitteis's *The State of the High Middle Ages* (1940) was an example of comparative constitutional history (*vergleichende Verfassungsgeschichte*). Tracing the development of state institutions in the feudal Europe of the tenth to the thirteenth century, he carefully noted the features of the individual countries he studied. These were the German Empire, Italy, France and England (the countries of eastern Europe, Scandinavia and the Iberian Peninsula received only cursory mention). In particular, he noted the limits of private jurisdiction in England compared to feudal immunity on the continent; the rarity in England – unlike in France – of internecine warfare or feuds; and the absence of castles that were not owned by the Crown from the time of Alfred the Great.[6] Thus, for Mitteis, comparison's main function was the individualization and identification of different versions within the general picture of the formation and development of medieval states.

Otto Hintze, who alongside Bloch was the leading pre-war comparativist, used comparative history of institutions for constructing typologies, some of which remain valid today. Thus, as Helmut Koenigsberger acknowledged, the only attempt at creating a general theory of political representation in European history was undertaken by Hintze in 1930 and 1931.[7] As mentioned earlier, Hintze had contrasted two types of representative institutions: the more ancient, bicameral parliament, found in England, which developed at the fringes of the Carolingian Empire, and the later form, comprising three chambers – like the French Estates-General – which characterized the area that had formed the nucleus of the former empire.[8] Of course, Hintze's proposed typology does not explain everything; in particular, Koenigsberger mentioned one country that certainly does not fit into this scheme: the Netherlands was at the very heart of the Carolingian Empire but in its various provinces there were bicameral, three-chamber and even single-chamber representative institutions.[9] Although Hintze's idea has its shortcomings, it has not been bettered even now.

After the Second World War the time period of comparative research in political history expanded significantly, encompassing the nineteenth and twentieth centuries, and there were many new themes: comparativists began to study phenomena such as revolutions, fascism and other dictatorships, absolutism and the welfare state.

[4] Petit-Dutaillis ([1933] 1936): 352, 353.
[5] Petit-Dutaillis ([1933] 1936): 372.
[6] Mitteis ([1940] 1962): 168–70.
[7] Koenigsberger (1986): 6.
[8] Hintze ([1930] 1970).
[9] Koenigsberger (1986): 7–8.

Building on the tradition of German comparative institutional or constitutional history (*vergleichende Verfassungsgeschichte*) in the mid-1960s, Theodor Schieder developed an original typology of the formation of nation states in Europe. Schieder believed that the first type, which he called 'national revolutionary' or 'national democratic' had arisen in England and France in the revolutionary era of the seventeenth to the eighteenth century. The essence of this process was the transformation of existing states according to the new principles of the will of the people and citizenship.[10] Schieder believed that the second type arose at another, later stage and in a different part of Europe, namely, in Germany and Italy: in this case, a national unification movement involved the creation of a nation state from the parts of a politically fragmented nation.[11] Finally, a third type of nation state formed later still and was typical of the areas of eastern Europe where the Habsburg, Ottoman and Russian empires – which seemed to be 'prisons of peoples' for the local national movements of the nineteenth century – held dominion. Here, the state was a hostile force that opposed national traditions. Therefore, all the nation states of eastern Europe – from Serbia, Greece, Bulgaria and Romania to the Baltic states – arose through separation from the great powers.[12]

Schieder himself well understood the tentative nature of the scheme he proposed. 'As always in history', he wrote, 'systematization lacks complete precision.'[13] Therefore, having described the three types of nation state and their three respective stages of formation in general terms, Schieder made a number of provisos, particularly emphasizing that the stages mentioned had overlapped more than once. Movements aimed at separating from the great powers were often simultaneously unifying movements, as was clearly the case with Poland, Yugoslavia or Bulgaria after its division at the Berlin Congress. Britain as a state was the product of a unionist movement, through which Scotland – and later, with the help of force – Ireland were drawn into the Union. With its demands for the repeal of the Union, Ireland provides a clear example of the formation of a nation state through separation, with all the features characteristic of this model, which were also seen in a milder form in Norway and, later, in Iceland.

Finally, according to Schieder's observations, Italy provides an instance of the nation state movement passing through all three phases. At the first stage, the Italians experienced the direct influence of the French Revolution: the concept of 'Italy' was first introduced by this revolution and from then on could not be suppressed. The basis of the Italian nation state itself, however, belongs to the second phase – that of the national unification movements of central Europe. However, since this did not achieve the aim of uniting all Italians within a nation state and the 'unliberated' part of Italy (*Italia irredenta*) remained under Austrian power, the Italians took part in the third phase, that of separation, along with the peoples of southern Europe. This involvement in three major stages in the history of the European nation state,

---

[10] Schieder (1966): 62–3.
[11] Schieder (1966): 63.
[12] Schieder (1966): 64–5.
[13] Schieder (1966): 65.

from Napoleon's Italian campaign of 1796-7 up to the Versailles peace talks in 1919, gave Italian national consciousness a multilayered structure, Schieder noted. This includes the national democratic elements of 1789, reflected in an unbroken liberal tradition within Italian politics but strong unitary features as well from the unification movement (*Risorgimento*) phase; from the third stage comes the irredentist leaning of Italian national consciousness, manifested in a strong reaction to questions of national borders and in an interest in the cultural and linguistic aspects of the Italian character (*Italianità*).[14]

From the 1960s, one of the central places in both sociological and historical comparison was occupied by comparative study of revolutions. The shift towards this topic was noted in Palmer's two-volume work *The Age of the Democratic Revolution: The Political History of Europe and America, 1760 – 1800*,[15] although as noted earlier (see p. 44), comparison does not play a key part in the book. On the other hand, comparison became an overarching theme of American historical sociology from the 1960s to the 1980s (for more detail see Part I, Chapter 6), where particular attention was devoted to the phenomenon of revolutions on a worldwide historical scale.

Thus, within his general idea of transition from an industrial to a modern society, Barrington Moore contrasted the English Civil War, the French Revolution and the American Civil War, which he regarded as 'the last capitalist revolution'.[16] His former student Skocpol made a comparative analysis of the French, Russian and Chinese revolutions with the aim of identifying the causes of successful social revolutions generally[17] (for a detailed analysis of this book, see Part I, Chapter 6).

At the beginning of the 1980s, the sociologist Jack Goldstone summarized preliminary results from the comparative historical study of revolutions. He focused particularly on the key question of why revolutions arise. Summarizing judgements about this in the literature, Goldstone concluded that a combination of factors led to revolutions. These comprise the paralysis of a state unable to deal with multiple problems, conflicts within the ruling elite, and also urban and rural uprisings.[18] But since the phenomena mentioned often occur in isolation from each other without being accompanied by revolutionary shocks, it is their simultaneous occurrence which gives rise to what Goldstone calls the 'revolutionary conjuncture'. Some scholars think that military defeat plays a crucial role in the development of a revolutionary crisis while others believe that economic changes are decisive. Goldstone himself discerned the roots of revolution in the lengthy waves of growth in population and food prices.[19] (Goldstone devoted a sizeable work to explaining the theory of demographic causes of revolutions; in this he compared political crises in Europe and Asia in early modern times.)[20]

[14] Schieder (1966): 66.
[15] Palmer (1959–1964).
[16] Moore (1966): chaps 1–3.
[17] Skocpol (1979).
[18] Goldstone (1982): 200.
[19] Goldstone (1982): 204–5.
[20] Goldstone (1991).

Historians also displayed enthusiasm for discovering the causes of revolutions. Thus, Lawrence Stone devoted a book published in 1972 to analysing the causes of the English Revolution of the seventeenth century. Interestingly, in subsequent discussions between Stone and his reviewer Helmut Koenigsberger, both actively used comparison to argue their cases. Questioning the significance that Stone gave to the lack of a standing army and of a local bureaucracy as factors in the weakening of the English monarchy, Koenigsberger adduced the experience of France and Spain where he believed that neither an army nor bureaucracy had been the main tools in establishing absolutism.[21] Maintaining his point of view, however, Stone emphasized the contrast between the French monarchy, which had beaten the Fronde thanks to the existence of large military and financial resources and the support of the local bureaucracy, and the English monarchy, which lost the civil war because of the lack of both.[22]

Like sociologists, historians in the 1960s and 1970s attempted to refine the concept of revolution using comparison, distinguishing the phenomenon from non-violent changes in society on the one hand and from ordinary revolts and uprisings, on the other; Zagorin's article illustrates these attempts.[23] Under the influence of the Cultural Revolution, however, interest in constructing an ideal model of revolution and seeking its causes in various countries later waned and comparison started to be used with different aims. A good example of the contemporary comparative history of revolutions is historian Stephen Smith's *Revolution and the People in Russia and China* (2008).

In the introduction to the book Smith emphasizes the differences between his approach to comparing revolutions and that which had previously dominated – primarily in the works of historical sociologists – which was focused on constructing a theory of revolution and models of causal explanation or on testing hypotheses about their origins and conditions, the roles of social classes and parties, and typical stages in the development of a revolution and its typical outcomes. Smith contrasts his own 'style' of comparative history – which is concerned more with culture, human activity and the micro-level contexts in which individuals act and develop than with the 'big structures, large processes, [and] huge comparisons' mentioned in the title of Tilly's book[24] – with these sorts of 'nomothetical attempts' based on a secondary literature that offers interpretations of other interpretations and often lacks the detailed social, political and cultural context that is important for historians. Instead of attempting to construct a comprehensive model of revolution, Smith tries to identify similarities and differences between the two revolutions, constructing local observations inductively, based on careful study of primary sources.[25]

A central category of analysis in Smith's work is the concept of identity: in Smith's opinion, the revolutions in Russia and China in significant part represented a conflict of identities. Who did the former peasants who had become workers in St Petersburg between the 1880s and 1917 or in Shanghai from the 1900s to 1949 feel themselves to be? What was the relationship among them between individualism and collectivism

[21] Koenigsberger (1974): 104–5.
[22] Stone (1974): 109.
[23] Zagorin (1976).
[24] Tilly (1984).
[25] Smith (2008): 8.

and between class and national consciousness? How did the position of women change? Smith addresses these and similar questions in his book.

Despite the obvious differences in culture and economic starting conditions in Russia and China in the twentieth century, sociocultural processes in both countries show many common features. Although the tendency towards individual self-expression was markedly more apparent in Russia by 1917 than in China by 1949, the traditions of hierarchical collectivism proved very persistent in both societies and later city-dwellers – former migrants who had only recently been emancipated from the guardianship of the patriarchal family or community, obtained protection in new collective structures created by the party and the state.[26] Collectivism ultimately triumphed over the individual in both communist regimes but as Smith convincingly demonstrates, class identity was a response not only to capitalist exploitation but also to a feeling of systematic lack of respect towards themselves that working people had experienced.[27]

There was also a noticeable similarity in other aspects of social life, particularly in gender relations where a collapse of the patriarchal family occurred and – more in words than in fact – equal rights for women were affirmed.[28] The intertwining of class and national identity was also typical among both Russian and Chinese workers.[29] As a whole, however, although there was far less scope for individual self-expression under communist regimes than under capitalism – be this in terms of consumption, high culture or religion – the development of workers' identity proceeded in directions that could not be determined by central policies, propaganda or repression: social and demographic processes beyond the reach of the state, new forms of urban life, cultural changes, including secularization and the cult of science; all this, Smith emphasizes, formed the identity of workers under communism. 'Communism, too, was the form of modernity,' Smith concludes.[30]

There is a sociocultural bent in a new theme of comparative political history which began to be elaborated actively in the 1990s – that of the welfare state. Researchers like Baldwin were interested in the class basis of welfare policy in various European countries; gender aspects of such policies, including support of the family and maternal and child health, attracted Klaus and Pedersen (see Part I, Chapter 4).

Along with a welfare state, however, the twentieth century engendered the sinister phenomenon of fascism. Fascism was, of course, an Italian term in origin, originally used to refer to Mussolini's regime. Can its use as a generalizing concept that encompasses German Nazism and the dictatorships of Hungary, Romania and several other countries therefore be justified? As Wolfgang Wippermann rightly notes, only comparative research can answer this question.[31] After researching twentieth-century movements that communists, liberals and conservatives alike considered fascist, Wippermann concluded that the general concept does, indeed, make sense

[26] Smith (2008): 108–9.
[27] Smith (2008): 110.
[28] Smith (2008): 149–50.
[29] Smith (2008): 190–1.
[30] Smith (2008): 235.
[31] Wippermann (1983): 20.

and maintains its heuristic value.³² He underlines deep similarities in the external appearance, aims, ideology and political tactics of fascist movements in different countries: characteristic of all of these was a hierarchical structure with a leader, a distinctive political style comprising uniforms, mass meetings and marches, the open approval and use of violence, and an ambivalent ideology in which anti-capitalist and anti-communist as well as anti-modernist and ultra-modern motives intertwined and extreme nationalism coexisted with transnational elements.³³

Despite a similarity of basic features, European fascism differed through a significant variety of forms. Wippermann distinguishes between three versions that attained power: a 'normal' Italian type, a 'radical' German form and the 'fascism from above' of the Baltic countries, Poland, Hungary, Romania, Spain and Portugal. A specific feature in eastern and southern Europe was the absence or extreme weakness of mass fascist parties; in these countries therefore, unlike in Italy and Germany, fascism relied on the army and police rather than a party, and was imposed from above instead of rising to power from below.

The wide prevalence of the phenomenon in Europe poses a number of complex problems for researchers: in particular, it is not possible to establish a correlation between the level of a country's socio-economic development and the emergence of fascism since, as Wippermann reminds us, fascist movements existed in both developed industrial and agrarian societies. Wippermann was therefore correct to observe that theories linking fascism to specific stages in the development of capitalism or the process of modernization were misleading.³⁴ Generally, he considers attempts to explain it with a single principle and to construct a global theory unpromising. In his view, it is more useful to continue the empirical comparative study of fascism.³⁵

Although twentieth-century issues occupy a central place in contemporary historical comparison, earlier eras are also addressed. Typology of the states of early modern times, as the period between the end of the Middle Ages and the French Revolution is known, is one of the themes that have been actively studied using a comparative approach in the last few decades.

In his 1974 work *Lineages of the Absolutist State*, Perry Anderson traced the developmental paths of European monarchies under the ancient régime. As a Marxist, he based his analysis on the class structure of these societies in the period of crisis in feudal relations. He revised the well-known thesis of historical materialism according to which absolutism is a product of a temporary balance of powers between the old landowning aristocracy and the ascendant bourgeoisie. In Anderson's opinion, the feudal aristocracy had remained the dominant class in both economics and politics throughout the early modern era. It had, however, needed to adapt to new trade and monetary relations in order to preserve its dominance over the peasantry and the urban bourgeoisie.³⁶

---

[32] Wippermann (1983): 197, 206.
[33] Wippermann (1983): 197–9.
[34] Wippermann (1983): 202.
[35] Wippermann (1983): 206.
[36] Anderson ([1974] 1996): 18–23.

According to Anderson, the model of European absolutism took two forms – western and eastern. The social basis of western European absolutism was the peasantry, which was already emancipated from serfdom and influential towns; but in eastern Europe absolutism was built on serfdom in the countryside and subjugated towns.[37] Apart from endogenous factors, Anderson attributed an important role in the genesis of eastern European absolutism to geopolitical causes, pointing to the decisive influence of western Europe on the formation of the state structures of its eastern neighbours. In his words, 'It was the international pressure of Western Absolutism, the political apparatus of a more powerful feudal aristocracy, ruling more advanced societies, which obliged the Eastern nobility to adopt an equivalently centralized state machine, to survive.'[38]

It can be seen that in turning from western to eastern Europe, the logic of Anderson's argument changes fundamentally: where he emphasizes internal, socio-economic causes – the feudal lords' attempt to retain their dominance in a market economy and in the face of a free peasantry – in his analysis of the origins of western absolutism, he turns to geopolitical argument – western military pressure on the less developed East – to explain the emergence of the same political superstructure.

However, the strength of the book does not lie in the general idea of the origin of European absolutism, which is highly susceptible to criticism and has not received wide support outside Marxist historiography; the book's success is, instead, largely due to Anderson's mastery of comparative analysis, exemplified in his expressive depictions of individual monarchies and emphasis on their particular features within a general model of absolutism. There is a memorable characterization of Spain as a complex state composed of two very different political bodies, the kingdoms of Castile and Aragon. There are striking examples from Sweden in which absolutism developed in a surprising manner on the basis of a free peasantry and weak towns, and also from the Poland of the Szlachta, whose collapse in Anderson's opinion was 'a graphic *a contrario* demonstration of the historical rationality of Absolutism for a noble class'.[39]

Anderson's throwaway remark that 'No Western monarchy ever enjoyed an absolute power over its subjects, in the sense of an untrammelled despotism'[40] anticipated a trend in later historiography on this theme. Nicholas Henshall's *The Myth of Absolutism: Change and Continuity in Early Modern Monarchy* (1992) was entirely devoted to substantiating the thesis laconically formulated by Anderson in the earlier remark. Comparison does not play a substantial role in Henshall's work so we will not focus on it in detail. It should nevertheless be noted that he made persistent efforts to re-examine accepted ideas about the contrast between French absolutism and English limited monarchy: drawing on research from the 1980s he emphasized the traditional nature of the power of French kings, including Louis XIV, and in 'normalizing' the model of the French monarchy played down the differences between this and the British crown.[41]

[37] Anderson ([1974] 1996): 179.
[38] Anderson ([1974] 1996): 197–8.
[39] Anderson ([1974] 1996): 279.
[40] Anderson ([1974] 1996): 49.
[41] Henshall (1992).

It is also important to briefly mention a large-scale project that involved European historians studying the origins of the modern state. The project, undoubtedly connected to the political and economic unification of Europe, began in 1984 and was initially supported by the French National Centre for Scientific Research (CNRS) and then by the European Science Foundation. From the mid-1980s to the mid-1990s, several round tables and conferences on the subject took place and the materials from these were published.[42] Between 1995 and 2000, seven volumes in a series entitled *Origins of the Modern State in Europe, 13th to 18th Centuries* were published by Oxford University Press.

Although from the outset the project was intended to be comparative,[43] there is little direct evidence of this in the volumes published. After comparing the representation of the people and the influence of petitions on the legislative process in Germany, England and Sweden in the period, Peter Blickle, Stephen Ellis and Eva Österberg concluded that in all three countries this influence was significant and the very right to submit petitions was a distinguishing feature of European statehood, which was unknown in the Ottoman Empire and in Asian countries.[44] As a whole, however, the vast material on many countries in western and eastern Europe that was collected in the course of the project has not yet been assimilated or fully contrasted.

The most recent trends in the comparative study of systems of government in the early modern period lie in a broadening of scale – from European to global – and in a gradual shift in emphasis from analysis of official institutions and administrative structures to informal mechanisms of rule and the role of individuals and social groups in this process. These trends are seen clearly in numerous works by the historian Jeroen Duindam.

Having begun with a critical commentary on Norbert Elias's classic work on court society,[45] Duindam then published a detailed comparative study of the French royal and Habsburg imperial courts, which shed new light on both institutions and enabled certain stereotypes to be questioned (in particular that of the supposed utter impotence and submissiveness of French court aristocracy in the seventeenth century).[46]

Duindam later incorporated his observations into a wider comparative context,[47] and his most recent monograph on dynasties between 1300 and 1800 is global in nature. Such a scale gives the book an anthropological dimension and the author's aspiration to overcome the traditional dichotomy between the East and the West and to question existing historiographical clichés (e.g. notions about the grandeur of the dynasty and the servility of the elite, fostered by official histories) and the current terminology (is the usual term 'court' and its equivalents in European languages appropriate as a catchall, worldwide term, for example?) is undoubtedly conducive to further progress in the study of this important subject.[48]

---

[42] See the project's biography in Genet (1990a): 308–50 and Genet (1997): 3–4.
[43] See Genet (1990a): 286.
[44] Blickle, Ellis and Österberg (1997): 151.
[45] Duindam (1995).
[46] Duindam (2003).
[47] Duindam, Artan and Kurt (2011).
[48] Duindam (2016).

13

Comparison in social history

Social history is one of the most actively growing areas of comparison and its themes are very varied. Kaelble's 1999 bibliography of works related to this area of research comprises over 250 items.[1]

Social history is far newer than political and even economic history; its rise began only in the post-war decades and the subject of social historians' endeavours is difficult to define. Peter Burke recalled G. M. Trevelyan's characterization of social history that held sway until recently as 'a history with politics left out'. Burke himself proposed his own more positive definition. In his words, 'The new social history might be defined . . . as the study of social change in specific communities, where "social change" means change in the social structure, the groups that make up society.'[2]

Naturally, since Burke proposed his definition in 1974 social history has continued to develop and expand. It now includes new themes such as the history of gender, social welfare, education and migration. Nevertheless, it would seem that Burke correctly grasped the essence of the field. Above all, it involves studying patterns in relations between social groups in a particular society. Putting comparative history of the family and kinship aside, I will focus in this chapter on works that compare the position of the major social groups – classes and other social strata – from the Middle Ages to the present day.

The sources of comparative analysis of medieval societies date back to the classic works of Weber, Hintze and Bloch.

Weber's legacy to subsequent generations of scholars was the model of the medieval city, and several works on comparative urban studies begin with a homage to Weber.[3]

In Weber's opinion, the western European city that emerged in the Middle Ages differed substantially from the city state of antiquity and from Asian cities. Unlike ancient Athens and Rome, the medieval western city was a union of individuals rather than families and unlike Asian cities, it was a community and – in a legal sense – a corporation of city-dwellers. Weber identified five attributes which he believed characterized such a city: a fortification; a market; its own court and laws; 'an associational structure'; and at least partial autonomy and self-government.[4] City

---

[1] Kaelble (1999): 163–79.
[2] Burke (1974): 9.
[3] See, for example, Nicholas (2003): 1.
[4] Weber ([1956] 1978), 2: 1226.

fortresses and markets did exist in the East also but Weber believed that the three other attributes were characteristic only of the urban community of the West.[5]

Weber's model, built as it was on a contrast between the 'medieval city of the West' and the 'Asian city' was not merely Eurocentric; it related to only part of western Europe ('the lands north of the Alps') where, in his words, the city 'developed in a form approximating the ideal type'.[6] The cities of eastern Europe, including Russia, did not particularly interest Weber. He mentioned Moscow 'before the abolition of serfdom' once or twice,[7] calling it a 'continental city' which reminded him of 'a large Oriental city of the time, say, of Diocletian: it was a place where rents derived from the ownership of land and souls, as well as office revenues, were consumed'.[8]

Contemporary researchers still use Weber's model of the medieval town, but have substantially expanded the geographical range of its application. After carrying out a comparison, on the one hand, of major late medieval cities in northern Italy (Milan, Sienna and Venice) and Germany (Nuremberg, Munich, Cologne, Lübeck and others) and, on the other, cities in eastern and south-eastern Europe, including Krakow, Lviv, Kiev, Novgorod, Pskov, Moscow, Ragusa and Bulgarian and Byzantine cities, Rudolf Mumenthaler came to the unexpected conclusion that Novgorod and Pskov met all the criteria that Weber had established for a western city.[9] He discovered many features common to both these *veche* republics of the North West and Italian city states. Mumenthaler classed the other Russian cities – like Bulgarian and Serbian cities – as of a 'princely residence' type, which lacked both autonomy and their own court and legal system and so forth.[10]

The lengthy independence of Novgorod and Pskov can scarcely be explained solely by the fact that they lacked their own princely dynasty, as Mumenthaler would have it. An economic dimension should probably also be taken into account, in particular the involvement of both Russian cities in intensive trade with the Baltics. Nevertheless, the expanded typology of medieval European cities that Mumenthaler proposed based on Weber's criteria certainly merits attention.

Common ideas in contemporary historiography about medieval social structure are firmly linked to the concept of feudalism, which was strongly influenced by Hintze and Bloch. As indicated earlier, neither scholar considered the feudal order an exclusively western European phenomenon, acknowledging the existence of similar systems in Japan but Hintze also found particular versions of feudalism in Islamic countries and in Muscovite Rus (see p. 26).

During the twentieth century, historians discovered feudalism in an increasing number of countries. In the 1930s, the idea of Russian feudalism was firmly and apparently permanently established in Soviet historiography. Soviet historians found feudalism not only in ancient Rus but also in the Baltic countries and in the

---

[5] Weber ([1956] 1978): 1227.
[6] Weber ([1956] 1978): 1236.
[7] Weber ([1956] 1978): 1215.
[8] Weber ([1956] 1978): 1342.
[9] Mumenthaler (1998): 67.
[10] Mumenthaler (1998): 67.

countries of the Caucasus.[11] This should not, however, be seen as a peculiarity of Soviet historiography; influenced by Marx and Bloch, historians from many other countries were searching for local versions of feudalism at the time. The literature contains descriptions of feudal systems in Japan, China, India and even Ethiopia (examples of these works are given in Reynolds's article).[12]

With the increase in versions of feudalism, its basic model was eroded. The doubts first expressed in the 1970s, however, were not inspired by African or Japanese studies: by then scholars had already recognized the internal variety and heterogeneity inherent in western European feudalism itself. Thus in 1970 the medievalist A. Y. Gurevich, as then little known outside the Soviet Union, drew attention to the disparity between Scandinavian, English, Byzantine and ancient Rus' realities and the traditional model of feudalism, which was based on northern French materials.[13] A few years later, in a high-profile article published in the *American Historical Review* entitled 'The Tyranny of the Construct' (1974), Elizabeth Brown questioned the usefulness and necessity of the term 'feudalism' itself.[14]

But the greatest blow to established ideas was dealt by Susan Reynolds's book *Fiefs and Vassals* in which Reynolds showed that the evidence of medieval sources did not fit the Procrustean bed of the theory of feudalism. Reynolds believed that the concept of vassalage obscures at least half a dozen distinct types of relationship: these included ruler and subject, patron and client, landlord and tenant, master and servant, and commander and warrior.[15] Reynolds considered the established notion of a certain period (dated variously by different historians) at which a 'union' occurred between vassalage and fief and interpersonal relations first acquired a territorial nature particularly erroneous.[16] As a whole, the concept of vassalage was both too indistinct and too narrow and did not fit with existing data, and Reynolds was convinced that it could not be a tool for further study of medieval society.[17]

The concept of the fief fared no better. As Reynolds noted, until the twelfth century and even later, this term (like 'benefice' and 'allodium') was not used as frequently as had been supposed. In England, for example, the word 'feodum' did not refer exclusively to a knightly holding, but meant any free and hereditary property.[18] English material generally plays an important role in Reynolds's reasoning. In particular, the experience of the English monarchy, with its early centralization and strong bureaucratic apparatus, manifestly contradicts widespread notions of 'feudal anarchy'.

Reynolds's significant conclusion is that the apparently coherent theory of feudal law together with the associated idea of the 'feudal pyramid' and the 'hierarchy of feudal holdings' lying at the foundation of academic notions of feudalism was the creation of academic lawyers (beginning with north Italian scholars of the twelfth

---

[11] See Novosel'tsev, Pashuto and Cherepnin (1972).
[12] Reynolds (2009): 197–8, 213, 216.
[13] Gurevich ([1970] 1999): 194–5.
[14] Brown ([1974] 1998).
[15] Reynolds (1994): 33.
[16] Reynolds (1994): 46.
[17] Reynolds (1994): 47.
[18] Reynolds (1994): 68, 394.

century, the authors of the treatise *Libri Feodorum*, and continuing until the 'feudalists' of the sixteenth to the seventeenth century) and royal bureaucrats,[19] and that this theory obscures the actual diversity of medieval life.

Reynolds's views on the influence of the traditional concept of feudalism on comparative research are of particular relevance for historical comparison: 'Calling the traditional model an ideal type and pointing to variations as exceptions or anomalies that do not affect its validity has', she believes, 'discouraged historians from investigating either uniformities or variations. Reliance on the model allows them to work within their separate national traditions with a minimum of comparisons, using the model to fill in gaps in their own evidence.'[20]

'Feudalism, however defined', Reynolds claims in a recently published article, 'has outlasted its usefulness as a tool of comparative history. Trying to fit one society into the Cinderella slipper of a composite model derived from another ... is surely not the best method of comparison.'[21] She recognizes that categories such as 'feudal' or 'capitalist' have their value, but believes they are incapable of encapsulating all significant features of societies. 'Labels tend to discourage close and critical study of what is under them,' she rightly observes. She recommends beginning by comparing individual aspects of various societies such as their economies, technology, political structures and ideas, legal systems and religions.[22] Thus, in essence Reynolds had come to appreciate the maxim which the theorists of the comparative method had previously formed (see Part II, Chapter 10): like other complex systems, societies should not be compared in their entirety; it is only possible to compare particular aspects.

We will now turn from debates about feudalism to consider the seventeenth century, a period that is considered feudal only within the Marxist tradition. A certain amount of comparative research has been devoted to this eventful period including Peter Burke's *Venice and Amsterdam* (1974), in which the elites of the two cities are studied in parallel over a period of 140 years from the late sixteenth century until approximately 1720. Burke compared sources of income, political functions, lifestyle, views and value systems, and the education of the Venetian nobility and Amsterdam's upper echelons. This comparison is especially interesting since social status in Venetian society was based on birth whereas in Amsterdam, very unusually for seventeenth-century Europe, it was based on financial position. In one city power and wealth were determined mainly by a person's social status while in the other, conversely, status depended on wealth and power.[23]

The book rests on contrast: in Venice clans dominated whereas in Amsterdam the basic unit of social life was the nuclear family; individualism and a focus on personal success were accentuated more strongly in Amsterdam.[24] The Venetians ruled a vast empire as well as their own city; the functions of the Amsterdam town council were more modest but because of the important role that the city played in the life

---

[19] Reynolds (1994): 3–8, 73–4, 256–7.
[20] Reynolds (1994): 479.
[21] Reynolds (2009): 215.
[22] Reynolds (2009): 215–16.
[23] Burke (1974): 16.
[24] Burke (1974): 27–32.

of the Netherlands, the council also discussed political questions. Even the external appearances of the 'fathers' of each city differed. Despite often being careful with money in their personal lives, the Venetian nobles spared no expense when it came to lavish public ceremonies. The Amsterdam burgomasters and town council members by contrast differed little from the other townspeople in their appearance and made do without ceremonies.[25] The development of these major republics of the seventeenth century and their elites had much in common, however; both the Venetian aristocracy and Amsterdam's wealthy burghers began to derive more of their income from land than they received from naval trade and a spirit of enterprise began gradually to give way to one of the rentier.[26]

Although the cities were the focus of power and wealth, traditionally the majority of the population lived in the countryside. The historian Roland Mousnier undertook comparative research on the peasantry and its social protest in the seventeenth century. He compared peasant uprisings in France, Russia and China, three countries that differed greatly in their social structure.

Without detailed knowledge of Chinese history and language, it is difficult to evaluate Mousnier's description of the Chinese peasantry (the chapters that deal with this are based entirely on literature in English and French). As far as Russia is concerned, despite his obvious dependence on a few works by Western historians specializing in Russia, the section on Russia is of undoubted interest thanks to the constant comparisons made with the French society of the early modern era, on which Mousnier was an expert.

The key metaphor Mousnier employed when talking about Russian society from the end of the sixteenth to the seventeenth century is that of a 'people which had been torn up by the roots'.[27] He saw the causes of this situation in the terror perpetrated by the *oprichniki* under Ivan the Terrible, the devastating Livonian War, the Tartar raids and other factors such as epidemics and harvest failures, which forced people to abandon their homes. This is the standpoint from which Mousnier examined the process of colonization as well as the development of a Cossack 'frontier' at the fringes. He contrasted this model of a country with a nomadic, tumbleweed-like population with his native France which 'by its very nature' was divided into particular regions whose inhabitants had put down roots over many generations in a land that was the soil of their forebears, and which all social groups were prepared to defend jointly. 'Russia', Mousnier believed, 'lacked those strong territorial communities, little fatherlands, which in France gave a local habitation to each revolt, uniting the social groups to defend local privileges and freedoms. The great Russian revolts could unfurl themselves over vast spaces, embracing masses of people who were not greatly different from each other, though hundreds of kilometers apart.'[28]

Mousnier was thus inclined to explain the span of popular movements in Russia in the seventeenth century – from that led by Ivan Bolotninkov to Stenka Razin's – by

---

[25] Burke (1974): 62, 65–6.
[26] Burke (1974): 104, 108.
[27] Mousnier ([1967] 1972): 156.
[28] Mousnier ([1967] 1972): 159.

the absence of regional particularism and in general by the weak differentiation of Russian society compared to French society of the same time.[29] It is possible that by following the long historiographical tradition engendered in Russian academia itself in the nineteenth century, Mousnier exaggerated the 'fluidity' of the Muscovite state's population and underestimated the extent to which local allegiances had developed among the inhabitants of individual historical regions in Russia, but the validity of the way in which he framed the issue, which was dictated by identifying serious differences in the two agrarian societies would appear beyond question.

In the concluding section of the book, summarizing the findings of his comparison of peasant uprisings in France, Russia and China in the seventeenth century, Mousnier concludes that the main cause in all three countries was state activity in the form of growth in taxes and the curtailment of citizens' rights and privileges.[30] He also observed that these disturbances were never initiated by the peasants, but by other social elements.[31] Finally, questioning the rebels' aims, Mousnier emphasized that they lacked any programme and believed that it was only in Russia, in Stenka Razin's time, that the Cossacks and peasants 'were . . . thinking of a revolution'.[32] He saw the causes of this 'revolutionary spirit' which distinguished the Russian peasants of the seventeenth century from their French and Chinese counterparts as the process of enslavement that had occurred in Russia and the limitation of social mobility.[33]

The Russian peasantry was the subject of a further piece of comparative research in Peter Kolchin's *Unfree Labor* (1987). In this, Kolchin contrasted American slavery and Russian serfdom – two forms of enforced labour that had existed simultaneously on different continents. Thus, these two significant topics, which had hitherto been studied separately and had acquired a solid historiography in the United States and Russia, respectively, were brought together for the first time. Kolchin's plan was to research and examine the two forms of servitude alongside each other and to then present each in a new light, challenge received ideas and put forward new hypotheses.

Kolchin makes active use of contrasting comparison in the book. He contrasts the way of life of planters, who remained on their farms continually, with the absenteeism of the Russian landlords who preferred to delegate the management of their estates so that the serfs rarely saw their master. He concludes that in Russia these relations were far more impersonal than they were between American planters and their slaves[34] and from this infers differences in the nature of the respective emancipations of the slaves and the peasants in the 1860s, which was violent in America and comparatively peaceful in Russia. The cohesion of the Russian peasant community contrasted with the disunity of the slaves, which Kolchin believes explained the frequency of peasant disturbances and rebellions in Russia and the rarity of open protest by American slaves. The serfs may have had an awareness of major events in the country such as the accession of a new tsar and felt part of a greater society; the American slaves, however,

---

[29] Mousnier ([1967] 1972): 178.
[30] Mousnier ([1967] 1972): 306–8, 332, 348.
[31] Mousnier ([1967] 1972): 327.
[32] Mousnier ([1967] 1972): 344.
[33] Mousnier ([1967] 1972): 345.
[34] Kolchin (1987): 58.

did not share this feeling nor did they follow national events.³⁵ Kolchin characterized the differences between the two social systems in the introduction to his book by saying that the world of the American South was that of the slave owner, while rural Russia was the world of the peasant.³⁶

Despite the differences, the similarities between these two institutions are significant. Kolchin observed that by the end of the eighteenth century, Russian serfdom was in essence very close to slavery in nature and the nobility's attitude to the peasants was reminiscent of racial hatred. Emphasizing the difference between the peasants and themselves, the landowners stopped just short of racial arguments and they regarded the peasants as different people.³⁷

Although it achieved a high profile, Kolchin's book received a mixed reception. Specialists in Russian history were highly critical and Michael Confino's verdict was particularly harsh. Not only did he question a number of Kolchin's specific conclusions (e.g. he believed that Russian landowners' absenteeism was far from typical of the Russian nobility)³⁸ but he also denied the very possibility of comparisons between slavery and serfdom and between the Russian peasant society of the eighteenth to the nineteenth century and the American South and its class and racial differences.³⁹

Americanists were more favourably disposed to the book: although he noted that it had not changed his ideas about the planters of the American South, Fredrickson acknowledged that the proposed new perspective on Russian serfdom appeared to be genuinely important.

It was the comparativists, however – and, indeed, those without a particular connection to either Russian or American history – who gave *Unfree Labor* the greatest plaudits. For example, Peter Baldwin, a specialist in nineteenth- and twentieth-century western European history, called the book 'one of the best examples of comparative history' and, in particular, noted Kolchin's ability to construct comparison in such a way that the cases compared illuminated and enriched one another.⁴⁰ Reynolds, a medievalist, had earlier found 'the comparison of unfreedom in two different societies with different economies, legal systems, etc.' in Kolchin's book 'extremely thought-provoking'.⁴¹

Kolchin's skill as a comparativist is considerable and Confino's harsh words would appear unjustified. As for Confino's questioning of the comparability of slave ownership in Russia and the American South, as was shown earlier (see Part II, Chapter 9), comparability is established by research rather than being inherent in its objects. Confino's scepticism would appear to merely show that Kolchin's arguments failed to convince him. Confino is mistaken in believing that Russian serfdom can be called slavery only in a metaphorical sense.⁴² A legalistic approach is not helpful

---

[35] Kolchin (1987): 326.
[36] Kolchin (1987): XII.
[37] Kolchin (1987): 170, 173, 180.
[38] Confino (1990): 1132–5.
[39] Confino (1990): 1136–9; Confino (2009): 107, 109–10.
[40] Baldwin (2004): 16.
[41] Reynolds (1994): 481, note 5.
[42] Confino (1990): 1137.

here, and it is essential to take account of the development of serfdom in Russia: while at its inception in the seventeenth century it may have been more akin to medieval *servage*, by the end of the eighteenth century it had acquired clear features of slavery; the attempts by serf owners to find 'racial' differences between themselves and the peasants that Kolchin mentioned very much reflect this. Although Kolchin did not adduce any new facts or archival documents, he raised new and important questions and suggested new interpretations of the phenomena he studied.

By any measure of economic effectiveness both the serf-owning landowners and planter slave owners seemed in the mid-nineteenth century to represent a dying era.[43] The leading figures of the new period were sharp, enterprising individuals and capitalist industrialists. In the 1980s, Kocka led a group of German historians who published a series of books on the European bourgeoisie of the nineteenth century from a comparative perspective and on the phenomenon of 'bourgeoisness' itself.[44] Ruble compared the development of three major cities, Chicago, Moscow and Osaka, in the period of industrial boom from the end of the nineteenth to the beginning of the twentieth century and found much in common in the policies of the leaders of these cities – the mayor of Chicago, Carter Harrison; Moscow Mayor Nikolai Alekseev; and the mayor of Osaka, Seki Hajime; he used the term 'pragmatic pluralism' to describe them.[45]

But change in the ruling class was far from immediate: Europe's aristocracy was in no hurry to give up its position to the newly moneyed bourgeoisie. Dominic Lieven set out to explore how the upper nobility survived the nineteenth century and how it adapted to the changes taking place. To this end he compared the fates of the English, Russian and German aristocracies in the period between the Congress of Vienna in 1815 and the beginning of the First World War. He was interested in the property situation of the upper echelons of the nobility and the sources of its well-being as well as in the aristocracy's way of life, upbringing and education, their military careers and involvement in politics.

A rather mixed picture emerged. Above all, it transpired that the concept of a 'European aristocracy' encompassed groups that varied greatly in their status and political and cultural influence. Thus, it was only the English lords occupying as they did seats in the House of Lords – the upper chamber of the British parliament – who could be called a 'ruling' class in the full sense of the word. By contrast, in Germany where an aristocratic elite had not yet emerged, the Prussian Junkers – a populous section of the rural nobility of modest means – enjoyed exceptional influence. A unique feature of the nobility in Russia was its high level of culture and the artistic

---

[43] Kolchin cites the Americanists' unanimous opinion that the economy of the Southern plantations was on an upswing on the eve of the Civil War (Kolchin (1987): 370). The question of the economic potential of Russian serfdom on the eve of its abolition is more contentious; in the most recent literature the suggestion has been put forward that estates based on serf labour brought owners an income right up to 1861 and were not experiencing a crisis (Mironov (2000), II: 123). In any case, however, by the middle of the nineteenth century both forms of enforced labour were considered anachronistic and both socially and ethically were entirely incompatible with the norms of the new capitalist era.
[44] See Kocka (1987).
[45] Ruble (2001).

talent of many of its members: no other European country's nobility produced so many outstanding writers and composers as the Russian aristocracy.[46]

The loss of the aristocracy's leading position in society was irreversible but occurred at different rates in different countries and areas of life. The British aristocracy was better able than most to adapt to the realities of the capitalist era, but by the beginning of the twentieth century it had lost its political power in significant measure. By contrast, the Prussian Junkers and the Russian landowning elite were less successful economically, but on the eve of the First World War their influence on the politics of their countries had, in fact, been growing for some time.[47]

The Industrial Revolution brought in its wake a rapid growth in the urban proletariat, who were to play a key role in a number of major events of the nineteenth to the twentieth century. Comparative labour history is now a flourishing trend in contemporary comparison.

Christiane Eisenberg has compared trade union movements in Germany and Britain in the nineteenth century and drawn conclusions that substantially amended earlier academic ideas. Scholars had long noted a certain asynchronicity in the development of the labour movement in these countries: in Britain, trade union organizations began to appear back in the eighteenth century but an actual workers' party – the Labour Party – was not founded until the beginning of the twentieth century. In Germany, by contrast, a social democratic party appeared in 1863 when German trade unions had barely begun to develop: a noticeable breakthrough in this came only in the 1890s. This development of the German labour movement, seen as 'anomalous' in the British context, is usually linked with the country's delayed industrialization (according to Gerschenkron's theory) and regarded as a manifestation of Germany's Sonderweg. Drawing on work done by comparativists in the 1980s, Eisenberg showed that the relatively early development of a social democratic party in Germany in 1863 could not be evidence of accelerated political development of German workers compared to their British counterparts. This early and immature party structure (as compared to the English Chartist movement of the 1840s) should rather be seen as representing the filling of a political vacuum brought about by the lack of trade unions in Germany, their development having long been inhibited by the continued existence of guild structures in the German states.[48]

Among recent research, Jan Lucassen's article on brickmakers in western Europe in the eighteenth to the nineteenth century and northern India in the nineteenth to the twentieth century deserves particular mention. Lucassen took a highly scholarly approach and endeavoured to observe the *ceteris paribus* principle, that is, to reduce the number of differences between the cases compared to a minimum, limiting them to those arising from geography and cultural factors. He therefore focused on manual brick production as a technology that was comparatively simple and uniform throughout the world, and for his comparison chose western Europe up to 1900 and India up to the beginning of the first decade of the twenty-first century as time periods

---

[46] Lieven (1992): 178.
[47] Lieven (1992): 220–1.
[48] Eisenberg (1989).

when technological improvements had not yet brought about fundamental changes in the production process.[49] In addition to archival and other available written sources, Lucassen used interviews with present-day Indian brickmakers. The theoretical significance of Lucassen's comparative research was that it established the fundamental comparability of the behaviour of workers in different cultures, which several well-regarded academics had doubted. In particular, Dipesh Chakrabarty had described the belief that modern capitalist employment relations throughout the world are based on the principles of citizenship, individualism and equality before the law as seriously mistaken. In his work on the jute factories of Calcutta at the end of the nineteenth to the mid-twentieth century, Dipesh Chakrabarty noted the 'hierarchical and inegalitarian nature of relationships of power' that the Indian workers found themselves in, and pointed to the 'undemocratic cultural codes of Indian society'.[50]

The results of Lucassen's comparative 'experiment' proved very fruitful. Having carefully studied the way in which brickmakers' work was organized and the forms of their collective protest in several western European countries and northern India, Lucassen found no fundamental differences: the organization of work and labour relations in these areas of the world that were very distant from each other proved to be similar in many respects.[51] As Lucassen rightly notes, this outcome could be 'a boost to global labour history and comparative history'.[52]

In conclusion, it is worth briefly mentioning social mobility as another promising topic of comparative research within social history. In the 1980s Kaelble contrasted indicators of mobility (accessing education and achieving a successful career) in various European countries and the United States in the nineteenth to the twentieth century.[53] In the 1990s comparative study of another form of mobility – migration – came to the fore. This included labour migration and the position of ethnic minorities in various cities and countries. Nancy Green, author of a book published in 1997 about female immigrant workers in clothing factories in Paris and New York in the late nineteenth and twentieth centuries, made a significant contribution to developing this topic and her reviews[54] offer a good introduction to the subject.

---

[49] Lukassen (2006): 514.
[50] Cited in Lukassen (2006): 514–15.
[51] Lukassen (2006): 569.
[52] Lukassen (2006): 569.
[53] Kaelble (1983).
[54] See Green (1990, 1994, 2004).

14

Comparative research on nationalism, empire and colonialism

In this chapter we will examine three interrelated topics of comparative historical research which, due to their scale, do not fit into any of the notional headings above. Indeed, the phenomenon of nationalism can be studied from various points of view including the political, social or cultural. This is equally true of empire and colonialization.

Several competing theories of nationalism exist. Christopher Bayly offered a critical review of these in his book *The Birth of the Modern World: Global Connections and Comparisons, 1780-1914* (2004), which stands out from similar overviews by the global comparative perspective from which Bayly examines the issue.

Theorists of nationalism disagree fundamentally about whether modern nations are real communities with roots in a previous historical period. Anthony Smith and 'primordialists' have insisted that nations grew naturally out of earlier ethnic groups. The 'constructivists' or 'modernists' on the other hand consider nations to be the invention of the nationalists of modernity, although they diverge on the reasons why nationalism arose. Some scholars, such as Ernest Gellner, attribute its development to the process of modernization, which transformed former agrarian societies into industrial ones; others such as John Breuilly and Eric Hobsbawm have ascribed a crucial role to the state and political factors. Others still emphasize the significance of the printed word, newspapers and books in the development of an 'imagined community' as Benedict Anderson puts it – the nation.

As Bayly rightly noted, all these ideas should be viewed as methods of interpretation rather than as theories in the strict sense of the word: they help shed light on particular instances of nationalism at the end of the nineteenth century, but are not predictive and none of them taken individually is capable of explaining either the nature of nationalism or why it arose when it did.[1]

Summarizing existing observations within the literature, Bayly acknowledges that several nations in nineteenth-century Europe (e.g. Britain and France) and beyond (Vietnam, Sri Lanka and Japan) had longer lineages than others. However, this in no way negates the fact that in many parts of the world, national feeling was at the same time formed by the state. Gellner's thesis about the link between nationalism

---

[1] Bayly (2004): 202.

and capitalist industrialization applies most closely to the situation in central and eastern Europe, and this is what Gellner had in mind when he formulated his theory: confrontation between Czechs, Germans and Hungarians in the Austro-Hungarian Empire did, indeed, take place in conditions of rapid urbanization – the population of Prague, for instance, grew from 157,000 in 1850 to 514, 000 in 1900. The same is true for Germany and partly for Italy – certainly in the new industrial centre of Piedmont. As Bayly reminds us, though, strong nationalist movements also arose in those societies where industrialization remained at a low level.[2] Anderson's idea, with its emphasis on the role of the imagination, shared feeling and printed material in the invention of nationalism was highly applicable to areas that had not yet been touched by capitalism and urbanization and did not have strong state power, but where people nevertheless advanced claims to the status of a nation. Therefore, in Bayly's opinion, Anderson's work on 'imagined communities', derived from the study of colonial Dutch Indonesia, became popular among historians specializing in nineteenth-century India and Africa.[3]

Bayly's observations bring to mind Bloch's warning to his colleagues to avoid attempting to explain phenomena occurring on a Pan-European scale with local causes.[4] Clearly, nationalism is a process that has encompassed the entire world over the last two centuries. Various factors – economic, political and religious – have played out according to local features in different countries, but the advance of nationalism around the world has nevertheless continued.

The lack of a single, comprehensive theory of nationalism does not, however, prevent historians from successfully studying individual aspects of this complex phenomenon, sometimes using the comparative method. Czech scholar Miroslav Hroch's work is one such example of successful comparative historical research which, perhaps oddly, did not come to Bayly's attention.

A professor at the Charles University in Prague, Miroslav Hroch (b. 1932) began his comparative study of nineteenth-century nationalist movements as early as the 1960s and came to prominence after the publication of *Social Preconditions of National Revival in Europe*.[5]

Unlike the constructivists, Hroch certainly did not consider nations to be the product of national consciousness. On the contrary, for him a nation was the 'fundamental reality', and nationalism derived from this.[6] In his book, Hroch focused on the 'awakening' of small or oppressed nations in central, eastern and northern Europe within the Habsburg and Romanov empires or other state entities. Hroch discerned three phases in the development of national movements. Phase A was a period of academic interest in the national language, folklore and so forth; Phase B was a period of patriotic agitation – Hroch accorded this phase crucial importance. Finally, Phase C involved the rise of a mass national movement. Hroch correlated these phases with the general process of transition from feudal to bourgeois relations, in which

[2] Bayly (2004): 203.
[3] Bayly (2004): 204.
[4] Bloch ([1928] 1953): 505, 506.
[5] Hroch (1985).
[6] Hroch (1985): 3.

he identified two stages, occurring before and after the establishment of capitalism.[7] Hroch obtained the basis for a typology of the movements he studied by arranging measures of national and socio-economic development in an overlapping manner.

Hroch believed that the first, 'integrated' type characterized the Czechs, Norwegians and Finns: in this case, the national agitation phase (Phase B) coincided with the Industrial Revolution and the mass national movement phase (Phase C), with bourgeois revolution. In this way, the newly developed modern nation rapidly acquired a full class structure. The second type, which Hroch called 'belated', was characterized by a delayed inception of Phase C, which occurred after the proletariat had already formed; this applied to the Slovaks and Lithuanians. Hroch located a third, 'mutinous' type in Macedonia and Bulgaria but did not study this separately in his work. Finally, a fourth, 'collapsing' type is described using the Flemish movement in Belgium as an example; this was distinguished by the fact that national agitation (Phase B) began only when a developed capitalist society already existed, and the mass movement phase (Phase C) began very late or not at all.[8]

The main strength of Hroch's work, however, is not this typology, which can be seen as a nod to the intellectual fashion of the 1960s (cf. Schieder's typology of nation states in Chapter 2). Its greatest value lies in the central section of the book, which contains a quantitative comparative analysis of the make-up of those involved in the national movements of Europe in the nineteenth century; this is based on lists of members of social organizations and subscribers to patriotic publications and similar documents. Hroch appears to have been surprised by the conclusions of his research. As it transpired, no single class or social group occupied a sufficiently stable place in the structures of patriotic communities to allow it to be claimed that the involvement of that group had been either constant or essential to the national movement concerned.[9] Thus, the success of Phase B, focused on a rise in national consciousness, did not depend on the exclusive involvement of any particular group and there was no typical combination of social groups.[10] This conclusion is consistent with Bayly's later observations mentioned earlier about the ubiquity of nationalism, which was fostered by various factors in different countries.

It was particularly surprising that Hroch, who undoubtedly remained a Marxist historian, should claim that the bourgeoisie played no major role whatsoever in the national movements of the oppressed peoples of Europe.[11] Carefully conducted empirical comparativist research had thus facilitated an escape from a number of historiographical myths and stereotypes. The book also contained positive conclusions, however, which were supported by a large amount of material. In particular, Hroch convincingly demonstrated the significance of the urban setting in the national 'awakening' of the peoples of central and eastern Europe; the leaders of the Czech, Norwegian and Flemish movements were drawn from the intelligentsia or the urban middle classes and it was only in Lithuania, Estonia and Belorussia, where the national

[7] Hroch (1985): 22–3.
[8] Hroch (1985): 25–8.
[9] Hroch (1985): 129.
[10] Hroch (1985): 155.
[11] Hroch (1985): 134.

awakening was greatly delayed, that the patriots had predominantly peasant roots.[12] And although the typology that Hroch proposed was disputed by a later generation of historians of European nationalism,[13] his book remains a remarkable model of comparative research.

The history of empire and imperial policy has been the theme of numerous comparative works in recent decades but scholars acknowledge that unlike the history of nationalism it suffers from a lack of theories capable of explaining the development of empires and their decline.[14] Indeed, the concept of empire itself, which has been applied to a very wide range of political entities from antiquity to the present, remains vague. It is unsurprising that having compared the

fates of the British, Ottoman, Austro-Hungarian and Russian empires, Dominic Lieven shied away from giving 'too rigorous and "scientific" a definition' of this key term. As Lieven puts it, 'Empire is a fine subject, peopled by leopards and other creatures of the wild. To reduce all this to definitions and formulas is to turn the leopard into a pussycat, and even into an incomplete but misshapen pussycat with three legs and no tail.'[15]

In practice, of course, all historians begin with their own understanding of the subject they are studying. Lieven thus puts the emphasis primarily on the foreign policy dimension. For him, empire is 'first and foremost, a very great power that has left its mark on the international relations of an era'.[16] He also takes account of the entirely undemocratic methods involved in administering large territories and multi-ethnic conglomerations that are typical of empire.[17] But for Alfred Rieber, who like Lieven is also a specialist in Russian history, the main feature of an empire is one ethnic group's control over others within the borders of a defined territory.[18]

As Alexei Miller recently noted, while comparison of the Romanov, Habsburg and Ottoman empires was previously intended to highlight their backwardness and the inevitable decline that took place over the last two centuries of their existence, new comparative research shifts the focus from the traditional features of these empires to models of how they adapted to the challenges of a new era.[19] Miller himself believes that the potential of these empires – with the possible exception of the Turkish – was far from exhausted by the beginning of the twentieth century, that their collapse was not predetermined, and that it was only the First World War that brought about their end.[20]

The longevity and viability of these continental empires were the subject of Rieber's comparative research. He names three factors that facilitated their long stability and gradual renewal: imperial ideology, bureaucracy and defence of borders.[21] Taking

---

[12] Hroch (1985): 157–60.
[13] Kocka and Haupt (2009): 7 and note 21.
[14] Rieber (2004): 33.
[15] Lieven (2000): 417.
[16] Lieven (2000): XIV.
[17] Lieven (2000): XIV.
[18] Rieber (2004): 34.
[19] Miller (2007): 19–20.
[20] Miller (2007): 32.
[21] Rieber (2004): 39.

the politics of Russia, Austro-Hungary and Turkey as an example, Rieber shows the dynamism of imperial ideology – interchanging secular and religious images, for instance – and the evolution of administrative structures. The typology of Eurasian borders that Rieber proposed, which comprises western European state borders, Islamic borders and 'dynamic' borders is particularly interesting.[22] Thus, the Habsburg and Romanov empires' borders with European states were of the first type. These were stable and clearly defined in accordance with international agreements. In the southeast, however, the Habsburgs had bordered the Islamic world for centuries and the Russian Empire had a 'dynamic' border, where the settled rural population moved southwards, encroaching on the territory of nomads and coming into contact with their culture. The borders of the Ottoman Empire, like those of the Persian one, were of the Islamic type.[23]

A method typically employed in the comparative history of empire is contrasting continental powers with naval ones, whose colonies were located far from the centre. As Rieber emphasizes, unlike their rivals with overseas colonies, continental empires were not able to establish different forms of government at the centre and the periphery; the introduction of a constitutional system in one part of a Eurasian empire demanded that it should be introduced in the rest of the state's territory. The implications of this were evident in the case of the Habsburg Empire after 1867, the Ottoman Empire after 1876 and the Russian Empire after 1905. A serious contradiction was immediately revealed between the 'absolute' power of the rulers and the constitutional power of the representative organ and between the unitary nature of the state and the demand for greater territorial autonomy at the periphery. Such autonomy was dangerous, because it increased susceptibility to economic penetration by more developed foreign powers and threatened to weaken political control by the centre over the vulnerable edges.[24]

But as Miller emphasizes, since the continental empires also bordered each other they had a strong mutual influence and formed a single macro-system. While Britain, for example, was able to incite the mountain dwellers of the Caucasus against the Russian powers as much as it wished without fear of difficulties from its own Muslim subjects, the position was entirely different in relation to neighbouring empires; if Austro-Hungary supported the Polish or Ukrainian movements in the Russian Empire, it would have had to change its policy in relation to its 'own' Poles or the Ruthenian Ukrainians.[25]

The existence of colonies is considered one of the hallmarks of empire. Among the numerous pieces of research that have involved comparison of the colonial policies of the great powers,[26] Oxford professor John Elliott's *Empires of the Atlantic World: Britain and Spain in America, 1492-1830* (2006) stands out. As Elliott points out, the American colonies of the two countries had already been contrasted in the eighteenth century[27] and since then attempts have repeatedly been made to characterize the differences

---

[22] Rieber (2004): 54.
[23] Rieber (2004): 55.
[24] Rieber (2004): 66.
[25] Miller (2007): 30–1.
[26] See, for example, Bayly and Kolff (1986); Hart (2003).
[27] Elliott (2006): 403–4.

between them. In particular, in the 1970s historian James Lang defined the Spanish and British possessions in America as an 'empire of conquest' and an 'empire of commerce', respectively. Elliott, however, considers this approach to the issue oversimplified. His observations are that from the earliest expeditions, the motives of the English and Spanish colonizers could not be classified in such a straightforward manner or placed under such neat headings.[28] Moreover, in Elliott's opinion, comparing the history and culture of large political bodies, which leads to a series of sharp contrasts, hardly takes the complexity of the past into account sufficiently.[29] Therefore, not seeing sense in reducing the diversity of historical experience to simple formulae, Elliott avoided any attempt to analyse the various aspects of the histories of British and Spanish America by enumerating their common features and differences. Instead, he endeavoured to show the development of the two great civilizations of the New World over three centuries, continually comparing, contrasting and intertwining their histories in his account in the hope that elucidating one would at the same time assist in understanding the other.[30]

In the parallel histories of Spanish and British colonialization that Elliott traced, comparison plays a 'profiling', particularizing role. Elliott formulated his understanding of comparison thus: 'The movements involved in writing comparative history are not unlike those involved in playing the accordion. The two societies under comparison are pushed together, but only to be pulled apart again. Resemblances prove after all to be not as close as they look at first sight; differences are discovered which at first lay concealed.'[31]

In accordance with this credo, Elliott builds a narrative on contrast: in the first chapter he presents a form of double portrait of the leaders of two expeditions – Hernán Cortés in 1519 and Christopher Newport in 1606 – who laid the foundations for the Spanish and British colonial empires, respectively. Both were adventurists, but of different sorts. One acted on the orders of the Governor of Cuba; the other was in the service of the private joint-stock company known as the Virginia Company. Elliott later repeatedly turns to contrast: he contrasts the slow and accidental actions that led the English towards creating an empire with the speed with which the Spanish colonies in America were formally incorporated into an effective imperial system.[32] While the Spanish colonial administration was subject to careful control by bureaucrats in Madrid, the English governor in America was not only free of fear of such checks but, in fact, experienced difficulties as a result of the lack of an imperial bureaucracy.[33] Liberation from colonial power also occurred in different ways. First, Spanish America obtained independence forty to fifty years later than British America and this was directly influenced by the American Revolution and the formation of the United States; second, the cruelty displayed at the time of the American War of Independence paled

---

[28] Elliott (2006): 16.
[29] Elliott (2006): XVI.
[30] Elliott (2006): XVIII.
[31] Elliott (2006): XVII.
[32] Elliott (2006): 119.
[33] Elliott (2006): 138, 140.

into insignificance alongside the terror of the civil war that raged in Spanish America, particularly in Venezuela.[34]

The chief value of Elliott's book lies in the nuanced way in which it treats the traditional subjects of colonial history such as motives and methods for capturing new lands, relations between the colonizers and the indigenous population, the mother country and the colonial administration, and the formation of local elites. Meanwhile, a new generation of historians has substantially widened the scope of the comparative study of colonialism, focusing on the subtle domestic boundaries that separated colonial societies in their everyday life in the area of gender and family relations. Ann Laura Stoler gives a good introduction to this theme in her 2001 article 'Tense and Tender Ties: The Politics of Comparison in North American History and (Post) Colonial Studies' and we will conclude this chapter with an overview of this.

Stoler, who had studied the Dutch East Indies of the nineteenth century over a number of years, underlined the role of children's institutions such as nurseries, kindergartens and boarding schools in perpetuating racial and class boundaries. These institutions were designed to 'save' European children from the influence of indigenous nannies, which was perceived as dangerous and harmful to their morality and health. Stoler draws a parallel between the fears of the colonizers and pedagogical ideas that were widespread in Europe and America at the time, according to which the children of aristocratic and bourgeois families needed to be shielded from the rough care of uneducated servants. Such ideas led to the appearance of the first kindergartens, at first in Germany and Britain in the late 1820s and then in Holland in the 1850s.[35]

Another typical example that Stoler gives were the craft schools for impoverished orphans of mixed marriages that the Dutch established in their East Indian colonies in the second half of the nineteenth century, and similar institutions – boarding schools for the children of native Americans – that then appeared in the United States. Both pedagogical experiments embodied the idea that physical labour inculcated correct ideas about morality and order in these children, who were seen as potential criminals.[36] The colonial structure was thus reproduced and racial distinctions maintained in different parts of the world.

---

[34] Elliott (2006): 391–2.
[35] Stoler (2001): 850–2.
[36] Stoler (2001): 853–6.

Conclusion

I began this book by enumerating several paradoxes of historical comparison, chief of which was the fact that although comparison in history has existed since Herodotus's time, its status remains unclear even now: many modern scholars do not acknowledge it as a method, speaking, instead, of a certain approach or perspective or even of a 'comparative imagination'. I do not share this scepticism; analysis of the theory and practice of historical research has led me to the conclusion that a methodology of comparative analysis is fully capable of being developed and, moreover, that the foundations for this have already been laid.

At this point, the heuristic and analytical possibilities of historical comparison have been well elucidated; several typologies have been proposed, which are based either on logic – individualization or generalization – or on the selection of the objects that are seen in parallel, cross-cultural or asymmetrical comparison. A specialized terminology is gradually developing.

Some will perhaps consider these achievements in the methodology clearly inadequate. It is true that current methodological recommendations by no means encompass all aspects of comparative research; many difficulties, potential errors and stumbling blocks remain to be identified and future comparativists will need to face and overcome these. This is partly explained by the fact that critical thought about methods of comparative analysis is a relatively recent development. While source criticism has been developing for over three centuries, systematic historical comparison, if Bloch's seminal article of 1928 is taken as a starting point, has existed for little over ninety years.

Moreover, the possibilities of theory should not be exaggerated when using historical methods. There is no qualitative (as opposed to quantitative) method that can be expressed as a formula: the so-called rules are simply recommendations based on successful research experience and applying them requires a creative approach. In my view, however, it is fundamentally important that if – as I do not doubt – the analytic process we have considered is by its nature a general method which can be applied to any theme or problem, a cumulative effect will emerge. Each generation of researchers will add to the sum of rules developed by their predecessors. Indeed, this is happening before our eyes: the theory of historical comparison has significantly advanced recently, primarily through the efforts of Kaelble, Kocka and Haupt. This book is, however, only the second summary of the theory (the first, Kaelble's *Historical Comparison*, was published in 1999).[1]

---

[1] Kaelble (1999).

There would appear to be grounds for cautious optimism about the prospects of historical comparison. Common complaints about its marginal position in academic history[2] are not consistent with the rise of comparative historical research that is now seen internationally. These complaints would appear to derive from the mistaken premise that comparison or as it is often known, 'comparative history,' is or should be a particular movement, specialism, or as Fredrickson proposed, a subdiscipline of history.[3] Meanwhile, with its highly diverse modern themes and forms, there are no signs of this happening.

Judging by prominent examples cited in seminal articles by its leading present-day exponents, comparison features far more frequently in historical research than one might think. As well as works in which it plays a systematizing role, there are others in which it is used 'surgically' in analysing individual aspects of a selected theme.

Ultimately, as Grew reminds us, 'In the broadest sense, then, comparison is unavoidable. The question', he continues, 'is not so much whether historians should make comparisons but whether the study of history benefits when those comparisons are done consciously and sometimes even systematically.'[4] Like Grew, I consider that systematic, carefully calibrated comparative analysis is far more effective than a casual, ill-considered analogy. Indeed, it was a conviction about the value of thinking seriously about methodology that gave rise to this book.

Apart from re-examining its research practice, hopes for further progress in historical comparison depend on a more active use of the experience of associated disciplines. Since the comparative method is cross-disciplinary and the boundary between history and the social sciences is highly notional and flexible, knowing the methods of sociology, political science and anthropology – which have long used comparison in their work with considerable success – is useful for historians, as I have tried to demonstrate.

Finally, it would be remiss to overlook the experimental nature of comparison, which entails innovation and inventiveness in solving problems; if this book is of assistance to those at the initial stages of discovering the exciting possibilities of historical comparison to enlighten, its aim will have been achieved.

---

[2] Cohen (2004): 57; Haupt and Kocka (2004): 25; Kocka and Haupt (2009): 1, 15.
[3] Fredrickson (2000): 36.
[4] Grew (1980): 769.

Bibliography

Abou-El-Haj, Rifa 'at 'Ali (1991), *Formation of the Modern State: The Ottoman Empire, Sixteenth to Eighteenth Centuries*. Albany, NY: State University of New York.
Abrams, Philip (1980), 'History, Sociology, Historical Sociology', *Past and Present*, 87: 3–16.
'AHR Conversation: On Transnational History' (2006), *The American Historical Review*, 111 (5): 1441–64.
Allen, Robert C. (2011), *Global Economic History: A Very Short Introduction*. Oxford and New York: Oxford University Press.
Anderson, Perry ([1974] 1996), *Lineages of the Absolutist State*. London and New York: Verso. 7th impression (first publ. by NLB 1974; Verso edition 1979).
Baldwin, Peter (1990), *The Politics of Social Solidarity: Class Bases of the European Welfare State, 1875 – 1975*. Cambridge: Cambridge University Press.
Baldwin, Peter (2004), 'Comparing and Generalizing: Why All History Is Comparative, Yet No History Is Sociology', in Deborah Cohen and Maura O'Connor (eds), *Comparison and History: Europe in Cross-National Perspective*, 1–22. New York and London: Routledge.
Barkey, Karen (1994), *Bandits and Bureaucrats: The Ottoman Route to State Centralization*. Ithaca and London: Cornell University Press.
Bayly, C. A. (2004), *The Birth of the Modern World, 1780 – 1914: Global Connections and Comparisons*. Malden, MA, and Oxford: Blackwell.
Bayly, C. A. and Kolff, D. H. A., eds (1986), *Two Colonial Empires: Comparative Essays on the History of India and Indonesia in the Nineteenth Century*. Dordrecht, Boston and Lancaster: Martinus Nijhoff Publishers.
Bendix, Reinhard (1978), *Kings or People: Power and the Mandate to Rule*. Berkeley, Los Angeles and London: University of California Press.
Bernheim, Ernst (1908), *Lehrbuch der historischen Methode und der Geschichtsphilosophie*, 5th and 6th edn. Leipzig: Verlag von Duncker & Humblot.
Blickle, Peter, Ellis, Steven and Österberg, Eva (1997), 'The Commons and the State: Representation, Influence, and the Legislative Process', in Peter Blickle (ed.), *Resistance, Representation, and Community*, 115–53. Oxford and New York: Oxford University Press (The Origins of the Modern State in Europe, 13th to 18th Centuries).
Bloch, Marc ([1924] 1973), *The Royal Touch: Sacred Monarchy and Scrofula in England and France*, transl. by J. E. Anderson. London: Routledge and Kegan Paul.
Bloch, Marc (1928), 'Pour une histoire comparée des sociétés européennes', *Revue de synthèse historique*, XLVI: 15–50.
Bloch, Marc ([1928] 1953), 'Toward a Comparative History of European Societies', transl. by J. C. Riemersma, in Frederick C. Lane and Jelle C. Riemersma (eds), *Enterprise and Secular Change: Readings in Economic History*, 494–521. London: George Allen and Unwin Ltd.
Bloch, Marc (1930), 'Comparaison', *Bulletin du Centre international de synthèse, section de synthèse historique*, 9: 31–9.

Bloch, Marc ([1931] 1973), *French Rural Society: An Essay on Its Basic Characteristics*, transl. from the French by Janet Sondheimer. Berkeley and Los Angeles: University of California Press.
Bloch, Marc ([1939-40] 1961), *Feudal Society*, transl. by L. A. Manyon, 2 vols. Chicago: The University of Chicago Press; London: Routledge & Kegan Paul Ltd.
Bloch, Marc ([1949] 1954), *The Historian's Craft*, transl. from the French by Peter Putnam. Manchester: Manchester University Press.
Blue G. R. (1998), 'Comparative History', in D. R. Woolf (ed.), *A Global Encyclopedia of Historical Writing*, 2 vols, I: 192-5. New York and London: Garland Publishing, Inc.
Boas, Franz ([1896] 2006), 'The Limitations of the Comparative Method of Anthropology', in Alan Sica (ed.), *Comparative Methods in the Social Sciences*, 4 vols, I: 150-9. London: Sage Publications.
Bonnell, Victoria (1980), 'The Uses of Theory, Concepts and Comparison in Historical Sociology', *Comparative Studies in Society and History*, 22 (2): 156-73.
Bovykin, V. I. (2003), 'Ekonomicheskaia politika tsarskogo pravitel'stva i industrial'noe razvitie Rossii. 1861-1900 gg.' [Economic Policy of the Tsarist Government and the Industrial Development of Russia, 1861-1900], *Ekonomicheskaia istoriia. Ezhegodnik [Economic History. A Yearbook]*. 2002, 9-32. Moscow: Rosspen.
Braembussche, Anton A. van den (1989), 'Historical Explanation and Comparative Method: Towards a Theory of the History of Society', *History and Theory*, 28 (1): 1-24.
Brown, Elizabeth ([1974] 1998), 'The Tyranny of a Construct: Feudalism and Historians of Medieval Europe', in Lester K. Little and Barbara H. Rosenwein (eds), *Debating the Middle Ages: Issues and Readings*, 148-69. Malden, MA and Oxford: Blackwell Publishers.
Buravoy, Michael (1989), 'Two Methods in Search of Science: Skocpol versus Trotsky', *Theory and Society*, 18 (6): 759-805.
Burke, Peter (1974), *Venice and Amsterdam: A Study of Seventeenth-Century Elites*. London: Temple Smith.
Burke, Peter (1992), *History and Social Theory*. Cambridge: Polity Press.
Burrow, John (2009), *A History of Histories: Epics, Chronicles, Romances and Inquiries from Herodotus and Thucydides to the Twentieth Century*. London: Penguin Books.
Clark, Gregory (2007), *A Farewell to Alms: A Brief Economic History of the World*. Princeton, NJ and Oxford: Princeton University Press.
Cohen, Deborah (2001), *The War Come Home: Disabled Veterans in Britain and Germany, 1914 - 1939*. Berkeley: University of California Press.
Cohen, Deborah (2004), 'Comparative History: Buyer Beware', in Deborah Cohen and Maura O'Connor (eds), *Comparison and History: Europe in Cross-National Perspective*, 57-69. New York and London: Routledge.
Cohen, Deborah and O'Connor, Maura, eds (2004), *Comparison and History: Europe in Cross-National Perspective*. New York and London: Routledge.
Collingwood, R. G. ([1946] 1961), *The Idea of History*. London: Oxford University Press.
Comparative History in Theory and Practice: A Discussion (1982), *The American Historical Review*, 87 (1): 123-43.
Confino, Michael (1990), 'Servage russe, esclavage américain (note critique)', *Annales ÉSC*, 45 (5): 1119-41.
Confino, Michael (2009), 'Questions of Comparability: Russian Serfdom and American Slavery', in Benjamin Z. Kedar (ed.), *Explorations in Comparative History*, 93-112. Jerusalem: The Hebrew University Magnes Press.

Conrad, Sebastian (2009), 'Double Marginalization: A Plea for a Transnational Perspective on German History', in Heinz-Gerhard Haupt and Jürgen Kocka (eds), *Comparative and Transnational History: Central European Approaches and New Perspectives*, 52–76. New York and Oxford: Berghahn Books.

Conrad, Sebastian and Osterhammel, Jürgen, eds (2004), *Das Kaiserreich transnational: Deutschland in der Welt 1871 – 1914*. Göttingen: Vandenhoeck & Ruprecht.

Crossick, Geoffrey (1996), 'And what should they know of England? Die vergleichende Geschichtsschreibung im heutigen Großbritannien', in Heinz-Gerhard Haupt and Jürgen Kocka (eds), *Geschichte und Vergleich. Ansätze und Ergebnisse international vergleichender Geschichtsschreibung*, 61–75. Frankfurt am Main and New York: Campus Verlag.

Dal Lago, Enrico and Halpern, Rick, eds (2002), *The American South and the Italian Mezzogiorno: Essays in Comparative History*. Houndmills, Basingstoke, Hampshire and New York: Palgrave.

Davillé, Louis (1913–1914), 'La comparaison et la méthode comparative, en particulier dans les études historiques', *Revue de synthèse historique*, 27 (1): 4–33; (3): 217–57; 28 (2): 201–29.

Degler, Carl N. (1968), 'Comparative History: An Essay Review', *The Journal of Southern History*, 34 (3): 425–30.

Detienne, Marcel ([2000] 2008), *Comparing the Incomparable*, transl. by Janet Lloyd. Stanford, CA: Stanford University Press.

Droysen, Johann Gustav (1937), *Historik. Vorlesungen über Enzyklopädie und Methodologie der Geschichte*, ed. by Rudolf Hübner. Munich and Berlin: Verlag von R. Oldenbourg.

Duindam, Jeroen (1995), *Myths of Power: Norbert Elias and the Early Modern European Court*. Amsterdam: Amsterdam University Press.

Duindam, Jeroen (2003), *Vienna and Versailles*. Cambridge and New York: Cambridge University Press.

Duindam, Jeroen (2016), *Dynasties: A Global History of Power*. Cambridge: Cambridge University Press.

Duindam, Jeroen, Artan, Tülay and Kunt, Metin, eds (2011), *Royal Courts in Dynastic States and Empires: A Global Perspective*. Leiden and Boston, MA: Brill.

Durkheim, Emile ([1895] 1966), *The Rules of Sociological Method*, transl. by Sarah A. Solovay and John H. Mueller, ed. by George E. G. Catlin, 8th edn. New York: The Free Press; London: Collier-Macmillan Ltd.

Eisenberg, C. (1989), 'The Comparative View in Labour History: Old and New Interpretations of the English and German Labour Movements before 1914', *International Review of Social History*, 34: 403–32.

Elliott, John (2006), *Empires of the Atlantic World: Britain and Spain in America, 1492-1830*. New Haven and London: Yale University Press.

Espagne, Michel (1994), 'Sur les limites du comparatisme en histoire culturelle', *Genèses*, 17: 112–21.

Evans-Pritchard, Edward E. (1961), *Anthropology and History*. Manchester: Manchester University Press.

Evans-Pritchard, Edward E. (1963), *The Comparative Method in Social Anthropology* (L.T. Hobhouse Memorial Lecture, 33). London: Athlone Press.

Evans-Pritchard, Edward (1981), *A History of Anthropological Thought*, ed. by André Singer. New York: Basic Books, Inc.

Febvre, Lucien (1936), 'De Spengler à Toynbee: quelques philosophies opportunistes de l'histoire', *Revue de Métaphysique et de Morale*, 43 (4): 573–602.
Fredrickson, George M. ([1980] 2000), 'The Status of Comparative History', reprinted in Fredrickson, *The Comparative Imagination: On the History of Racism, Nationalism, and Social Movements*, 23–36. Berkeley, Los Angeles and London: University of California Press.
Fredrickson, George M. (1981), *White Supremacy: A Comparative Study in American and South African History*. Oxford and New York: Oxford University Press.
Fredrickson, George M. (1995a), *Black Liberation: A Comparative History of Black Ideologies in the United States and South Africa*. Oxford and New York: Oxford University Press.
Fredrickson, George M. (1995b), 'From Exceptionalism to Variability: Recent Developments in Cross-National Comparative History', *The Journal of American History*, 82 (2): 587–604.
Fredrickson, George M. (2000), *The Comparative Imagination: On the History of Racism, Nationalism, and Social Movements*. Berkeley, Los Angeles and London: University of California Press.
Freeman, Edward A. (1873), *The Comparative Politics: Six Lectures Read before the Royal Institution in January and February, 1873, with The Unity of History. The Rede Lecture Read before the University of Cambridge, May 29, 1872*. London: Macmillan and Co.
Freeman, Edward A. (1886), *The Methods of Historical Study: Eight Lectures Read in the University of Oxford in Michaelmas Term, 1884*. London: Macmillan and Co.
Gay, Peter (1968), 'The Enlightenment', in C. Vann Woodward (ed.), *The Comparative Approach to American History*, 34–46. New York and London: Basic Books Inc.
Genet, Jean-Philippe, ed. (1990a), *L'État moderne: Bilans et perspectives. Actes du Colloque tenu au CNRS à Paris les 19 - 20 septembre 1988*. Paris: Éditions du Centre national de la recherche scientifique.
Genet, Jean-Philippe (1990b), 'L'Etat moderne : un modèle opératoire?' in Jean-Philippe Genet (ed.), *L'État moderne: Bilans et perspectives. Actes du Colloque tenu au CNRS à Paris les 19 - 20 septembre 1988*, 261–81. Paris: Éditions du Centre national de la recherche scientifique.
Genet, Jean-Philippe (1997), 'La genèse de l'État moderne. Les enjeux d'un programme de recherche', *Actes de la recherche en sciences sociales*, 118: 3–18.
Gerschenkron, Alexander (1962), *Economic Backwardness in Historical Perspective*. Cambridge, MA: The Belknap Press of Harvard University Press.
Gerschenkron, Alexander (1970), *Europe in the Russian Mirror: Four Lectures in Economic History*. Cambridge: Cambridge University Press.
Goffman, Daniel (2002), *The Ottoman Empire and Early Modern Europe*. Cambridge: Cambridge University Press.
Goldstone, Jack (1982), 'The Comparative and Historical Study of Revolutions', *Annual Review of Sociology*, 8: 187–207.
Goldstone, Jack (1991), *Revolution and Rebellion in the Early Modern World*. Berkeley, Los Angeles and London: University of California Press.
Goldthorpe, John H. (2006), 'Current Issues in Comparative Macrosociology: A Debate on Methodological Issues', in Alan Sica (ed.), *Comparative Methods in the Social Sciences*, 4 vols, I: 390–429. London: Sage Publications.
Green, Nancy L. (1990), 'L'histoire comparative et le champ des études migratoire', *Annales ESC*, 45 (6): 1335–50.

Green, Nancy L. (1994). 'The Comparative Method and Poststructural Structuralism: New Perspectives for Migration Studies', *Journal of American Ethnic History*, 13 (4): 3–22.
Green, Nancy L. (2004), 'Forms of Comparison', in Deborah Cohen and Maura O'Connor (eds), *Comparison and History: Europe in Cross-National Perspective*, 41–56. New York and London: Routledge.
Gregory, Paul R. (1977), 'Russian Industrialization and Economic Growth: Results and Perspectives of Western Research', *Jahrbücher für Geschichte Osteuropas*, 25 (2): 207–14.
Grew, Raymond (1980), 'The Case for Comparing Histories', *The American Historical Review*, 85 (4): 763–78.
Grew, Raymond (1985), 'The Comparative Weakness of American History', *The Journal of Interdisciplinary History*, 16 (1): 87–101.
Grew, Raymond (2006), 'On Rereading an Earlier Essay', in Aram A. Yengoyan (ed.), *Modes of Comparison: Theory and Practice*, 118–36. Ann Arbor: The University of Michigan Press.
Guarneri, Carl J. (1995), 'Reconsidering C. Vann Woodward's *The Comparative Approach to American History*', *Reviews in American History*, 23 (3): 552–63.
Guenée, Bernard (1980), *Histoire et culture historique dans l'Occident médiéval*. Paris: Aubier Montaigne.
Gurevich, A. Ya. ([1970] 1999), *Problemy genezisa feodalizma v Zapadnoi Evrope* [*The Problems of the Genesis of Feudalism in Western Europe*], reprinted in Gurevich, *Izbrannye trudy* [*Selected Works*], 4 vols, I: 189–342. Moscow and St. Petersburg: Universitetskaia kniga.
Hart, Jonathan (2003), *Comparing Empires: European Colonialism from Portuguese Expansion to the Spanish-American War*. Gordonsville, VA: Palgrave Macmillan.
Hatton, Timothy J., O'Rourke, Kevin H. and Taylor, Alan M. (2007), 'Introduction: The New Comparative Economic History', in Timothy J. Hatton, Kevin H. O'Rourke and Alan M. Taylor (eds), *The New Comparative Economic History: Essays in Honor of Jeffrey G. Williamson*, 1–8. Cambridge, MA: MIT Press.
Haupt, Heinz-Gerhard (1996), 'Eine schwierige Öffnung nach außen: Die international vergleichende Geschichtswissenschaft in Frankreich', in Heinz-Gerhard Haupt and Jürgen Kocka (eds), *Geschichte und Vergleich. Ansätze und Ergebnisse international vergleichender Geschichtsschreibung*, 77–90. Frankfurt am Main and New York: Campus Verlag.
Haupt, Heinz-Gerhard (2001), 'Comparative History', in Neil J. Smelser and Paul B. Baltes (eds-in-chief), *International Encyclopedia of the Social and Behavioral Sciences*, 26 vols, 4: 2397–403. Oxford: Elsevier.
Haupt, Heinz-Gerhard and Kocka, Jürgen, eds (1996a), *Geschichte und Vergleich. Ansätze und Ergebnisse international vergleichender Geschichtsschreibung*. Frankfurt am Main and New York: Campus Verlag.
Haupt, Heinz-Gerhard and Kocka, Jürgen (1996b), 'Historischer Vergleich: Methoden, Aufgaben, Probleme. Eine Einleitung', in Heinz-Gerhard Haupt and Jürgen Kocka (eds), *Geschichte und Vergleich. Ansätze und Ergebnisse international vergleichender Geschichtsschreibung*, 9–45. Frankfurt am Main and New York: Campus Verlag.
Haupt, Heinz-Gerhard and Kocka, Jürgen (2004), 'Comparative History: Methods, Aims, Problems', in Deborah Cohen and Maura O'Connor (eds), *Comparison and History. Europe in Cross-National Perspective*, 23–37. New York and London: Routledge.
Haupt, Heinz-Gerhard and Kocka, Jürgen, eds (2009), *Comparative and Transnational History: Central European Approaches and New Perspectives*. New York and Oxford: Berghahn Books.

Heaton, Herbert (1957), 'Summary of Discussion', *The Journal of Economic History*, 17 (4): 596–602.
Henshall, Nicholas (1992), *The Myth of Absolutism: Change and Continuity in Early Modern European Monarchy*. London and New York: Longman.
Herder, Johann Gottfried v. ([1784–91] 1966), *Outlines of a Philosophy of the History of Man*, transl. from the German by T. Churchill. New York: Bergman Publishers.
Herodotus ([1954] 1966), *The Histories*, newly transl. with an Introduction by Aubrey de Selincourt. Harmondsworth, Middlesex and England: Penguin Books (first published 1954, reprint 1966).
Hill, Alette Olin and Hill, Boyd H., Jr. (1980), 'Marc Bloch and Comparative History', *The American Historical Review*, 85 (4): 828–46.
Hintze, Otto ([1929] 1970), 'Wesen und Verbreitung des Feudalismus', in Hintze, *Staat und Verfassung. Gesammelte Abhandlungen zur allgemeinen Verfassungsgeschichte*, ed. by Gerhard Oestreich (Gesammelte Abhandlungen, vol. I), 3rd edn, 84–119. Göttingen: Vandenhoeck & Ruprecht.
Hintze, Otto ([1930] 1970), 'Typologie der ständischen Verfassungen des Abendlandes', in Hintze, *Staat und Verfassung. Gesammelte Abhandlungen zur allgemeinen Verfassungsgeschichte*, ed. by Gerhard Oestreich (Gesammelte Abhandlungen, vol. I), 3rd edn, 120–39. Göttingen: Vandenhoeck & Ruprecht.
Hintze, Otto ([1931] 1975), 'The Preconditions of Representative Government in the Context of World History', in *The Historical Essays of Otto Hintze*, ed. with an Introduction by Felix Gilbert, 305–53. New York: Oxford University Press.
Hroch, Miroslav (1985), *Social Preconditions of National Revival in Europe: A Comparative Analysis of the Social Composition of Patriotic Groups among the Smaller European Nations*. Cambridge: Cambridge University Press.
Iriye, Akira (2004), 'Transnational History', *Contemporary European History*, 13 (2): 211–22.
Kaelble, Hartmut (1983), *Soziale Mobilität und Chancengleichheit im 19. und 20. Jahrhundert*. Göttingen: Vandenhoeck & Ruprecht.
Kaelble, Hartmut (1999), *Der historische Vergleich. Eine Einführung zum 19. und 20. Jahrhundert*. Frankfurt am Main and New York: Campus Verlag.
Kaelble, Hartmut (2002), 'Vergleich, historische', in Stefan Jordan (ed.), *Lexikon Geschichtswissenschaft: hundert Grundbegriffe*, 303–6. Stuttgart: Reclam.
Kaelble, Hartmut (2009), 'Between Comparison and Transfers – and What Now? A French-German Debate', in Heinz-Gerhard Haupt and Jürgen Kocka (eds), *Comparative and Transnational History: Central European Approaches and New Perspectives*, 33–8. New York and Oxford: Berghahn Books.
Kareev, N. I. ([1913] 2010), 'Sravnitel'no-istoricheskii metod' ['The Comparative Historical Method'], in Kareev, *Teoriia istoricheskogo znaniia [A Theory of Historical Knowledge]*, 2nd edn. Moscow: Krasand.
Kashtanov, S. M. ([1992] 2015), 'O tipe Russkogo gosudarstva v XIV-XVI vekakh' [On the Type of the Russian State in the Fourteenth through Sixteenth Centuries], reprinted in Kashtanov, *Moskovskoe tsarstvo i Zapad: Istoriograficheskie ocherki [The Muscovite Tsardom and the West: Historiographical Essays]*, 439–45. Moscow: Russkii fond sodeistviia obrazovaniiu i nauke.
Kashtanov, S. M. (1999), 'Istoricheskie paralleli: Ivan III i Karl Martell' [Historical Parallels: Ivan III and Charles Martel], in *Rossiia v IX – XX vekakh: Problemy istorii, istoriografii i istochnikovedeniia [Russia in the Ninth through the Twentieth Centuries: Problems of History, Historiography and Source Criticism]*, 180–1. Moscow: Russkii mir.

Kedar, Benjamin Z., ed. (2009a), *Explorations in Comparative History*. Jerusalem: The Hebrew University Magnes Press.
Kedar, Benjamin Z. (2009b), 'Outlines for Comparative History Proposed by Practicing Historians', in Benjamin Z. Kedar (ed.), *Explorations in Comparative History*, 1–28. Jerusalem: The Hebrew University Magnes Press.
Kivelson, Valerie (1997), 'Merciful Father, Impersonal State: Russian Autocracy in Comparative Perspective', *Modern Asian Studies*, 31 (3): 635–63.
Kocka, Jürgen, ed. (1987), *Bürger und Bürgerlichkeit im 19. Jahrhundert*. Göttingen: Vandenhoeck & Ruprecht.
Kocka, Jürgen (1988), 'German History before Hitler: The Debate about the German Sonderweg', *Journal of Contemporary History*, 23 (1): 3–16.
Kocka, Jürgen (1993), 'Comparative Historical Research: German Examples', *International Review of Social History*, 38: 369–79.
Kocka, Jürgen (1996), 'Historische Komparatistik in Deutschland', in Heinz-Gerhard Haupt and Jürgen Kocka (eds), *Geschichte und Vergleich. Ansätze und Ergebnisse international vergleichender Geschichtsschreibung*, 47–60. Frankfurt am Main and New York: Campus Verlag.
Kocka, Jürgen (1999), 'Asymmetrical Historical Comparison: The Case of the German Sonderweg', *History and Theory*, 38 (1): 40–50.
Kocka, Jürgen (2003), 'Comparison and Beyond', *History and Theory*, 42 (1): 39–44.
Kocka, Jürgen and Haupt, Heinz-Gerhard (2009), 'Comparison and Beyond: Traditions, Scope, and Perspectives of Comparative History', in Heinz-Gerhard Haupt and Jürgen Kocka (eds), *Comparative and Transnational History: Central European Approaches and New Perspectives*, 1–30. New York and Oxford: Berghahn Books.
Koenigsberger, H. G. (1974), 'Review of The Causes of the English Revolution, 1529–1642, by Lawrence Stone', *The Journal of Modern History*, 46 (1): 99–106.
Koenigsberger, H. G. (1986), *Politicians and Virtuosi: Essays in Early Modern History*. London and Ronceverte: The Hambledon Press.
Kolchin, Peter (1982), 'Comparing American History', *Reviews in American History*, 10 (4): 64–81.
Kolchin, Peter (1987), *Unfree Labor: American Slavery and Russian Serfdom*. Cambridge, MA, and London: The Belknap Press of Harvard University Press.
Krom, Mikhail (2009), 'Formen der Patronage im Russland des 16. und 17. Jahrhunderts: Perspektiven der vergleichenden Forschung im europäischen Kontext', *Jahrbücher für Geschichte Osteuropas*, 57 (3): 321–45.
Krom, Mikhail M. (2010a), *Istoricheskaia antropologiia: uchebnoe posobie [Historical Anthropology: A Student's Guide]*, 3rd edn. St. Petersburg and Moscow: The European University at St. Petersburg Press and Kvadriga.
Krom, Mikhail M. (2010b), *Vdovstvuiushee tsarstvo: politicheskii krizis v Rossii 30–40-kh godov XVI veka [The Widowed Tsardom: The Political Crisis in Russia in the 1530s and 1540s]*. Moscow: Novoe literaturnoe obozrenie.
Krom, Mikhail M. (2011), 'Institut regentstva na zapade i vostoke Evropy: opyt sravnitel'no-istoricheskogo issledovaniia' [The Institute of Regency in the West and East of Europe: An Essay in Comparative History], in I. G. Galkova et al. (eds), *Obrazy proshlogo: sbornik pamiati A. Y. Gurevicha [Images of the Past: Collected Studies in Memory of A. Y. Gurevich]*, 411–26. St. Petersburg: Tsentr gumanitarnykh initsiativ.
Krom, Mikhail M. (2018), *Rozhdenie gosudarstva: Moskovskaia Rus' XV-XVI vekov [The Birth of the State: Muscovite Rus' in the 15th and 16th Centuries]*. Moscow: Novoe literaturnoe obozrenie.

Krom, Mikhail M. and Pimenova, L. A., eds (2013), *Fenomen reform na zapade i vostoke Evropy v nachale Novogo vremeni (XVI-XVIII vv.) [A Phenomenon of Reforms in Western and Eastern Europe in the Early Modern Age, 16th through 18th Centuries]*. St. Petersburg: The European University at St. Petersburg Press.

Langlois, Charles V. (1890), 'The Comparative History of England and France during the Middle Ages', *The English Historical Review*, 5 (18): 259–63.

Langlois, Ch.-V. and Seignobos, Ch. ([1898] 1912), *Introduction to the Study of History*, transl. by G. G. Berry. 2nd impression. London: Duckworth and Co.; New York: Henry Holt and Co.

Le Goff, Jacques (1990), 'La genèse du miracle royal', in Hartmut Atsma and André Burguière (eds), *Marc Bloch aujourd'hui: histoire comparée et sciences sociales*, 147–56. Paris: Éditions de l'École des hautes études en sciences sociales.

Levi, Giovanni (2012), 'Microhistory and the Recovery of Complexity', in Susanna Fellman and Marjatta Rahikainen (eds), *Historical Knowledge: In Quest of Theory, Method and Evidence*, 121–32. Newcastle upon Tyne: Cambridge Scholars Publishing.

Lieven, Dominic (1992), *The Aristocracy in Europe, 1815–1914*. Basingstoke: Macmillan.

Lieven, Dominic (2000), *Empire: The Russian Empire and Its Rivals*. London: John Murray.

Liubarskii, G. Y. (2000), *Morfologiia istorii: sravnitelnyi metod i istoricheskoe razvitie [The Morphology of History: A Comparative Method and Historical Development]*. Moscow: KMK Press.

Lukassen, Jan (2006), 'Brickmakers in Western Europe (1700 – 1900) and Northern India (1800 – 2000): Some Comparisons', in Jan Lukassen (ed.), *Global Labour History: A State of the Art*, 513–71. Bern: Peter Lang.

Mahoney, James (2003), 'Knowledge Accumulation in Comparative Research: The Case of Democracy and Authoritarianism', in James Mahoney and Dietrich Rueschemeyer (eds), *Comparative Historical Analysis in the Social Sciences*, 131–74. Cambridge and New York: Cambridge University Press.

Mahoney, James and Rueschemeyer, Dietrich, eds (2003), *Comparative Historical Analysis in the Social Sciences*. Cambridge and New York: Cambridge University Press.

Mahoney, James and Thelen, Kathleen, eds (2015), *Advances in Comparative-Historical Analysis*. Cambridge: Cambridge University Press.

Maine, Henry Sumner ([1861] 1908), *Ancient Law, Its Connection with the Early History of Society and Its Relation to Modern Ideas*. London: John Murray.

Meillet, Antoine ([1925] 1967), *The Comparative Method in Historical Linguistics*, transl. by Gordon B. Ford. Paris: Librarie Honoré Champion.

Mill, John Stuart ([1843] 1874), *A System of Logic, Ratiocinative and Inductive: Being a Connected View of the Principles of Evidence and the Methods of Scientific Investigation*, 8th edn. New York and London: Harper and Brothers Publishers.

Miller, Alexei (2007), 'The Value and the Limits of a Comparative Approach to the History of Contiguous Empires on the European Periphery', in Kimitaka Matsuzato (ed.), *Imperiology: From Empirical Knowledge to Discussing the Russian Empire*. Sapporo: Hokkaido University, Slavic Research Center.

Miller, Michael (2004), 'Comparative and Cross-National History: Approaches, Differences, Problems', in Deborah Cohen and Maura O'Connor (eds), *Comparison and History: Europe in Cross-National Perspective*, 115–32. New York and London: Routledge.

Mironov, Boris N., with Ekloff, Ben (2000), *The Social History of Imperial Russia, 1700 – 1917*, 2 vols. Boulder and Oxford: Westview Press.

Mitteis, Heinrich ([1940] 1962), *Der Staat des hohen Mittelalters: Grundlinien einer vergleichenden Verfassungsgeschichte des Lehnszeitalters*, 7th edn. Weimar: Böhlau.

Montesquieu, Charles de Secondat baron de ([1748] 1989), *The Spirit of the Laws*, transl. and ed. by Anne M. Cohler, Basia C. Miller and Harold S. Stone. Cambridge: Cambridge University Press.

Moore, Barrington, Jr. (1966), *Social Origins of Dictatorship and Democracy: Lord and Peasant in the Making of the Modern World*. Boston, MA: Beacon Press.

Mousnier, Roland ([1967] 1972), *Peasant Uprisings in Seventeenth-Century France, Russia, and China*, transl. from the French by Brian Pearce. New York, Evanston, San Francisco and London: Harper and Low (Harper Torchbooks).

Mumenthaler, Rudolf (1998), 'Spätmittelalterliche Städte West- und Osteuropas im Vergleich: Versuch einer verfassungsgeschichtlichen Typologie', *Jahrbücher für Geschichte Osteuropas*, N.F., 46 (1): 39–67.

Nicholas, David (2003), *Urban Europe, 1100 – 1700*. Houndmills, Basingstoke and New York: Palgrave Macmillan.

Novoseltsev, A. P., Pashuto, V. T. and Cherepnin, L. V. (1972), *Puti razvitiia feodalizma (Zakavkaz'ie, Sredniaia Aziia, Rus', Pribaltika) [The Paths of Development of Feudalism (Transcaucasia, Central Asia, Rus', the Baltic Countries)]*. Moscow: Nauka.

O'Brien, P. K. (2001), 'Industrialization, Typologies and History', in Neil J. Smelser and Paul B. Baltes (eds-in-chief), *International Encyclopedia of the Social and Behavioral Sciences*, 26 vols, 11: 7360–67. Oxford: Elsevier.

Palmer, R. R. (1959–1964), *The Age of the Democratic Revolution: The Political History of Europe and America, 1760 – 1800*, 2 vols. Princeton, NJ: Princeton University Press.

Paulmann, Johann (1998), 'Internationaler Vergleich und interkultureller Transfer', *Historische Zeitschrift*, 267 (3): 649–85.

Pedersen, Susan (1993), *Family, Dependence, and the Origins of the Welfare State: Britain and France, 1914 – 1945*. Cambridge and New York: Cambridge University Press (pbk ed. 1995).

Petit-Dutaillis, Charles ([1933] 1936), *The Feudal Monarchy in France and England from the Tenth to the Thirteenth Century*, transl. from the French by E. D. Hunt. London: Kegan Paul, Trench, Trubner & Co., Ltd.

Petrusewicz, Marta (2004), 'The Modernization of the European Periphery; Ireland, Poland, and the Two Sicilies, 1820 – 1870: Parallel and Connected, Distinct and Comparable', in Deborah Cohen and Maura O'Connor (eds), *Comparison and History: Europe in Cross-National Perspective*, 145–63. New York and London: Routledge.

Pirenne, Henri ([1925] 1969), *Medieval Cities, Their Origins and the Revival of Trade*, transl. from the French by Frank D. Halsey. Princeton, NJ: Princeton University Press.

Polybius ([1922–1927] 1998–2012), *The Histories*, with an English translation by W. R. Paton, 6 vols. Cambridge, MA: Harvard University Press; London: W. Heinemann (Loeb classical library).

Pomeranz, Kenneth (2000), *The Great Divergence: China, Europe, and the Making of the Modern World Economy*. Princeton, NJ and Oxford: Princeton University Press.

Prost, Antoine (1996), *Douze leçons sur l'histoire*. Paris: Éditions du Seuil.

Ragin, Charles C. (1987), *The Comparative Method: Moving Beyond Qualitative and Quantitative Strategies*. Berkeley, Los Angeles and London: University of California Press.

Randeria, Shalini (2009), 'Entangled Histories of Uneven Modernities: Civil Society, Caste Councils, and Legal Pluralism in Post-Colonial India', in Heinz-Gerhard Haupt and Jürgen Kocka (eds), *Comparative and Transnational History: Central European Approaches and New Perspectives*, 77–104. New York and Oxford: Berghahn Books.

Redlich, Fritz (1958), 'Toward Comparative Historiography: Background and Problems', *Kyklos: International Review for Social Studies*, 11 (3): 362–89.

Reynolds, Susan (1994), *Fiefs and Vassals: The Medieval Evidence Reinterpreted*. Oxford and New York: Oxford University Press.

Reynolds, Susan (2009), 'The Use of Feudalism in Comparative History', in Benjamin Z. Kedar (ed.), *Explorations in Comparative History*, 191–217. Jerusalem: The Hebrew University Magnes Press.

Rickert, Heinrich (1896), *Die Grenzen der naturwissenschaftlichen Begriffsbildung. Eine logische Einleitung in die historischen Wissenschaften*. Freiburg i. B. & Leipzig: Akademische Verlagsbuchhandlung von J. C. B. Mohr (Paul Siebeck).

Rickert, Heinrich (1926), *Kulturwissenschaft und Naturwissenschaft*, 6th and 7th edn. Tübingen: Verlag von J. C. B. Mohr (Paul Siebeck).

Rieber, Alfred (2004), 'Sravnivaia kontinentalnye imperii' ['Comparing Continental Empires'], in Alexei Miller (ed.), *Rossiiskaia imperiia v sravnitel'noi perspektive [The Russian Empire in a Comparative Perspective]*, 33–70. Moscow: Novoe izdatel'stvo.

Rostow, W. W. (1960), *The Stages of Economic Growth*. Cambridge and New York: Cambridge University Press.

Rozhkov, N. A. (1919–1926), *Russkaia istoriia v sravnitel'no-istoricheskom osveschenii. (Osnovy sotsialnoi dinamiki). [The Russian History from a Comparative Historical Perspective. (The Foundations of Social Dynamics)]*, 12 vols. Petrograd and Moscow: Kniga.

Ruble, Blair A. (2001), *Second Metropolis Pragmatic Pluralism in Gilded Age Chicago, Silver Age Moscow, and Meiji Osaka*. Cambridge, New York, Melbourne and Washington, DC: Woodrow Wilson Center Press and Cambridge University Press.

Salvati, Mariuccia (1996), 'Histoire contemporaine et analyse comparative en Italie', *Genèses*, 22: 146–59.

Schieder, Theodor (1966), 'Typologie und Erscheinungsformen des Nationalstaats in Europa', *Historische Zeitschrift*, 202 (1): 58–81.

Schieder, Theodor (1968), 'Möglichkeiten und Grenzen vergleichender Methoden in der Geschichtswissenschaft', in Schieder, *Geschichte als Wissenschaft. Eine Einführung*, 2nd rev. edn, 195–219, 234–8. Munich and Vienna: R. Oldenbourg.

Sewell, William H., Jr. (1967), 'Marc Bloch and the Logic of Comparative History', *History and Theory*, 6 (2): 208–18.

Sewell, William H., Jr. and Thrupp, Sylvia L. (1980), 'Comments', *The American Historical Review*, 85 (4): 847–53.

Shannon, David A. (1968), 'Socialism and Labor', in C. Vann Woodward (ed.), *The Comparative Approach to American History*, 238–52. New York and London: Basic Books Inc.

Sica, Alan, ed. (2006), *Comparative Methods in the Social Sciences*, 4 vols. London: Sage Publications.

Skocpol, Theda (1979), *States and Social Revolutions: A Comparative Analysis of France, Russia, and China*. Cambridge and New York: Cambridge University Press.

Skocpol, Theda and Somers, Margaret (1980), 'The Uses of Comparative History in Macrosociological Inquiry', *Comparative Studies in Society and History*, 22 (2): 174–98.

Smith, S. A. (2008), *Revolution and the People in Russia and China: A Comparative History*. Cambridge and New York: Cambridge University Press.

Spengler, Oswald ([1918] 1927), *The Decline of the West: Form and Actuality*, authorized transl. with notes by Charles Francis Atkinson. New York: Alfred A. Knopf, 6th printing.
Stoler, Ann Laura (2001), 'Tense and Tender Ties: The Politics of Comparison in North American History and (Post) Colonial Studies', *The Journal of American History*, 88 (3): 829–65.
Stone, Lawrence (1967), 'News from Everywhere', *The New York Review of Books*, 9 (3): 32–4.
Stone, Lawrence (1974), 'A Reply [to H. G. Koenigsberger]', *The Journal of Modern History*, 46 (1): 106–10.
Strayer, Joseph R. (1970), *On the Medieval Origins of the Modern State*. Princeton, NJ: Princeton University Press.
Thrupp, Sylvia L. (1957), 'The Role of Comparison in the Development of Economic Theory', *The Journal of Economic History*, 17 (4): 554–70.
Thrupp, Sylvia L. (1958), 'Editorial', *Comparative Studies in Society and History*, 1 (1): 1–4.
Tilly, Charles (1984), *Big Structures, Large Processes, Huge Comparisons*. New York: Russell Sage Foundation.
Tilly, Charles (1992), *Coercion, Capital, and European States, AD 990–1992*. Cambridge, MA and Oxford: Blackwell Publishers.
Toynbee, Arnold J. ([1946] 1987), *A Study of History*, abridgement of volumes I–VI by D. C. Somervell. New York and Oxford: Oxford University Press.
Troeltsch, Ernst (1922), *Der Historismus und seine Probleme. Erstes Buch: Das logische Problem der Geschichtsphilosophie*. Tübingen: Verlag von J. C. B. Mohr (Paul Siebeck).
Tylor, Edward B. ([1871] 1920), *Primitive Culture: Researches into the Development of Mythology, Philosophy, Religion, Art, and Custom*, 2 vols, 6th edn. London: John Murray.
Tyrrell, Ian (1991a), 'American Exceptionalism in an Age of International History', *The American Historical Review*, 96 (4): 1031–55.
Tyrrell, Ian (1991b), 'Ian Tyrrell Responds', *The American Historical Review*, 96 (4): 1068–72.
Vico, Giambattista ([1744] 1968), *The New Science*, transl. from the third edition (1744) by Thomas Goddard Bergin and Max Harold Fisch. Ithaca and New York: Cornell University Press.
Voltaire ([1765] 1901), 'Histoire', in *The Works of Voltaire, A Contemporary Version*, transl. by William F. Fleming, 22 vols, 5 (pt. 2): 61–99. New York: St. Hubert Guild.
Walker, Lawrence D. (1980), 'A Note on Historical Linguistics and Marc Bloch's Comparative Method', *History and Theory*, 19 (2): 154–64.
Weber, Max ([1904] 1949), '"Objectivity" in Social Science and Social Policy', in Weber, *On the Methodology of Social Sciences*, transl. and ed. by Edward A. Shils and Henry A. Finch, 50–112. Glencoe and Illinois: The Free Press.
Weber, Max ([1905] 2002), *The Protestant Ethic and the Spirit of Capitalism*, transl. by Talcott Parsons. London and New York: Routledge.
Weber, Max ([1956] 1978), *Economy and Society: An Outline of Interpretive Sociology*, transl. Ephraim Fischoff, Hans Gerth et al., ed. by Guenther Roth and Claus Wittich, 2 vols. Berkeley, Los Angeles and London: University of California Press.
Welskopp, Thomas (1995), 'Stolpersteine auf dem Königsweg: Methodenkritische Anmerkungen zum internationalen Vergleich in der Gesellschaftsgeschichte', *Archiv für Sozialgeschichte*, 35: 339–67.

Werner, Michael and Zimmermann, Bénédicte, eds (2004), *De comparaison à l'histoire croisée*. Paris: Éditions du Seuil.
Werner, Michael and Zimmermann, Bénédicte (2006), 'Beyond Comparison: Histoire Croisée and the Challenge of Reflexivity', *History and Theory*, 45 (1): 30–50.
Winks, Robin W. (1968), 'Imperialism', in C. Vann Woodward (ed.), *The Comparative Approach to American History*, 253–70. New York and London: Basic Books Inc.
Wippermann, Wolfgang (1983), *Europäischer Faschismus im Vergleich (1922 – 1982)*. Frankfurt am Main: Suhrkamp.
Zagorin, Perez (1976), 'Prolegomena to the Comparative History of Revolution in Early Modern Europe', *Comparative Studies in Society and History*, 18 (2): 151–74.
Zimmermann, Bénédicte, Didry, Claude and Wagner, Peter, eds (1999), *Le travail et la nation. Histoire croisée de la France et de l'Allemagne*. Paris: Éditions de la Maison des sciences de l'homme.

Index

Note: Page numbers followed by "n" refer to notes.

absolutism   62, 86, 98, 110, 113
   European   116
   French   116
   Prussian   64
   Swedish   116
   western   116
Alekseev, Nikolai   125
Allen, Robert   107, 108
American Association of Economic History   40
American Historical Association   46
American Historical Review   46, 59, 74, 120
Amsterdam   121–2
analogy   12, 15, 17, 18, 28, 33, 72, 73, 85, 86, 136
Anderson, Benedict   128, 129
Anderson, Perry   115–16
   Lineages of the Absolute State   88, 115
Annales (historical journal)   54
anthropology   19, 21, 39, 91, 136
   evolutionary theory in   15
   historical   76 n.36, 77
   social   87
archaeology   14
Argentina   63
aristocracy   11, 44, 61–3, 115–17, 122, 125, 126
Asia   11
Athens   118
Austria   49, 63
   role of banks in financing industry   41
Austro-Hungarian Empire. *See* empire

Baden School (of philosophy)   21
   'nomothetic' *vs.* 'idiographic' methods   21
   'nomothetic' *vs.* 'idiographical' disciplines   86

Baldwin, Peter   51, 52, 84, 88–9, 96, 108, 124
   Contagion and the State in Europe, 1830–1930   49
   Disease and Democracy: The Industrial World Faces AIDS   49
   Narcissism of Minor Differences: How America and Europe Are Alike, The   49
   Politics of Social Solidarity: Class Bases of the European Welfare State, 1875–1975   48, 57
Bayly, Christopher   129
   Birth of the Modern World: Global Connections and Comparisons, 1780–1914, The   128
Beckert, Sven   59
Belgium   40
   Flemish movement in   130
   role of banks in financing industry   41
Belorussia   130
Below, Georg von   17 n.20
Bendix, Reinhard   88
   Kings or People: Power and the Mandate to Rule   63–4
   Social Origins of Dictatorship and Democracy   63
Berlin Congress   111
Bern   92
Bernheim, Ernst   23, 24, 71
   Introduction to Historical Science, An   18
Berr, Henri   23, 27
   Revue de synthèse historique   35
Bielefeld School of historical social science (*historische Sozialwissenschaft*)   50
Blickle, Peter   117

Bloch, Marc 23–37, 44, 49, 52, 73, 74, 77, 78, 80–2, 86, 90–1, 119, 120
  'Comparison' 35
  Feudal Society 36, 48, 93, 94
  French Rural History: An Essay on Its Basic Characteristics 36
  Historian's Craft, The 82
  Royal Touch: Sacred Monarchy and Scrofula in England and France, The 34, 36, 57, 77, 81, 93, 109
  'Toward a Comparative History of European Societies' 31, 32, 81
Boas, Franz 16
Bodin, Jean
  Method for the Easy Comprehension of History 9
Bolotninkov, Ivan 122
Bonn 92
Bonnell, Victoria 66
Bopp, Franz 14
bourgeois democracy 61
bourgeoisness 125
Braembussche, Anton van den 89 n.46
Brandenburg 18
Breuilly, John 128
Britain 54, 61, 64, 83, 85, 90, 109, 120, 128, 134
  agrarian relations 62
  bicameral parliament 110
  industrialization 41, 106
  industrial revolution 107
  influence of petitions on the legislative process 117
  landed aristocracy in 63
  trade union movements in 126
  welfare state in 48
Brown, Elizabeth
  'Tyranny of the Construct, The' 120
Bulgaria 111, 130
Burke, Peter 31, 118
  Venice and Amsterdam 121

Calcutta 127
canon law 34
capitalism 43, 62, 83, 84, 115, 129, 130
  industrial 24, 41
  modern 24
  spirit of 42, 43 n.28
capitalist form of enterprise 43 n.28

Carolingian empire. *See* empire
Caucasus 120
Central Europe. *See* Europe
ceteris paribus 126
Chakrabarty, Dipesh 127
Chicago 125
child welfare policy 47–8
China 3, 10, 64, 90, 113, 114
  Chinese Revolution of 1911 64
  communist dictatorship in 62
  industrialization 106
  land, labour and capital markets in 107
  peasant uprisings in 122, 123
Cicero 9
civilization 15, 24, 27–31, 40, 44, 56, 91, 96, 100, 136
Clark, Gregory 108
  Farewell to Alms, A 107
clientelism 81
Cohen, Deborah 52, 78, 83, 84, 94, 108
collectivism 113, 114
Collingwood, R. G. 28, 30
colonialism 128–34
communism 114
comparability, problem of 91–2
comparative constitutional history (*vergleichende Verfassungsgeschichte*) 110, 111
comparative ethnology 18
comparative historical sociology 61–7
comparative historiography 39
comparative history 1–3, 18, 22, 25, 31, 33, 35, 45, 46, 47, 51–3, 55, 56, 59, 71–4, 76, 78, 83, 84, 89, 100, 110, 113, 118, 121, 124, 127, 132, 133, 136
comparative institutional history 25
comparative linguistics 2, 13, 14 n.4, 19, 73, 74
comparative method in history 1, 2, 13–24, 27, 29–37, 40, 44, 50, 61, 63, 64, 67, 80, 82, 84, 85, 87, 89–91, 97, 99, 105, 121, 129, 136
  development of 32, 74
  existence of 2, 7, 71–9
comparative political science 2
comparative religion 74

comparative sociology 16, 47
Comparative Studies in Society and History
    (journal) 1–2, 38, 39, 45, 46,
    73, 74
comparison
    analogical 17, 72. *See also* analogy
    contrasting 24, 84–6, 89, 123
    criticism of traditional 54–60
    cross-cultural 7, 76, 93–5, 135
    definition of 80
    encompassing 89
    generalizing 12, 30, 72, 89
    heuristic effect of 95
    long-range 90
    'making strange' effect of 85, 95
    object selection for 90–6
    particularizing 22, 24–6, 31, 64, 72,
        84–6, 89
    universalizing 89
    variation-finding 89
Comte, Auguste 13, 16
    Foundations of Sociology 15
Confino, Michael 91–2, 95, 124
Congress of Vienna 125
Conrad, Sebastian 58, 59
contemporaneity 28, 29
Cortes 34–5
Cortés, Hernán 133
Cossacks 122, 123
critical method 24
critical method of source analysis 19
cultural history 52, 55, 76, 77, 84, 108
Cultural Revolution 113
cultural transfers 55–6
curia regis 109, 110
Cuvier, Georges 13

Danilevskii, Nikolai 28
Davillé, Louis 23–4, 32, 71
decolonization 39
Degler, Carl N. 45, 47
    *Neither Black nor White: Slavery and
        Race Relations in Brazil and the
        United States* 47
democracy 44, 63, 66
    bourgeois 61
    parliamentary 62
democratic development, historical
    conditions for 61–2

democratization 39
Denmark, welfare state in 48
Detienne, Marcel 91
dictatorship 61–3, 66, 114
Diderot
    Encyclopédie 10
difference of environment, as a condition
    for comparison 33
Dilthey, Wilhelm 22
discovery of laws 30
'divided history' (*geteilte Geschichte*) 58
Droysen, Johann Gustav 85
    *Encyclopaedia and Methodology of
        History* 17–18
    History of Prussian Politics 20
Dublin 92
Duindam, Jeroen 117
Durkheim, Émile 16, 17, 32, 89, 99

Eastern Europe. *See* Europe
Eck, Alexandre 27
economic growth 40–1
economic history, comparison in 105–8
Eisenberg, Christiane 94, 126
Eisenstadt, Shmuel
    Political Systems of Empire 88
Elias, Norbert 3, 117
    Civilizing Process, The 61
Elliott, John 132–4
    *Empires of the Atlantic World:
        Britain and Spain in America,
        1492–1830* 132–3
Ellis, Stephen 117
empire 128–34
    Austro-Hungarian Empire 129
    Carolingian 25, 26, 27 n.21, 98, 110
    German Empire 110
    Habsburg Empire 132
    Ottoman Empire 86, 117, 132
England. *See* Britain
English Civil War 112
Enlightenment 9, 10, 19, 27, 28, 72, 85
    American 45
entangled histories 58, 60, 109
Espagne, Michel 54–6
    'On the Limits of Comparison in
        Cultural History' 54
Estonia 130
Eurasia 106

Europe 3, 10, 24, 83, 130
   Central 34, 44
   Eastern 3, 49, 111, 115, 119
   industrialization 41, 42
   nation states, formation of 111
   Western 27 n.21, 34, 44, 105, 126
European University Institute 51
Evans-Pritchard, Edward Evan 14
   'Anthropology and History' 87
evolutionary theory in anthropology 15
explanatory hypothesis 91

fascism 62, 114, 115
Febvre, Lucien 30
feudalism 25–6, 86, 119–21
   European 26, 36
   factors determining 25
   Japanese 93
   Russian 119–20
   western European 26, 120
First World War 22, 25, 27, 38, 49, 83, 94, 125, 126, 131
folklore studies 2
France 18, 23, 26, 27, 40, 54, 61, 64, 90, 110, 113, 122, 128
   agrarian history of 34
   chambre des comptes 109
   equality of opportunity in 51
   Estates-General 110
   États 34
   French Revolution 62, 64, 111, 112
   gender-based approach to historical research 48
   maternal and child welfare policy 47, 48
   parlement 109
   peasant uprisings in 122, 123
   role of banks in financing industry 41
   role of the church 55
   social mobility in 51
   social politics in 94
   social solidarity policies in 49
   welfare state in 48
Franks 26
Frazer, James George 32, 36, 71
   Golden Bough 33
Fredrickson, George M. 46, 47, 53, 94, 100–1, 124
   Comparative Imagination, The 75–6

Freeman, Edward
   Comparative Politics 18
   Methods of Historical Study 18
Freiburg School. *See* Baden School (of philosophy)
French School of Sociology 16

Galton, Francis 16
Galton's problem 16
Gaul 109
Gay, Peter 45
Gellner, Ernest 128–9
gender-based approach to historical research 48
gender history 52
Germany 2, 20, 24, 27, 44, 49, 54, 83, 111, 134
   conservative modernization in 62
   equality of opportunity in 51
   gender-based approach to historical research 48
   German Empire 110
   historicism 50
   industrialization 73
   influence of petitions on the legislative process 117
   landed aristocracy in 63
   role of banks in financing industry 41
   role of the church 55
   social mobility in 51
   social solidarity policies in 49
   trade union movements in 126
   welfare state in 48–9
   Western 26, 49, 50, 92
Gerschenkron, Alexander 41–4, 52, 66, 95, 100, 105, 126
   Economic Backwardness in Historical Perspective 41, 57, 77
   Europe in the Russian Mirror 42
Ghent 27
Giddens, Anthony 87
Ginzburg, Carlo 1
global history 26, 53, 59, 105
globalization 38, 39, 44, 58, 105, 107–8
Glotz, Gustave 23, 24, 31, 71
Goldstone, Jack 3, 112
Graeco-Persian Wars 8
Greece 7, 10, 111
Green, Nancy L. 39, 96, 97, 127

Grew, Raymond   1–2, 45, 74–6, 75 n.26, 80, 96, 136
  'Comparative Weakness of American History, The'   46
Grimm, Jacob   14
Guarneri, Carl   45–6
Gurevich, A. Y.   120

Habsburg Empire   132
Hague   92
Hajime, Seki   125
Hammurabi, laws of   26
Harrison, Carter   125
Hatton, Timothy J.
  New Comparative Economic History, The   105
Haupt, Heinz-Gerhard   1, 37, 49, 60, 76, 81, 83–5, 92, 94, 95, 98, 100, 135
Hellas. *See* Greece
Henshall, Nicholas
  Myth of Absolutism: Change and Continuity in Early Modern Monarchy, The   116
Herder, Johann Gottfried v.   12
  Outline of a Philosophical History of Humanity   10
Herodotus   1, 7–8, 52
  Histories   8
Hill, Alette Olin   32, 74
  'Marc Bloch and Comparative History'   73
Hill, Boyd H., Jr.   32, 74
  'Marc Bloch and Comparative History'   73
Hintze, Otto   22, 25–7, 31, 37, 48, 52, 73, 77, 84, 109, 110, 119
  'Commissary and his Significance in General Administrative History, the'   25
  'Nature and Spread of Feudalism, The'   25
  'Origins of the Modern Ministerial System, the'   25
  'Preconditions of Representative Government in the Context of World History, The'   25
  'Typology of the Forms of the Estates System in Western Europe'   25
histoire croisée   54, 56–60, 76, 96, 109
historical anthropology   76 n.36, 77

historical comparison
  and causal analysis   9, 18, 64, 66, 83, 88, 89
  conditions for   33, 61–2, 97
  forms of   3, 22, 28, 33–4, 71–2, 89, 95
  functions of   80–9
    analytical   82, 83, 135. *See also* hypothesis testing
    contrasting   24, 84–6, 89, 123, 133
    descriptive   9, 16, 84, 87
    heuristic   34, 41, 71, 78, 81, 84, 86, 88, 95, 115, 135
    paradigmatic   10, 12, 57, 59, 72, 84, 85, 89
    particularizing   21, 22, 24–6, 31, 35, 64, 72, 84–6, 89, 133
  paradoxes of   1–3, 98, 135
  types of   90–6
    asymmetrical   94–5, 135
    diachronic   56, 95, 98, 107
    paired   94
    parallel   18, 27, 33–4, 40, 45, 48, 82, 90, 93–5, 97
historical linguistics   14, 32, 73
historical positivism   30
historical research   24
  methods of *vs.* scientific research   21
historical scholarship   79
historical sociology. *See* sociology
historicism   13–22
history of law   14, 22
Hitler, Adolf   49
Hobsbawm, Eric   128
holistic approach   98, 99
homology   28
Hroch, Miroslav   93 n.17, 129–31
  Social Preconditions of National Revival in Europe   129
humankind, historical development of   13, 22
Humboldt, Wilhelm von
  On the Comparative Study of Languages in Connection with Various Stages of their Development   14
Hungary   115
  role of banks in financing industry   41
hypothesis testing, logic of   16–17, 34, 42, 63, 72, 74, 82, 83, 86, 89

idealistic theory of history 21
ideal type. *See* Weber, Max
'idiographic' *vs.* 'nomothetic' methods. *See* Baden school (of philosophy)
imagined community 128
India 3
    industrialization 106
    textile industry in 108
individualism 113, 121, 127
industrial capitalism 24, 41
industrialization 39, 41–2, 106
Industrial Revolution 40, 126
institutionalization 17
interview method 78, 79
Irish Catholics 45
Iriye, Akira 59
Italy 110, 115
    industrialization 106
    nation state 111–12
    Parlamenti 35
    unification movement (*Risorgimento*) 112

Japan 3, 26, 64, 105, 128
    conservative modernization in 62
    economic development 40
    industrialization 73
    landed aristocracy in 63
    land, labour and capital markets in 107
    socialist movement in 45
Jean Bodin Society of Comparative History of Institutions 27
Jena, University of 12

Kaelble, Hartmut 44, 51, 57, 80, 83, 87, 92, 103, 118, 135
    Social Mobility and Equality of Opportunity in the Nineteenth to Twentieth Centuries 51
Kareev, Nikolai 71, 86
Kashtanov, Sergei 98–9
Kedar, Benjamin 23, 27, 32, 35, 39, 79
Kiev 119
Klaus, Alisa 47–8, 94, 114
Kocka, Jürgen 50–2, 60, 76, 81, 83–5, 92, 94–5, 97, 100, 135
Koenigsberger, Helmut 110, 113

Kolchin, Peter 2, 46, 75, 92, 94, 123–5, 125 n.43
    Unfree Labor 47, 91, 123
Krakow 119
Križanić, Juraj 43

Lang, James 133
Langlois, Charles-Victor 20, 23, 24, 31, 32, 82, 90, 91
    Introduction to the Study of History 18–19, 71
Latin America 3, 93, 105
Libri Feodorum 121
Lieven, Dominic 131
linguistics
    comparative 2, 13, 14 n.4, 19, 73, 74
    historical 14, 32, 73
Lithuania 130
Liubarskii, Georgii 91, 92
Livonian War 122
Livy 9
London 92
Lucassen, Jan 126–7
Lviv 119

Macedonia 130
McLennan, John
    Primitive Marriage 14–15
macro-analytical method 88
macro-causal analysis 88
Maddison, Angus
    Contours of the World Economy 1-2030 AD: Essays in Macro-Economic History 105
Madrid 133
Mahoney, James 63
Maine, Henry 14
Martel, Charles 98, 99
Marx, Karl 120
maternal welfare policy 47–8
meaning of comparative method 72
Mecklenburg 18
Meillet, Antoine 32 n.48, 71
    Comparative Method in Historical Linguistics, The 32
methodological pluralism 59
methodology of the natural sciences 21
methods *vs.* approaches 76–7

Michelet, Jules
    History of France 20
Miller, Alexei 131, 132
Mill, John Stuart 74
    canons 65, 66, 80
    method of agreement 13, 74–5
    method of concomitant variations 14
    method of difference 13, 74–5
    method of residues 14
    methods of induction 16
    System of Logic, A 13–14, 64
Mitteis, Heinrich 109
    *State of the High Middle Ages,
        The* 110
modern capitalism 24
modernization 41, 58, 61, 62, 106, 108, 115, 128
modern state 2, 86, 98, 117
Montesquieu, Charles de Secondat baron de 10–12
    Spirit of the Laws, The 10, 11, 87
Moore, Barrington, Jr. 3, 63, 64, 66, 67, 112
    Social Origins of Dictatorship and Democracy 61–2, 88
Morozov family 42
Moscow 98, 119, 125
Mousnier, Roland 122–3
Mumenthaler, Rudolf 119
Muscovite Rus/Muscovy 26, 81, 98

Napoleon's Italian campaign of 1796-7 112
nationalism 20, 27, 115, 128–34
    methodological 58
National Socialism 49
nation-state 105, 111
Nazism 49, 114
Neo-Kantians 21, 86
Netherlands/Holland 92, 110, 121–2, 134
    economic development 40
    industrialization 106
newcomers to historical comparison, recommendations for 97–101
new cultural history 52
Newport, Christopher 133
New York 96, 127
Novgorod 98, 119

O'Brien, Patrick 42, 106
oral history 79
Origins of the Modern State in Europe, 13th to 18th Centuries (Oxford University Press) 117
O'Rourke, Kevin H.
    New Comparative Economic History, The 105
Osaka 125
Österberg, Eva 117
Osterhammel, Jürgen 59
Ottoman Empire. *See* empire

Palmer, Robert 45
    Age of the Democratic Revolution: The Political History of Europe and America, 1760–1800, The 44, 112
parallel demonstration of theory 88
Paris 92, 96
Parlamenti 35
parliamentary democracy 62
Passeron, Jean-Claude 87
patronage 81
Paulmann, Johann 55
Pedersen, Susan 114
    Family, Dependence and the Origins of the Welfare State: Britain and France, 1914–1945 48
Pederson, Susan 94
Peloponnesian War 8
Persia 10
Petit-Dutaillis, Charles
    Feudal Monarchy in France and England, from the Tenth to the Thirteenth Century, The 109–10
Petrusewicz, Marta 2
Petty, William 43
philosophy of history 12, 19, 31
Pirenne, Henri 31, 32, 45
    Medieval Towns and the Revival of Trade 27 n.21
    'On the Comparative Method in History' 27
Plutarch
    Parallel Lives 9
Poland 111, 115, 116
political history comparison 39, 109–17

Polybius 8–9, 28
Pomerania 18
Pomeranz, Kenneth 105–7
  Great Divergence: China, Europe, and the Making of the Modern World Economy, The 106
Portugal 49, 115
positive philosophy 15
pragmatic pluralism 125
Prague 129
Prost, Antoine 87
Protestant ethic 42, 66
Prussian Junkers 125
pseudo-similarities 85
Pskov 98, 119
Puerto Ricans 45

qualitative method 78
quantitative method 18, 78
Quellenkunde. See source criticism

Ragusa 119
Randeria, Shalini 58
Ranke, Leopold von 17, 20
Rask, Rasmus 14
Razin, Stenka 122
Redlich, Fritz 39, 100
reductionism 31, 40
regency 85
revolutionary conjuncture 112
Reynolds, Susan 120–1, 124
  Fiefs and Vassals 120
Rickert, Heinrich 21
Rieber, Alfred 131–2
right-wing radicalism 62
Romania 111, 115
Rome 10, 28, 118
Rostow, Walt 40–1, 105, 106
  Stages of Economic Growth 40
  theory of the stages of economic growth 105–6
Rozhkov, Nikolai 99–100
Russia 2, 3, 10, 27 n.21, 64, 81, 85, 95, 113, 114
  communist dictatorship in 62
  economic development 40
  historiography 119–20
  industrialization 42
  peasant uprisings in 122, 123
  role of banks in financing industry 41
  Russian Revolution of 1917 64
  textile industry 43
Ryabushinsky family 42

Schieder, Theodor 10–12, 30, 38–9, 50, 71–2, 80, 89, 111–12
  classification of forms of historical comparison 72, 89
  'Possibilities and Limitations of Comparative Methods in Historical Science, The' 73
  scientific method *vs.* methods of historical research 21
Scotland 111
Second World War 38, 39, 61, 92, 110
secularization 114
Sée, Henri 27, 32
Seignobos, Charles
  Introduction to the Study of History 18–19, 71
Serbia 111
serfdom 47, 84, 91, 93, 98, 116, 119, 123–5, 125 n.43
Sewell, William H. 72–5, 80, 90, 91
Shannon, David A. 45
shared history 58
Skocpol, Theda 61, 64–6, 112
  States and Social Revolutions 64, 88
slavery 41, 91, 93, 94, 123–5
Smith, Adam 107
Smith, Anthony 128
Smith, Stephen 114
  Revolution and the People in Russia and China 113
social anthropology 87
social history comparison 118–27
social insurance 47, 48
social security 47
social solidarity policies in 48–9
socio-economic history 34
sociological theory 17
sociology 13, 15, 16, 19, 21, 23, 24, 31, 32, 39, 47, 58, 71, 86, 87, 87 n.39, 136
  historical 61–7, 88, 89, 108, 112
Soloviev, S. M.
  History of Russia from Ancient Times 20

Somers, Margaret   88
Sonderweg (special path)   20, 49, 50
Sorbonne   23
source criticism   52, 78
South Africa   94
　race relations in   100
Spain   49, 113, 115, 116
　Cortes   34–5
Spencer, Herbert   15, 16
Spengler, Oswald   27–9, 96
　Decline of the West, The   28
Sri Lanka   128
Stoler, Ann Laura
　'Tense and Tender Ties: The Politics of Comparison in North American History and (Post) Colonial Studies'   134
Stone, Lawrence   113
　News from Everywhere, The   63
Sweden
　economic development   40
　influence of petitions on the legislative process   117
　socialist movement in   45
　welfare state in   48
Switzerland   49, 63, 92
　role of banks in financing industry   41
synthetic functions of comparison   73

Tacitus   9
Taylor, Alan M.
　New Comparative Economic History, The   105
tertium comparationis   54, 93, 99
theories of natural science   90
theory of stages of economic development. See Rostow, Walt
Thrupp, Sylvia L.   38, 40, 44, 73, 74, 76, 105
Tilly, Charles   3, 61, 89, 108
　Coercion, Capital, and European States AD 990–1992   66
　typology of comparison   89
Toynbee, Arnold   29–31, 37, 96
　'challenge and response'   29–31
　Study of History, The   29, 30
　'withdrawal and return'   30, 31

trade unions   48, 50, 126
transfer history   58
transnational history   33, 59, 60
Trevelyan, G. M.   118
Troeltsch, Ernst   21–2
　Historicism and Its Problems   22
Turkey   10, 26
Tylor, Edward Burnett   15–16
　Primitive Culture   15
typification   26
Tyrrell, Ian   59

United States   3, 44, 52, 61, 85, 105
　American Civil War   112
　American Enlightenment   45
　American Exceptionalism   59
　British possessions in   133
　Declaration of Independence   45
　development of comparative historical research   46
　economic development   40
　equality of opportunity in   51
　historiography   75
　landed aristocracy in   63
　maternal and child welfare policy   47, 48
　race relations in   100
　socialist movement in   45
　social mobility in   51
　social politics in   94
universalizing function of comparison   89

Vann Woodward, C.
　Comparative Approach to American History, The   44–5
Vedda   16
Venezuela   134
Verfassungsgeschichte (constitutional history)   25
Vico, Giambattista   11–12, 28
　Principles of the New Science about the Common Nature of Nations   11, 12
Vietnam   128
villeinage   84
Virginia Company   133
Voltaire   10, 12

Weber, Max   3, 22–37, 42, 43, 43 n.28, 61, 73, 77, 84, 118–19
   ideal type, concept of   24, 25, 43 n.28, 73, 76
Wehler, Hans-Ulrich   50
Weimar Republic   83
welfare state   48, 114
   European   50, 84, 94
Welskopp, Thomas   76
Werner, Michael   57
   'Beyond Comparison: Histoire Croisée and the Challenge of Reflexivity'   56
   Transfers: Intercultural Relations in the Franco-German Space   54

Western Europe. *See* Europe
Western Germany. *See* Germany
Windelband, Wilhelm   21
Winks, Robin W.   45
Wippermann, Wolfgang   114–15

Xerxes, King   8

Yugoslavia   111

Zagorin, Perez   113
Zimmermann, Bénédicte   54, 57
   'Beyond Comparison: Histoire Croisée and the Challenge of Reflexivity'   56

www.ingramcontent.com/pod-product-compliance
Lightning Source LLC
Chambersburg PA
CBHW070642300426
44111CB00013B/2225